Multithreaded Programming
with Win32

ISBN 0-13-010912-6

90000

Multithreaded Programming with Win32

Thuan Q. Pham
Pankaj K. Garg

Prentice Hall, PTR
Upper Saddle River, New Jersey 07458
http://www.phptr.com

Library of Congress Cataloging-in-Publication Data
Pham, Thuan Q.
    Multithreaded programming with Win32 / Thuan Q. Pham and Pankaj K.
 Garg.
        p.   cm.
    Includes bibliographical references (p.   ) and index.
    ISBN 0-13-010912-6
    1. Parallel programming (Computer science) 2. Threads (Computer
 programs 3. Microsoft Win32.   I. Garg, Pankaj K.   II. Title.
 QA76.642.P518   1998
 004'.35--dc21   98-37582
                                                                   CIP

Editorial/Production Supervision: Craig Little
Acquisitions Editor: Mary Franz
Manufacturing Manager: Alexis R. Heydt
Marketing Manager: Miles Williams
Cover Design Director: Jerry Votta
Cover Design: Scott Weiss

 © 1999 by Prentice Hall PTR
Prentice-Hall Inc.
A Simon & Schuster Company
Upper Saddle River, NJ 07458

All product names mentioned herein are the property of their respective owners.

Prentice Hall books are widely used by corporations and government agencies for training, marketing, and resale.

The publisher offers discounts on this book when ordered in bulk quantities.
For more information, contact the Corporate Sales Department at 800-382-3419, fax: 201-236-7141,
email: corpsales@prenhall.com or write Corporate Sales Department, Prentice Hall PTR,
One Lake Street, Upper Saddle River, New Jersey 07458.

Printed in the United States of America
10 9 8   7   6   5   4   3   2   1

ISBN   0-13-010912-6

Prentice-Hall International (UK) Limited, *London*
Prentice-Hall of Australia Pty. Limited, *Sydney*
Prentice-Hall Canada Inc., *Toronto*
Prentice-Hall Hispanoamericana, S.A., *Mexico*
Prentice-Hall of India Private Limited, *New Delhi*
Prentice-Hall of Japan, Inc., *Tokyo*
Simon & Schuster Asia Pte. Ltd., *Singapore*
Editora Prentice-Hall do Brasil, Ltda., *Rio de Janeiro*

Contents

List of Figures

List of Tables

Preface

*I*n this book, we describe techniques for designing and implementing multithreaded software applications. Multithreaded programming can effectively improve efficiency and performance in an application program by introducing *concurrency* or *parallelism*. Until recently, concurrent programming required multiple processes, each with a single thread of execution, running concurrently on a multitasking operating system. In the past, concurrent programming was a tool used mostly by researchers and system implementors, that is, programmers of operating systems, networking, and other systems software.

Modern operating systems like Solaris, AIX, DEC-UNIX, Windows 98, Windows NT, HP-UX, and Linux, all support multiple threads of control within the same address space. With the wide availability of multiprocessor computers in the coming years, multithreaded programming will be a viable and important technique for application programmers to master. With threads, a process can have multiple instruction streams executing simultaneously with much lower overhead than concurrent processes. Threads within the same address space inherently share that process's memory, which makes communication and data sharing among threads efficient. In addition, multithreading technology is absolutely essential for domains such as real-time multimedia and distributed systems.

Andrew Birrell, in his excellent tutorial, *Programming with Threads*,[1] lists five main benefits of multithreaded programming: (1) greater speed from multiprocessor computers, (2) improved program efficiency by avoiding waits associated with slow-speed I/O devices, (3) multiple inputs from a user at the same time, (4) simpler server programs, and (5) responsive programs with computations judiciously spread over time. Developing programs that exploit these benefits of multithreading, however, is a challenge; the presence of parallelism introduces a new set of problems like resource sharing, deadlocks, race conditions, and so forth.

The purpose of this book is both to introduce you to the concept of multithreaded programming, and to demonstrate how some of these challenges can be overcome. We have tried to cover all the important aspects of multithreaded programming, and to create a book that you will want to read as a primer book and use later as a reference guide.

Outline of Chapters

Chapter 1 introduces the *basic concepts, history, benefits*, and *challenges* of multithreaded programming. To provide an immediate hands-on experience, this chapter presents a small multithreaded program for you to experiment with right away.

Chapter 2 introduces the *Win32 thread interface* and discusses its use. Here we also discuss the concepts of processes and threads, illustrate thread management functions, describe thread priorities and scheduling, and examine synchronization objects.

In Chapter 3 we discuss the fundamental techniques for *synchronizing* threads of a multithreaded application. Using classic concurrency problems of producer-consumer, bounded-buffer, and readers-writers, we demonstrate synchronization techniques using the threads interface described in Chapter 2.

Chapters 4 and 5 introduce *monitors*, an important abstraction and tool for multithreaded programming. While Chapter 4 describes the structure and properties of monitors, Chapter 5 simulates monitors using a combination of C++ classes and Win32 synchronization objects. Once again, we use concurrency problems of producer-consumer, bounded-buffer, and readers-writers to illustrate and demonstrate the usefulness of monitors in these chapters.

Chapter 6 covers *system deadlock* in detail. In this chapter, we describe conditions for deadlock and explore techniques for avoiding it. Using the classic dining philosophers' problem, we demonstrate how to apply several deadlock- handling techniques like deadlock detection and recovery, prevention, and avoidance to application programs.

Chapter 7 surveys a variety of *thread package architectures*, including user-level threads, kernel threads, multiplexed threads, and scheduler activations. We describe the impact of each thread architecture on the design and implementation of multithreaded programs.

Chapter 8 covers the important topic of how to break up an application into multiple threads. We present illustrative *programming models*, including work groups, manager-worker, deferred computation, pipeline, and WorkCrew. Each model is illustrated using a sample program.

In Chapter 9 we describe how threads can be used in the client and server components of a *distributed application*. Multithreaded programming plays an important role in this

---

[1.] Birrell, A., "An Introduction to Programming with Threads," in *Systems Programming with Modula-3*, G. Nelson, ed. Prentice Hall, 1991, pp. 88–118.

domain. We show the basic steps for constructing a distributed application using Microsofts' Remote Procedure Call (RPC) and Distributed Component Object Model (DCOM).

The concurrent programming techniques covered in this book are well known in the computer science research community and are discussed in technical publications and several operating system textbooks. These concepts have, however, only recently become available for application programmers.

The target audience for this book are application developers who want to experiment with multithreaded programming, and who have a working knowledge of the C programming language. Some parts of the book require a knowledge of the C++ language and the Visual C++ programming environement. We do not describe the threads API of the Microsoft Foundation Classes (MFC). The examples have been implemented on Intel Pentium machines running the Windows NT 4.0 Workstation operating system. Also, for clarity and brevity of exposition, we have removed error-checking code from the listings presented in the book except where such code is essential to the content under discussion.

Acknowledgments

Scott Marovich provided invaluable assistance with the preparation of this book: he carefully went through several versions, pointing out numerous corrections and improvements. Scott, thank you! We thank Anthony T. Nguyen for his early discussions with us on the book. We thank Nawaf Bitar for his valuable review and feedback for this book's proposal. We thank Debbie Caswell for her review of earlier versions of the book and encouraging comments about it. We thank Mary Franz, our editor at Prentice Hall, for initially suggesting the project, for patiently guiding us through the process, and for her eternal optimism. We thank Derrick Burns, Jill Huchital, Mehdi Jazayeri, John Krystynak, Srikanth Nadhamuni, and Thu Nguyen for their comments on earlier versions of the book. We thank Craig Little, our production editor, for patiently working with us on this project, and Scott Disanno for his careful copyediting of the book.

Thuan thanks his wonderful wife, Nicole Anh-Dao, for all the support, encouragement, patience, and understanding that has made this project possible.

Pankaj thanks his parents, Shri Harish Chand Garg and Smt. Savitri Garg for their love, affection and care. He thanks Puna, for her caring and wonderful companionship, his sister, Priti, and brother-in-law, Ajay, and all his friends for their encouragement and support.

Introduction

Welcome to the world of multithreaded programming! What you are about to learn is an exciting and effective programming method for writing parallel application programs. Traditionally, a program is a single sequence of instructions with possible jumps, loops, and subroutine calls. Such programs have only one thread of control, that is, only one program instruction is available for execution at any given time. With Win32 API, however, we can write programs with many threads of control,[1] each executing in parallel with the others. By using multiple threads of control in an application program we can solve many problems, especially in systems with concurrent events, naturally and elegantly. In addition, a multithreaded program efficiently utilizes multiple system resources (e.g., processors and input/output devices); even more so in multiprocessor and distributed architectures.

In this introductory chapter, we'll take you through a whirlwind tour of multithreaded programming. Our tour starts with a definition of multithreaded programming and a brief history of the main concepts behind it, establishing a foundation for you to understand and appreciate the progression of programming technology that has led to multithreaded

---

[1.] For personal computers, some other operating systems that support multithreaded processes are OS/2, Linux, Solaris x86, etc.

programming. Next, we highlight benefits of multithreaded programming. We present a simple multithreaded program example, and preview important concepts and techniques to be covered in subsequent chapters. Lastly, we give an overview of the technical challenges of multithreaded programming.

We assume you have some programming experience, so we will liberally use terms like *process, thread of execution, code,* and *data* before defining them more precisely in later chapters.

1.1   What is Multithreaded Programming?

Multithreading is a form of concurrent programming—a way to design and implement parallel application programs. Traditionally, a concurrent application has multiple concurrently executing processes. For example, a retail store's merchandise management system may have a process to manage the names, UPC codes, and inventory of products; another to maintain prices and supply sources; another to schedule the orders and deliveries; and so forth. In operation, these processes may be dynamically created and terminated by a main process. The processes all execute concurrently, sharing data and collaborating with each other to make the entire merchandise management system work. The practice of designing and implementing such parallel systems is called concurrent programming.

With threads, we can apply concurrent programming concepts and techniques within the address space of a single process as well. Multiple threads enable us to write efficient parallel programs and naturally model programming problems that are inherently parallel. In the following sections, we describe the advantages and challenges of multithreaded programming, and illustrate its power and elegance with a demonstration program.

1.2   A Bit of History

Over three decades of operating system and programming language research and practice have laid the foundation of ideas and technology relevant for multithreaded programming. We now describe the evolution of the "thread" concept in operating systems, and present a brief history of synchronization concepts for concurrent programming.

1.2.1   Processes and Threads

In the early 1940s, when computers were first defined and built, programmers adopted a "von Neumann" architecture [Burks et al., 1946]. In this architecture, a computer program is a sequence of steps to change values in a sequentially organized memory of data. This basic model of a program is directly visible to the computer user or programmer. There was neither hope nor any need for parallelism in this simplistic model.

The computers of those early days were basically enormous programmable calculators (some up to 100 feet long). Programming those machines was a tedious job of setting switches and plugging cables, and each user program consumed the entire machine.

Not long after this, programmers invented bootstrap programs to facilitate the loading of other programs through external devices (e.g., punched card readers). This innovation enabled a smoother transition between jobs and maximal utilization of the computer's running time, which led to the concept of batch processing that was widely used in the 1950s and early 1960s. Eventually, the bootstrap programs led to the birth of the first operating system—a program that loads and executes other user programs while managing the hardware resources.

The leap towards multiple concurrent programs occurred in the 1960s with the invention of *process*, *multiprogramming*, and *timesharing*. Basically, a process is a *program in execution*. A process executes as if it is the only one running on the computer. The operating system supports concurrent execution of several processes by multiplexing (time-sharing) the computer's resources among them. The major timesharing computer systems of this period were the Compatible Time-Sharing System (CTSS) [Corbató, 1963; Crisman, 1964] and the subsequent Multics system [Bensoussan et al., 1972] of MIT, and the TSS [Lett and Konigsford, 1968] and CP/CMS systems of IBM. The Multics project developed some of the basic understandings of the process concept [Saltzer, 1966].

Today, multithreaded programs can effectively take advantage of the multiple CPUs of multiprocessor machines. Each thread of execution can run on a different processor, in parallel, to improve the overall speed of a program. Multics designers understood the need and importance of simultaneously using multiple hardware components [Corbató and Vyssotsky, 1965]:

> … it is clear that systems with multiple processors and multiple memory units are needed to provide greater capacity [p. 187].

> Further features which should ultimately appear in the system are:
> 1. the ability to have one process spawn other processes which run asynchronously on several processors (thus improving the real-time response of the overall process);
> 2. the ability for the data bases to be shared among simultaneously operating programs [p. 192].

The concept of a process as conceived by Multics designers and several others in the 1960s (e.g., Dijkstra), however, did not contain the idea of multiple threads of execution in the same process. In those days, a process had a single thread of execution operating on a single sequence of memory (called the "address space" of the process); the process was a software abstraction of the von Neumann hardware architecture. For example, the Multics designers developed a strong association between a "thread of execution" and an "address space." The following quotation from [Vyssotsky et al., 1965] is evidence of this association:

> We define a process to be all those actions performed by a CPU with some given segment as descriptor segment, from the first time that segment becomes the descriptor segment until the last time the segment ceases to be the descriptor segment. Thus a process has a very definite beginning; if it ends, it has an equally definite end [p. 206].

Multiple threads of execution cannot share the same address space when an address space is exclusively linked to one thread. To develop a parallel program in such a situation, we are forced to use several address spaces. Multiple address spaces cause two problems: (1) each address space is expensive for the operating system to maintain, and (2) inter-address space communication is expensive. Until the late 1970s, most popular operating systems, like

DEC's TOPS-10, IBM's MVS, and Bell Lab's UNIX©, only supported the process abstraction (without threads). To write a parallel program in such operating systems, one was forced to use multiple processes; they exchanged information using interprocess communication (IPC) or pipes.

It was not until 1979—more than a decade after the introduction of the process concept—that David Cheriton and colleagues, while building the Toth operating system, defined a *lightweight process;* a process devoid of the baggage of an address space. This definition provided a fundamental breakthrough on the road to multithreaded programming. Cheriton and colleagues explained their goals for the Toth operating system as follows [Cheriton et al., 1979]:

> The design of Toth strives for more than portability. A second design goal is to provide a system in which programs may be structured using many small concurrent processes. We have aimed for efficient interprocess communication and inexpensive processes to make this structuring technique attractive [p. 105].
>
> ...
>
> Each process belongs to a team which is a set of processes sharing a common address space and a common free list of memory resources [p. 107].

Several operating system researchers adopted the lightweight process after it was introduced in the Toth system. Although researchers used the Toth system at the University of Waterloo, Canada, commercial computer companies did not adopt it. The UNIX operating system, developed at Bell Telephone Laboratories, on the other hand, was gaining more and more popularity—and Toth was not compatible with the UNIX system. The idea of a lightweight process, therefore, had to wait another decade for the arrival of the Mach operating system from Carnegie Mellon University. As part of a Strategic Computing Initiative (SCI) from the U.S Department of Defense Advanced Research Program Agency (DARPA), Rick Rashid and colleagues built the Mach operating system in the mid-80s. Mach was popular because its designers provided UNIX compatibility:

> The basic abstractions of Mach are intended not simply as extensions to normal Unix facilities but as a new foundation upon which to build further Unix facilities and develop Unix-like systems for new architectures [Rashid, 1986, p. 38].

This objective of Mach, along with others like robustness, usability, and efficiency, ensured that it was quickly useful in many situations. Mach provided a clean separation between the concepts of processes (which were called tasks) and threads:

> A task is an execution environment in which threads may run. As the basic unit of resource allocation, a task includes a paged virtual address space and protected access to system resources (such as processors, port capabilities, and virtual memory). The Unix notion of a process thus is represented in Mach by a task that has a single thread of control.
> A thread is a basic unit of CPU utilization. It is roughly equivalent to an independent program counter operating within a task. All threads within a task share access to all task resources. [p. 39]

We see a similar separation in most commercial operating systems, including Windows 95, Windows 98, Windows NT, Solaris, DEC-UNIX, AIX, etc.

We are now at the end of the historical road from a process in Multics to Win32 threads. Next, we can turn our attention to the synchronization concepts in multithreaded programming.

1.2.2 Synchronization Concepts

Writing parallel programs using multiple threads of control is much more complicated than writing a single-threaded program. In addition to taking care of the program logic, you must ensure that the threads synchronize with each other so that they do not inadvertently corrupt each other's work. For example, two threads sharing a variable must ensure that they read and write the variable in proper order without losing updates. Threads that depend upon each other's work should not wait indefinitely for each other in a state of deadlock. Researchers developed synchronization techniques for solving such concurrent programming problems in the 1960s. E. W. Dijkstra, then at the Technical University of Eindhoven, Netherlands, wrote a seminal paper on this subject entitled *Cooperating Sequential Processes* [Dijkstra, 1968].

Dijkstra recognized an important general problem of *mutual exclusion* in concurrent programs with N processes:

> given N cyclic processes, each with a critical section, can we construct them in a way that at any moment at most one of them is engaged in its critical section? [p. 59]

He presented several solutions to this problem. First, he assumed the existence of a test-and-set instruction whereby a single indivisible program step could read and change the value of a variable. Solutions utilizing this simple assumption were, however, complex to implement. So he recommended an abstraction, called *semaphore,* for a process to indicate its intention of accessing shared data. A programmer can utilize such indications to ensure mutual exclusion between accesses. Dijkstra associated two basic operations (indications) with a semaphore object: one to indicate that a process wanted to access shared data, and another to signal that it had finished accessing the data.

> In other words: the previous set of communication facilities must be regarded as inadequate for the problem at hand, and we should look for more appropriate alternatives.
> Such an alternative is provided by introducing:
> (a) among the common variables special-purpose integers, which we shall call "semaphores,"
> (b) among the repertoire of actions, from which the individual processes have to be constructed, two new primitives, which we call the "P-operation" and the "V-operation" respectively [p. 67].

The semaphore abstraction was a significant contribution of its time; we see its widespread use in modern multithreaded programming environments.

A *monitor* is another important abstraction for synchronizing threads. Unlike a semaphore, a monitor *encapsulates* data to be shared among multiple threads. Code using shared data is thereby considerably simpler with improved understandability and robustness. The monitor concept was developed by Per Brinch Hansen and C. A. R. Hoare in the early 1970s (reportedly in close communication with E. W. Dijkstra) [Hoare, 1974; Hansen, 1975]. (Interestingly, the language SIMULA67 [Dahl, 1972] contributed to the development of the monitor concept, in addition to its major contribution to object-oriented languages like C++ [Stroustrup, 1994] and Smalltalk [Goldberg and Robson, 1983].)

We conclude our history of threads and their synchronization with one message: the techniques of multithreaded programming, now available to you, represent a culmination of research begun three decades ago!

Next, we look at several of the advantages of multithreaded programming.

1.3 Advantages of Threads

1.3.1 Economy and Speed

Concurrent programs using multiple threads are faster than similar programs with multiple processes. Using multiple processes to achieve concurrency is expensive because process creation is slow, often requiring initialization of process table entries, virtual memory address space, file descriptors, and so forth. Also, concurrent execution requires switching the processor from executing one process to another, which is slow due to the extensive resources held by each process. On the other hand, creation, switching, and destruction of threads are faster because they all share the same process's resources and have little unique context. For this reason, some implementors also refer to threads as *lightweight processes*.

1.3.2 Shared Memory and Resources

A significant advantage of threads is their ability to share memory and resources within a process. All threads in a process share its entire address space. Since concurrent programs often require communication and data sharing among constituent sequential tasks, these needs can be met efficiently with threads. Communication can be implemented efficiently using shared memory: If one thread A wants to share data with a thread B, it can simply write the data to a location known to B and then signal B if necessary. Similarly, resources such as file descriptors, or handles to graphic devices and other system objects, can be shared efficiently. In later chapters, we will demonstrate tools and techniques to synchronize resource sharing among threads.

1.3.3 Efficient Hardware Utilization

An important advantage of multithreaded programming is the possibility of performing I/O and computations concurrently, thereby better utilizing different components of a computer's hardware (CPU, disk, and peripherals). For instance, a database server using threads can perform checkpointing (writing information to a transaction log on disk) while continuing to service client queries and other transactions without interruption.

Using multiprocessor computers, multiple threads can truly run in parallel, allowing a process to use more than one processor simultaneously. While this increase in raw computing power improves the performance of all multithreaded applications, it especially benefits problems, such as sorting and searching, that can be naturally parallelized.

1.3.4 Responsive Application

While processing power can increase the speed of any program, we can make even an application on a slow computer seem responsive by using different threads for foreground and background processing. In a multithreaded spreadsheet application, for example, one thread can handle input and display while other threads handle computation. With this organization, the spreadsheet will remain responsive, allowing the user to move the cursor or type in data, while background computations are done concurrently. As another application of this technique, imagine a multimedia application where the user can preview and order movies on demand. Since it can take up to a few seconds to bring a movie from the server to the client's screen when switching between movies, the application can mitigate the delay effects by using a separate thread to pre-fetch parts of the new movie.

1.3.5 Remote Services

In distributed computing, threads are essential for remote service requests, because there is no guarantee that the results will be available immediately. A server machine may be slow, deadlocked, or even disabled. If a single-threaded client process uses a synchronous communication mechanism, such as Remote Procedure Call (RPC), the entire client process can hang indefinitely while waiting for a result. If we use asynchronous communication methods, the client program must stay in a polling loop while waiting for replies; then it must perform the complex task of matching the server's response with a previous request. Using a multithreaded program, a client program can dispatch a thread to service each remote request, and continue doing other useful work. With this technique, we achieve the flexibility and performance benefit of asynchronous communication with the simplicity of synchronous communication.

Similarly, we can structure a server process cleanly by having a main thread watch the queue of incoming service requests, then dispatch a thread to handle each request. While the server is busy servicing client requests, it will still be available to accept and process additional requests.

1.3.6 Concurrent Programming Abstraction

Applications with multiple threads of control are naturally concurrent. Concurrent programming was developed as a technique for addressing the complexity of writing large programs (e.g., an operating system) by allowing a designer to break it up into smaller units and deal with each one independently. With multithreaded programing, similar benefits are now available to application programmers. Consider an application that must maintain multiple objects on the computer screen which have to be updated occasionally. Rather than having one thread update and keep track of the multiple objects, we can substantially simplify the program logic by having a separate thread manage each object or a group of similar objects. We will see an example of this technique in the next section and later in this book.

1.4 A Multithreaded Program Example

To give you a taste of multithreaded programming, we now present a simple ping-pong game program. In our version of the game there are five objects, four paddles and a ball, each controlled by a separate thread. When the game starts, the ball bounces around the screen, and each paddle adjusts its position to meet the ball at its edge of the screen. Figure 1–1 shows a screen image of the game.

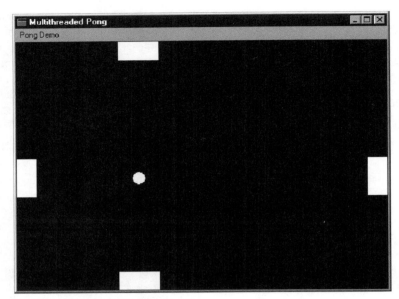

Figure 1–1. Multithreaded Pong Program Screen.

The following is the program code:

```
1    ////////////////////////////////////////////////////////////////
2    // PROGRAM: Pong.c
3    // PURPOSE: To demonstrate thread creation and management API
4    ////////////////////////////////////////////////////////////////
5
6    #include <stdio.h>
7    #include <windows.h>
8    #include <stdlib.h>
9    #include "pong.h"
10
11   #define BALL 0
12   #define TOP 1
13   #define BOTTOM 2
14   #define LEFT 3
15   #define RIGHT 4
16   #define NUM_THREADS 5
17
18   #define WIDTH 30
19   #define LENGTH 60
20   #define DRAW 1
21   #define ERASE 0
22
23   HANDLE hInst;
24   HANDLE hWnd;
25   HANDLE hBlackBrush, hRedBrush, hGreenBrush, hBlueBrush;
26
```

```
27   // structure to be used for coordinate and movement direction
28   struct Pong {
29     int x, y;
30   };
31
32   // these shared data need protection
33   struct Pong PongPos;
34   struct Pong PongDir;
35   int nCurrent, nLast; // current and last position of ball
36
37   // mutex Lock use to protect shared data
38   HANDLE hLock;
39
40   // command messages to direct a thread to self terminate
41   #define NOP 0
42   #define TERMINATE 1
43   int nCmdMsg[NUM_THREADS];
44
45
46   ////////////////////////////////////////////////////////////////////
47   // FUNCTION: WinMain
48   // PURPOSE: calls initialization function, processes message loop
49   ////////////////////////////////////////////////////////////////////
50
51   int APIENTRY WinMain (HANDLE hInstance,
52              HANDLE hPrevInstance,
53              LPSTR  lpCmdLine,
54              int    nCmdShow)
55   {
56     MSG  msg;
57     WNDCLASS wc;
58
59     UNREFERENCED_PARAMETER( lpCmdLine );
60     UNREFERENCED_PARAMETER( hPrevInstance );
61
62     hInst = hInstance;
63
64     wc.style = CS_VREDRAW | CS_HREDRAW;
65     wc.lpfnWndProc = (WNDPROC)MainWndProc;
66     wc.cbClsExtra = 0;
67     wc.cbWndExtra = 0;
68     wc.hInstance = hInstance;
69     wc.hIcon = LoadIcon (NULL, IDI_APPLICATION);
70     wc.hCursor = LoadCursor (NULL, IDC_ARROW);
71     wc.hbrBackground = GetStockObject (BLACK_BRUSH);
72     wc.lpszMenuName = "Pong_Menu";
73     wc.lpszClassName = "ThreadsWClass";
74
75     RegisterClass(&wc);
76     hWnd = CreateWindow ("ThreadsWClass",
77              "Multithreaded Pong",
78              WS_OVERLAPPEDWINDOW,
79              CW_USEDEFAULT,
80              CW_USEDEFAULT,
```

```
81                CW_USEDEFAULT,
82                CW_USEDEFAULT,
83                NULL,
84                NULL,
85                hInstance,
86                NULL);
87     ShowWindow(hWnd, nCmdShow);
88
89     while (GetMessage (&msg, NULL, 0, 0))
90       DispatchMessage (&msg);    // Dispatch message to window.
91
92     return (msg.wParam); // Returns value from PostQuitMessage.
93   }
94
95   /////////////////////////////////////////////////////////////////
96   // FUNCTION: MainWndProc
97   // PURPOSE:  Process windows messages, create Mutex,
98   //           create and terminate threads.
99   /////////////////////////////////////////////////////////////////
100
101  LONG APIENTRY MainWndProc (HWND hwnd,
102              UINT message,
103              UINT wParam,
104              LONG lParam)
105  {
106    PAINTSTRUCT ps;
107    DWORD  ThreadID;
108    static HANDLE hPong, hTopPaddle, hBottomPaddle,
109                  hLeftPaddle, hRightPaddle;
110    static int started = 0;
111    int i = 0;
112
113    switch (message)
114      {
115      case WM_PAINT:
116        BeginPaint (hwnd, &ps);
117        EndPaint (hwnd, &ps);
118        return (0);
119
120      case WM_CREATE :
121        // create the color drawing brushes
122        hBlackBrush = CreateSolidBrush((COLORREF) BLACK);
123        hRedBrush = CreateSolidBrush((COLORREF) RED);
124        hGreenBrush = CreateSolidBrush((COLORREF) GREEN);
125        hBlueBrush = CreateSolidBrush((COLORREF) BLUE);
126        // create mutex lock to protect shared data
127        hLock = CreateMutex(NULL,FALSE,NULL);
128
129      ResetPongPos(); // set initial ball position
130        return(0);
131
132      case WM_COMMAND:
133        switch(LOWORD(wParam)){
134        case IDM_START_DEMO:
```

```
135          // start only if it doesn't exist
136          if (!started){
137            // initialize the nCmdMsg array
138            for (i=0;i<NUM_THREADS;i++){
139              nCmdMsg[i] = NOP;
140            }
141
142            hPong = CreateThread(NULL,0,
143                    (LPTHREAD_START_ROUTINE)PongProc,
144                    (LPVOID)BALL,0,(LPDWORD)&ThreadID);
145            hTopPaddle = CreateThread(NULL,0,
146                    (LPTHREAD_START_ROUTINE)PaddleProc,
147                    (LPVOID)TOP,0,(LPDWORD)&ThreadID);
148            hBottomPaddle = CreateThread(NULL,0,
149                    (LPTHREAD_START_ROUTINE)PaddleProc,
150                    (LPVOID)BOTTOM,0,(LPDWORD)&ThreadID);
151            hLeftPaddle = CreateThread(NULL,0,
152                    (LPTHREAD_START_ROUTINE)PaddleProc,
153                    (LPVOID)LEFT,0,(LPDWORD)&ThreadID);
154            hRightPaddle = CreateThread(NULL,0,
155                    (LPTHREAD_START_ROUTINE)PaddleProc,
156                    (LPVOID)RIGHT,0,(LPDWORD)&ThreadID);
157            started = 1;
158          }
159          return(0);
160
161        case IDM_STOP_DEMO:
162          if (started){
163            // send a message to terminate the threads
164            WaitForSingleObject(hLock,INFINITE);
165            for (i=0;i<NUM_THREADS;i++){
166              nCmdMsg[i] = TERMINATE;
167            }
168            started = 0;
169            ReleaseMutex(hLock);
170          }
171          return(0);
172
173        default:
174          return(0);
175        }
176
177        // Terminate the threads and exit
178      case WM_DESTROY:
179        PostQuitMessage (0);
180        return (0);
181      }
182    return DefWindowProc (hwnd, message, wParam, lParam);
183 }
184
185
186 ////////////////////////////////////////////////////////////////////
187 // FUNCTION: PaddleProc
188 // PURPOSE:  Get position of paddle and draws it on screen.
189 //           Each paddle thread will execute this procedure.
```

```
190 ///////////////////////////////////////////////////////////////////
191
192 VOID PaddleProc(LPVOID nLocation)
193 {
194   RECT rect;
195   HDC hDC;
196   int x=0,y=0; // top left coordinate of paddle
197   int myID = (int) nLocation;
198
199   while(1){
200     WaitForSingleObject(hLock,INFINITE);
201
202     // check to see if we need to terminate
203     if (nCmdMsg[myID] == TERMINATE){
204       ReleaseMutex(hLock);
205       return;
206     }
207
208     // move paddle to new position and draw it
209     hDC = GetDC(hWnd);
210     GetClientRect(hWnd, &rect);
211     switch(myID){
212     case TOP:
213       // erase last paddle position
214       SelectObject(hDC, hBlackBrush);
215       Rectangle(hDC,x,y,x+LENGTH,y+WIDTH);
216
217       y = 0;
218       // paddle will correctly stop at left/right edge of screen
219       if (PongPos.x < LENGTH/2)
220         x = 0;
221       else if (rect.right - PongPos.x < LENGTH/2)
222         x = rect.right - LENGTH;
223       else
224         x = PongPos.x - LENGTH/2;
225       //draw paddle
226       SelectObject(hDC, hRedBrush);
227       Rectangle(hDC,x,y,x+LENGTH,y+WIDTH);
228       break;
229
230     case BOTTOM:
231       // erase last paddle position
232       SelectObject(hDC, hBlackBrush);
233       Rectangle(hDC,x,y,x+LENGTH,y+WIDTH);
234
235       y = rect.bottom - WIDTH;
236       if (PongPos.x < LENGTH/2)
237         x = 0;
238       else if (rect.right - PongPos.x < LENGTH/2)
239         x = rect.right - LENGTH;
240       else
241         x = PongPos.x - LENGTH/2;
242       //draw paddle
243       SelectObject(hDC, hRedBrush);
```

```
244          Rectangle(hDC,x,y,x+LENGTH,y+WIDTH);
245          break;
246
247      case LEFT:
248          // erase last paddle position
249          SelectObject(hDC, hBlackBrush);
250          Rectangle(hDC,x,y,x+WIDTH,y+LENGTH);
251
252          x = 0;
253          if (PongPos.y < LENGTH/2)
254            y = 0;
255          else if (rect.bottom - PongPos.y < LENGTH/2)
256            y = rect.bottom - LENGTH;
257          else
258            y = PongPos.y - LENGTH/2;
259          //draw paddle
260          SelectObject(hDC, hBlueBrush);
261          Rectangle(hDC,x,y,x+WIDTH,y+LENGTH);
262          break;
263
264      case RIGHT:
265          // erase last paddle position
266          SelectObject(hDC, hBlackBrush);
267          Rectangle(hDC,x,y,x+WIDTH,y+LENGTH);
268
269          x = rect.right - WIDTH;
270          if (PongPos.y < LENGTH/2)
271            y = 0;
272          else if (rect.bottom - PongPos.y < LENGTH/2)
273            y = rect.bottom - LENGTH;
274          else
275            y = PongPos.y - LENGTH/2;
276          //draw paddle
277          SelectObject(hDC, hBlueBrush);
278          Rectangle(hDC,x,y,x+WIDTH,y+LENGTH);
279          break;
280      }
281      ReleaseDC(hWnd, hDC);
282      ReleaseMutex(hLock);
283    }
284 }
285
286 ////////////////////////////////////////////////////////////////////////
287 // FUNCTION: PongProc
288 // PURPOSE:  Move the ball.
289 ////////////////////////////////////////////////////////////////////////
290
291 VOID PongProc(LPVOID nLocation)
292 {
293    RECT rect;
294    int myID = (int) nLocation;
295
296    while(1){
297      WaitForSingleObject(hLock,INFINITE);
```

```
298
299     // check to see if we need to terminate
300     if (nCmdMsg[myID] == TERMINATE){
301       ReleaseMutex(hLock);
302       ExitThread(1); // yet another way to end a thread's life
303     }
304
305     // erase current ball position
306     DrawPong(ERASE);
307
308     // move ball to new position
309     GetClientRect (hWnd, &rect);
310     // only need to draw ball if it's in window
311     if (InRange(rect)){
312       // move ball to new position
313       PongPos.x += PongDir.x;
314       // if reach edge, change L/R direction for next move
315       if ((PongPos.x == rect.left + WIDTH) ||
316           (PongPos.x == rect.right - WIDTH))
317         PongDir.x = -PongDir.x;
318       PongPos.y += PongDir.y;
319       // if reach edge, change U/D direction for next move
320       if ((PongPos.y == rect.top + WIDTH) ||
321           (PongPos.y == rect.bottom - WIDTH))
322         PongDir.y = -PongDir.y;
323
324       // draw ball at new position
325       DrawPong(DRAW);
326     }
327     ReleaseMutex(hLock);
328   }
329 }
330
331 ////////////////////////////////////////////////////////////////////
332 // FUNCTION: InRange
333 // PURPOSE:  Check and reset ball position in the event of
334 //           window resizing
335 ////////////////////////////////////////////////////////////////////
336
337 int InRange(RECT rect)
338 {
339   int InRange = 1;
340
341   // check to see if pong got out of windows because of resize
342   if (PongPos.x < WIDTH){
343     PongPos.x = WIDTH;
344     PongDir.x = 1;
345     InRange = 0;
346   }
347   else if (PongPos.x > rect.right - WIDTH){
348     PongPos.x = rect.right - WIDTH;
349     PongDir.x = -1;
350     InRange = 0;
351   }
```

```
352    if (PongPos.y < WIDTH){
353      PongPos.y = WIDTH;
354      PongDir.y = 1;
355      InRange = 0;
356    }
357    else if (PongPos.y > rect.bottom - WIDTH){
358      PongPos.y = rect.bottom - WIDTH;
359      PongDir.y = -1;
360      InRange = 0;
361    }
362    return(InRange);
363 }
364
365 ///////////////////////////////////////////////////////////////////
366 // FUNCTION: DrawPong
367 // PURPOSE:  Draw and erase the Pong ball on screen.
368 ///////////////////////////////////////////////////////////////////
369
370 VOID DrawPong(int action)
371 {
372    HDC hDC = GetDC(hWnd);
373
374    if (action == DRAW)
375      SelectObject(hDC, hGreenBrush);
376    else if (action == ERASE)
377      SelectObject(hDC, hBlackBrush);
378
379    Ellipse(hDC,PongPos.x-10,PongPos.y-10,PongPos.x+10,PongPos.y+10);
380    ReleaseDC(hWnd, hDC);
381 }
382
383 ///////////////////////////////////////////////////////////////////
384 // FUNCTION: ResetPongPos
385 // PURPOSE:  Reset the position of Pong when windows is resized.
386 ///////////////////////////////////////////////////////////////////
387
388 VOID ResetPongPos(VOID)
389 {
390    RECT rect;
391    static first_time = 1;
392
393    // When resize windows, reset Pong position
394    WaitForSingleObject(hLock,INFINITE);
395    GetClientRect (hWnd, &rect);
396    PongPos.x = (rect.right/2);
397    PongPos.y = (rect.bottom/2);
398
399    if (first_time){
400      PongDir.x = 1;
401      PongDir.y = 1;
402      first_time = 0;
403    }
404    ReleaseMutex(hLock);
405 }
```

This program has six threads running concurrently: the main window thread, one pong thread, and four paddle threads. When we start the program, lines 122–127 initialize the drawing brushes and a mutex lock (to protect shared data) and set the initial ball position and direction on the screen. When the user starts the game using the pulldown menu, lines 141–155 create five threads for the five game objects. Line 141 starts the ball thread in the function PongProc to move the ball around the screen. This function has no argument and loops indefinitely unless it receives a directive to break out of the loop and end the thread. Lines 144, 147, 150, and 153 each starts an independent paddle thread. They are started with the same function PaddleProc, but the starting argument (TOP, BOTTOM, LEFT, or RIGHT) causes each thread to assume a different position on screen and different behavior. All the threads then execute their own simple piece of code in parallel to make up the program.

The five game threads collaborate with each other by sharing data in memory: the coordinate of the ping-pong ball. Since the ball's position is continuously being read and updated, it must be properly protected from being corrupted by concurrent accesses. For this purpose, a mutex lock is created in line 127, and each thread must obtain this lock before it is able to read or update any shared data (lines 199, 296, and 393). Of course, when a thread finishes using the shared data, it must release the mutex lock so that other threads can access the data as well (lines 281, 326, and 403).

Multithreaded programs can be elegant and efficient, but this programming technique has its own challenges, such as thread synchronization, priority inversion, and deadlock. In the next section, we will briefly describe such challenges, and in the rest of this book we will describe techniques to solve them.

1.5   Challenges of Multithreaded Programming

Concurrency is why multithreaded programming is hard. Unlike sequential programming, where there is only one thread of execution, multithreaded programming involves many threads executing in parallel, and you have to worry about all possible interactions between them. For example, when sharing data between different threads, we have to ensure that one thread doesn't inadvertently corrupt data in another thread. Or, if one thread's activity depends upon those of others, you must synchronize the threads' execution to honor this dependency.

To design a multithreaded application, you have to determine the number of threads in the application. Sometimes, a programming problem suggests a natural division of work, and the number of threads is self-evident. If the cost of creating a thread is high—this depends upon the implementation underlying the thread package—you can create too many threads resulting in poor performance. Moreover, you always have to consider communication and synchronization costs.

Another important issue is to ensure that the multiple threads do not wait for each other in a *deadlock*, without making progress. This can happen when two or more threads hold resources while waiting for other threads to release theirs. Similarly, a condition called *livelock* can occur, where threads execute and keep the CPU busy, but the application as a whole makes no forward progress.

You should also be careful that the application's design results in *fairness:* all threads get a chance to do their work. The application should not get into a state where particular threads *starve* other threads indefinitely regardless of the speed at which the different threads execute or their scheduling order. Since preemptive threads produce nondeterministic behavior, reproducing a problem is difficult with such programs. Debugging a multithreaded program is harder.

To complicate things further, implementors of different operating systems provide varying degrees of thread support. If you are concerned about application portability across platforms, you must understand the thread package architectures of all target platforms in order to design the application for portability.

1.6 Summary

Multithreaded programming is an effective approach to writing concurrent and parallel application programs. Within a multithreaded program, multiple threads of control execute in parallel and share all software or hardware resources available to the program. The concept of a thread has evolved from the concept of a process, which was developed to support time-sharing operating systems. The concepts of thread synchronization have evolved from research in programming languages to supporting concurrent programs. Multithreaded programming has several benefits: speed, efficient resource sharing, efficient hardware utilization, responsive applications, easy access to remote services, and concurrent programming abstraction. These benefits, however, are not easy to achieve. Developing multithreaded programs requires careful consideration of possible parallelism in order to avoid critical synchronization problems. The rest of this book will describe techniques and tools to aid you in overcoming such problems.

1.7 Exercises

1. How is multithreaded programming different from writing a conventional sequential application?

2. What is a process and its address space?

3. Which operating system introduced the idea of separating a *thread of execution* from its *address space*?

4. In the program example, how many threads share the same PaddleProc procedure? How do the threads avoid stepping over each other while sharing this procedure?

5. Who invented the concept of a *semaphore*? What is a semaphore useful for?

6. How is a *monitor* different from a semaphore?

7. List five benefits of multithreaded programming over conventional sequential programming.

8. What makes multithreaded programming hard?

1.8 References

1. Bensoussan, A., Clingen, C. T., and Daley, R. C. (1972). The Multics Virtual Memory: Concepts and Design. *Communications of the ACM*, 15(5):308–318.
2. Burks, A. W., Goldstine, H. H., and von Neumann, J. (1946). Preliminary discussion of the logical design of an electronic computing instrument. Report to the U.S. Army Ordnance Department. Also appears in *Papers of John von Neumann*, W. Aspray and A. Burds, eds., The MIT Press, Cambridge, MA, and Tomash Publishers, Los Angeles, CA, 1987, pp. 97–146.
3. Cheriton, D. R., Malcolm, M. A., Melen, L. S., and Sager, G. R. (1979). Toth, a Portable Real-Time Operating System. *Communications of the ACM*, 22(2):105–115.
4. Corbató, F. J., editor (1963). *The Compatible Time-Sharing System: A Programmer's Guide*. MIT Press, Cambridge, MA.
5. Corbató, F. J. and Vyssotsky, V. A. (1965). Introduction and Overview of the Multics System. In *Proceedings of the AFIPS Fall Joint Computer Conference*, pp. 185–196.
6. Crisman, P. A., editor (1964). *The Compatible Time-Sharing System*. MIT Press, Cambridge, MA.
7. Dahl, O. J. (1972). Hierarchical Program Structures. In *Structured Programming*. Academic Press, New York.
8. Dijkstra, E. W. (1968). Cooperating sequential processes. In Genuys, F., ed., *Programming Languages*. Academic Press, New York.
9. Goldberg, A. and Robson, D. (1983). *Smalltalk-80: The Language and its Implementation*. Addison-Wesley, Reading, MA.
10. Hansen, P. B. (1975). The Programming Language Concurrent Pascal. *IEEE Transactions on Software Engineering*, SE-1(2):199–207.
11. Hoare, C. A. R. (1974). Monitors: An Operating System Structuring Concept. *Communications of the ACM*, 17(10):549–557.
12. Lett, A. S. and Konigsford, W. L. (1968). TSS/360: A Time-Shared Operating System. In *Proceedings of the AFIPS Fall Joint Computer Conference*, volume 33, pp. 15–28, Montvale, NJ.
13. Rashid, R. F. (1986). Threads of a new system. *Unix Review*, pp. 37–49.
14. Saltzer, J. H. (1966). *Traffic Control in a Multiplexed Computer System*. Ph.D thesis, Massachusetts Institute of Technology.
15. Stroustrup, B. (1994). *The Design and Evolution of C++*. Addison-Wesley Publishing Company, Reading, MA.
16. Vyssotsky, V. A., Corbató, F. J., and Graham, R. M. (1965). Structure of the Multics Supervisor. In *Proceedings of the AFIPS Fall Joint Computer Conference*, pp. 203–212.

Win32 Thread Interface

*I*n this chapter, we introduce the Win32 thread API and illustrate its use with a simple example program. We start by discussing some basic operating system concepts: threads, processes and their management, and scheduling. Then we describe the concepts of thread synchronization, and demonstrate their utility via the Win32 synchronization objects.

Using the concepts explained in this chapter, you can immediately start to write simple multithreaded programs for the Win32 platforms.

2.1 Processes and Threads

In Windows operating system, a *process* is a collection of system resources like memory address space, file and device handles, security attributes, synchronization objects, plus at least one *thread of execution*. Each *thread* in a process also has private resources: kernel and user stacks, a set of registers and object attributes, and a program counter. Threads in a process access and share all the resources of the process; for example, all threads can access the same memory space. A process is an operating system object with several properties: security attributes, execution context, scheduling priority, and processor affinity; these properties affect all threads running in the process's address space (see Figure 2-1).

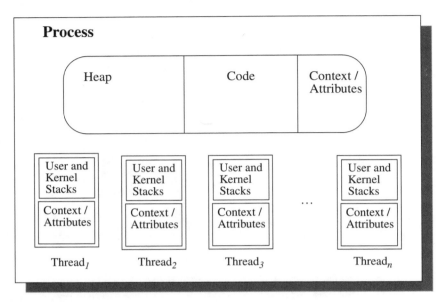

Figure 2-1. Process and Threads.

2.2 Thread Management Concepts

A thread is the basic unit of execution. At any given time, one thread gets to execute on a processor while others wait for resources or a chance to run. The operating system decides which thread gets the processor, and for how long, based upon its internal scheduling algorithms and policies.

2.2.1 Thread States

Usually, we think of a thread's state as being either running or not running, runable or not runable. In Windows NT, a thread can be in one of six states: **ready**, **standby**, **running**, **waiting**, **transition**, or **terminated**.

In the **ready** state, a thread may be scheduled for execution. The kernel keeps track of the number of ready threads and their priorities. When the dispatcher is ready to pick a thread to run next, it chooses the thread with the highest priority from the set of **ready** threads. The state of the selected thread changes to **standby**, and the thread waits its turn to run on a processor at the next context switch.

In the **standby** state, a thread designated to run on a particular processor waits for the processor to become available. Naturally, there can only be one **standby** thread per processor. If the priority of a standby thread is not high enough to preempt the running thread, it must wait for the next context switch. When the running thread blocks or finishes its time slice, a context switch occurs, and the standby thread begins to run on the processor. At this point, its state changes to **running**.

The **running** state indicates that a thread is executing instructions on the processor until its time slice runs out, or it is preempted, blocked, or terminated. If a running thread is preempted, or if its time slice runs out, it goes back to the **ready** state and is later ready to be scheduled to run again. If the thread is terminated, its state becomes **terminated**. If it awaits the occurrence of some event, it enters the **waiting** state.

In the **waiting** state, a thread is suspended while waiting for something to happen, such as keyboard or mouse input, the signaling of a synchronization object, and so forth. When the event happens, the thread can directly enter the **ready** state if the resources it needs to run are available. Otherwise, it goes to the **transition** state to wait while the system fetches the required resources, and then to the **ready** state.

In the **transition** state, a thread is ready to run but the resources it needs are not readily available. When the resources are available, the thread goes to the **ready** state, and is enabled for scheduling.

In the **terminate** state, the thread ceases execution. A thread can terminate itself, be terminated by other threads, or die when its parent process is terminated. At this point, the thread is removed from the system if there are no pending handles to it. When all handles to a terminated thread are closed, the system may reclaim the thread resources and reinitialize it for another thread creation.

Figure 2-2 is a state transition diagram showing possible states during a thread's life cycle.

2.2.2   Thread Scheduling

The modern Windows operating systems (Windows 95, 98, and NT) are truly multitasking environments because they allow many processes and applications to be run concurrently. The scheduling policy of these operating system is *preemptive multitasking*. Each program believes it has the whole machine to itself, while behind this abstraction, the actual hardware is limited to the number of processors, the available physical memory, and other system resources.

In order to emulate a virtual machine for each process, the operating system provides each process with a virtual address space, and it simulates parallelism by dividing processor time among running threads. A unit of time during which a thread can execute on a processor is called a *time slice* or *time quantum*.

Normally, each thread waits for its turn to utilize a processor. When the time quantum of a running thread runs out, that thread is temporarily taken off the processor to allow another thread to execute. The first thread has been *preempted*. When it is time for the preempted thread to use the processor again, the operating system restores the state of the thread and allows it to continue executing.

Preemption can also occur if a thread with higher priority needs the processor. We will discuss thread priorities in detail shortly. For now, it suffices to say that the operating system uses preemption to schedule higher-priority threads before lower-priority ones. If we have many high-priority threads running in the system, they can potentially deprive lower-priority threads of processor time, so the latter cannot make progress. This condition is called *starvation*. When working with threads and priorities, therefore, we must use discretion when raising a thread or process's priority above the normal level, because it can potentially disrupt other threads and processes.

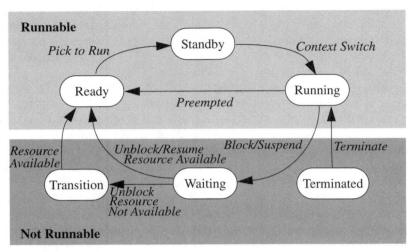

Figure 2-2. Possible Thread States.

When a thread is preempted, the operating system must perform a *context switch* to run a new thread.

2.2.3   Context Switch

A *context switch* is a sequence of events in which a running thread is temporarily stopped and removed from the processor in favor of executing another thread.   In order to resume the preempted thread later, all information relevant to its execution (the thread's *context*), such as the program counter, register values, address space pointer, kernel and user stack pointers, and so on, is saved by the kernel. When it is time to resume the preempted thread's execution, the kernel performs another context switch (swapping out the running thread) to reinstall its context.

Preemption by a higher-priority thread is one reason that causes a context switch. A thread can also cause a context switch to occur when it voluntarily yields the processor, or when it waits for events or synchronization. The processor can thus be reallocated to let other threads make progress.

For example, suppose a keyboard input event occurs that satisfies a blocked thread. The kernel changes the thread's status and triggers the *dispatcher*. The dispatcher then checks the ready threads to determine whether a context switch is necessary. If the priority of a ready thread is higher than that of the running thread, the dispatcher performs a context switch to the former, preempting the latter.

2.3 Thread Management Interface

The Win32 API provides several functions to create and manipulate threads in a multithreaded program: `CreateThread`, `ExitThread`, `TerminateThread`, `SuspendThread`, and `ResumeThread`. A thread is an operating system object with a handle. Many routines operate on a thread handle to manipulate the thread or to synchronize with it.

2.3.1   Thread Creation

A process begins with a single thread of execution. From this initial thread, other threads can be started by calling `CreateThread`:

```
HANDLE CreateThread(
          LPSECURITY_ATTRIBUTES lpsa,
                              // pointer to security attribute struct
          DWORD cbStack,  // stack size (optional)
          LPTHREAD_START_ROUTINE lpStartAddr, // thread start address
          LPVOID lpvThreadParm,  // thread argument
          DWORD fdwCreate,  // flag: 0 or CREATE_SUSPENDED
          LPDWORD lpIDThread // pointer to thread ID
          );
```

The first argument, `lpsa`, is a pointer to a `LPSECURITY_ATTRIBUTE` structure that contains a *security descriptor.* You can use fields of the security descriptor to create handles with limited privileges. For instance, you can choose to create a thread and return a handle such that no other thread can use that handle to suspend the thread. A security descriptor also contains a flag indicating whether a thread handle will be inherited by any subprocesses created within this process. If the security descriptor is NULL, the resulting thread handle has all access privileges granted to it, and it will not be inherited by any subprocesses.

The second argument specifies the size of the new thread's stack in bytes. If this argument is NULL, the new thread's stack size defaults to that of the process's initial thread.

The third argument is the address of a function from which the new thread begins execution. This function must have one argument, and it should return an exit code upon termination.

The fourth argument is data to be passed to this function. If the function requires more than one argument, we must bundle them in a single data structure and then pass a pointer to it.

The fifth argument, `fdwCreate`, specifies whether the thread should begin execution immediately. This argument can have one of two values: 0 or CREATE_SUSPENDED. If the argument is 0, the thread is run immediately upon creation; if the argument is CREATE_SUSPENDED, the thread is created but immediately suspended, and it does not run until the function `ResumeThread` is called on its handle.

The last argument, `lpIDThread`, is given the thread ID when the thread is created. The programmer must create a DWORD memory location and pass a pointer to it. This thread ID can also be obtained by a running thread via the function `GetCurrentThreadId`.

```
DWORD GetCurrentThreadId(VOID); // return the current thread ID
```

The `CreateThread` function returns a valid thread handle if it successfully created a thread, or 0 if it failed. If 0 is returned, the user can call the function `GetLastError` to learn more about the error. For example:

```
HANDLE hThread1, hRedPen;
DWORD ThreadID1, ErrorCode;
VOID ThreadProc (HANDLE hDrawPen);

hThread1 = CreateThread (NULL,  // no security attribute,
```

```
                                    // handle cannot be inherited
                    0, // use default stack size
                    (LPTHREAD_START_ROUTINE)ThreadProc, // thread starts here
                     hRedPen, // argument to starting thread
                     0, // start off running
                    (LPDWORD)&ThreadID1 // thread ID put here
                    );
    if (hThread1 == 0){
        ErrorCode = GetLastError();
        // handle error
    }
```

Another function to create threads is `CreateRemoteThread`. As its name suggests, this function creates a thread that runs in another process's address space. The interface for this function is almost identical to `CreateThread`, except for an additional first argument, `hprocess`:

```
HANDLE CreateRemoteThread(
            HANDLE hProcess, // handle to a process to create in
            LPSECURITY_ATTRIBUTES lpsa, // pointer to security
                                // attribute struct
            DWORD cbStack,   // stack size (optional)
            LPTHREAD_START_ROUTINE lpStartAddr, // thread start address
            LPVOID lpvThreadParm,  // thread argument
            DWORD fdwCreate,   // flag: 0 or CREATE_SUSPENDED
            LPDWORD lpIDThread // pointer to thread ID
            );
```

The first argument, `hProcess`, is the handle of the process in which the new thread is to be started. If successful, the function returns a handle for the new thread that you can subsequently use to obtain services from the thread. If `CreateRemoteThread` fails, `NULL` is returned.

In order for this to work, the process handle must have `PROCESS_CREATE_THREAD` access privilege to the process. Moreover, the process requesting creation of the new thread must have knowledge of the target process's address space; for example, it will need to know the address of the function that is to be invoked when the thread is started.

Since the new thread runs in the address space of another process, it will have access to all resources of that process. This can be useful for writing program debuggers and analyzers. A debugger process can fork the process to be debugged, then wait for user commands. To execute a user command (for example, to print out a data structure's contents) the debugger process can start a thread in the target process and collect information necessary for the command.

2.3.2   Thread Handles

The handle of a thread object can be used as an argument to any function that works with threads. Furthermore, a handle can be duplicated for another process's use with the function `DuplicateHandle`. This function returns `TRUE` if successful and `FALSE` otherwise.

```
BOOL DuplicateHandle(
            HANDLE hSourceProcess, // source process handle
            HANDLE hSource, // handle to duplicate
```

```
HANDLE hTargetProcess, // destination process
LPHANDLE lphTarget, // address of new handle
DWORD fdwAccess, // access level for new handle
BOOL fInherit, // inheritable by child process?
DWORD fdwOptions // optional actions
);
```

When a thread handle is no longer needed, it can be closed by calling `CloseHandle`. This function returns `TRUE` or `FALSE` to indicate its success status.

```
BOOL CloseHandle (HANDLE hObject); // close the object handle
```

Each thread object has a reference count to keep track of its active handles. When a thread is first created, the reference count is 1. Every time a thread handle is duplicated, its reference count increases by 1. On the other hand, if a thread terminates or a handle to it is closed, its reference count decreases by 1. When a thread's reference count reaches 0, the system removes the thread. For efficiency, the system may reinitialize the data structures of a terminated thread to host another thread.

The simplest way for a running thread to obtain its handle is by calling the function `GetCurrentThread`. This function returns a pseudo thread handle that can be used as an argument to any function requiring a thread handle.

```
HANDLE GetCurrentThread(VOID); // return a pseudo-handle to
                               // the current thread
```

A pseudo handle is almost the same as a regular thread handle. It carries the same access privileges as a real thread handle, and can be used as an argument to any function that expects a thread handle. One difference is that creating a pseudo handle does not increment the thread's reference count. Correspondingly, calling `CloseHandle` on a pseudo handle has no effect on the reference count.

Another difference is that a pseudo handle always points to the current thread. For example, if a thread calls the function `GetCurrentThread`, the returned pseudo handle points to the calling thread. If this thread creates a new thread and passes the pseudo handle to the child thread, then, in the context of the child thread, the pseudo handle points to the child, not to the parent.

2.3.3 Thread Termination

A thread can end its own execution by calling `ExitThread` with an exit code. This function is implicitly called when a thread ends by returning from the thread's initial procedure. Its interface is:

```
VOID ExitThread(DWORD dwExitCode);
```

When the last thread in a process terminates, the process also terminates.

Alternately, any thread in a process can terminate itself or another thread in that process by calling `TerminateThread`:

```
BOOL TerminateThread(HANDLE hThread, DWORD dwExitCode);
```

The first argument of this function is the handle of the thread to be terminated. The second argument is an exit code, just like that of the `ExitThread` function. If the function is successful, it returns TRUE; if not, it returns FALSE, and you can call GetLastError to obtain more detailed error information.

When a thread calls TerminateThread, the target thread is terminated immediately and unconditionally, with no chance to clean up. As discussed above, even when the thread is terminated, it would not be purged from the system until its reference count reaches 0. Also, once a thread is terminated it takes on a *signaled* state, satisfying all subsequent *wait* operations on it. We will discuss synchronization of threads later in this chapter.

Since threads belong to their parent processes, terminating a process also means ending all its threads. Thus, another way to terminate all threads in a process is by calling Exit-Process or TerminateProcess functions:

```
VOID ExitProcess (UINT fuExitCode);
BOOL TerminateProcess(HANDLE hProcess, UINT uExitCode);
```

Calling the function ExitThread is the most controlled way of ending a thread, and it is the preferred method.

2.3.4   Thread Suspension and Resumption

A thread's execution can be suspended by calling the function SuspendThread, and resumed by calling ResumeThread. These have the following interfaces:

```
DWORD SuspendThread(HANDLE hThread);
DWORD ResumeThread(HANDLE hThread);
```

Each function takes a thread handle as an argument and returns the thread's previous *suspend count* if it is successful. If the function fails, it returns -1 to indicate an error. The suspend count is a reference count indicating how many times the thread has been suspended since it last ran. For example, a running thread has a suspend count of 0. A call to SuspendThread on a running thread increases its suspend count to 1, causing the thread to be suspended. If you call SuspendThread again and again without calling ResumeThread, the suspend count can increase up to the predefined value MAXIMUM_SUSPEND_COUNT. As long as the suspend count remains larger than zero, the thread continues to be suspended.

A call to ResumeThread has the reverse effect: decreasing the suspend count. Every call to ResumeThread decreases a thread's suspend count by 1, and returns the previous suspend count value. When the suspend count reaches 0, the thread becomes eligible to run; otherwise, it remains suspended. Calling ResumeThread when the suspend count is 0 has no effect. For example:

```
HANDLE hThread;

for (i=0; i<10; i++)
   SuspendThread(hThread);
...
// resume thread
while(ResumeThread(hThread));
```

In this example, we suspended a thread 10 times, then later resumed its execution. Note that the while loop calls ResumeThread 11 times, since the value returned by the function is the *previous* suspend count. But since extraneous ResumeThread calls have no effect, no harm is done.

2.3.5 Threads and C Runtime Libraries

The `CreateThread` and `ExitThread` functions of the Win32 API work well if your application does not use the C runtime library. If your multithreaded application make use of functions and data structures in the C runtime library (i.e., strtok, printf, scanf, errno, etc.), you'll need to call the function _beginthreadex instead of `CreateThread`, allowing it to initialize certain per-thread C runtime datablock and variables. Correspondingly, you'll need to call the function _endthreadex instead of `ExitThread`, as it would need to clean up the per-thread data structures created by _beginthreadex. Microsoft provides a multithreaded version of the C runtime library, `libcmt.lib`, that you should use for multithreaded programs.

The signature of _beginthreadex and _endthread are very similar to those of `CreateThread` and `ExitThread`:

```
unsigned long _beginthreadex(
                void *security,
                unsigned stack_size,
                unsigned (__stdcall *start_address)(void *),
                void *arglist,
                unsigned initflag,
                unsigned *thrdaddr);


void _endthreadex(unsigned retval);
```

In addition, the C runtime library also contains two simpler siblings to the above functions called _beginthread and _endthread, which are older and in many ways more limited:

```
unsigned long _beginthread(
                void(__cdecl *start_address)(void*),
                unsigned stack_size,
                void *arglist );


void _endthread(void);
```

The function _beginthread does not have the arguments *security, stack_size, initflag,* and *thraddr*, so there is no way to specify the security attribute, create the thread in suspended mode, or retrieve the thread ID. The function _endthread does not take an argument, so there is no way for a thread to send back the thread exit code. Furthermore, _endthread closes the thread handle (whereas _endthreadex and `ExitThread` do not!), so when using this function, the user should not explicitly close the thread handle by calling `CloseHandle` from the Win32 API.

As the reader can see, the functions _beginthread and _endthread deviate quite a bit from the signature and behavior of _beginthreadex, _endthreadex, `CreateThread`, and `ExitThread`, we recommend that the readers use the functions _beginthreadex and _endthreadex. Again, these functions are only necessary when your program uses the C runtime library. Otherwise, the functions `CreateThread` and `ExitThread` in the Win32 API are perfectly adequate for your needs.

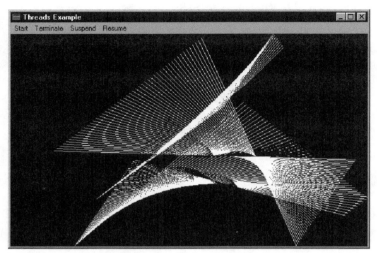

Figure 2-3. Screen Image of the LineSweep Application.

2.4 Example Program: LineSweep

Using functions described so far, we can create, terminate, suspend, and resume threads. Let's see how they work in the following "LineSweep" application that draws sweeping lines across the screen in seemingly random paths.

The program lets a user pull down menus to create, suspend, resume, and terminate three threads. Each thread draws a different line pattern on the screen, and uses a separate color: red, green, or blue. Figure 2-3 shows a screen image of this application.

In this program, the `WinMain` function initializes the windows, interacts with a user, and dispatches event messages based upon user selection.

```
1    ///////////////////////////////////////////////////////////////////
2    // PROGRAM: lines.c
3    // PURPOSE: To demonstrate thread creation and management API
4    ///////////////////////////////////////////////////////////////////
5
6    #include <stdio.h>
7    #include <windows.h>
8    #include <stdlib.h>
9    #include "lines.h"
10
11   #define NUM_THREADS 3
12   #define ACTIVE 1
13   #define SUSPENDED 2
14   #define TERMINATED 3
15
16   HANDLE hInst;
17   HANDLE hWnd;
18   HANDLE hBlackPen, hRedPen, hGreenPen, hBluePen;
19   HANDLE hTermRed, hTermGreen, hTermBlue;
```

```
20
21   int THR_RED = 0;
22   int THR_GREEN = 1;
23   int THR_BLUE = 2;
24
25   int nThreadState[NUM_THREADS];
26
27   ThrArgs RedArgs, GreenArgs, BlueArgs;
28
29   ///////////////////////////////////////////////////////////////////////
30   // FUNCTION: WinMain
31   // PURPOSE: calls initialization function, processes message loop
32   ///////////////////////////////////////////////////////////////////////
33
34   int APIENTRY WinMain (HANDLE hInstance,
35                HANDLE hPrevInstance,
36                LPSTR  lpCmdLine,
37                int    nCmdShow)
38   {
39     MSG  msg;
40     WNDCLASS wc;
41
42     UNREFERENCED_PARAMETER( lpCmdLine );
43     UNREFERENCED_PARAMETER( hPrevInstance );
44
45     hInst = hInstance;
46
47     wc.style = CS_VREDRAW | CS_HREDRAW;
48     wc.lpfnWndProc = (WNDPROC)MainWndProc;
49     wc.cbClsExtra = 0;
50     wc.cbWndExtra = 0;
51     wc.hInstance = hInstance;
52     wc.hIcon = LoadIcon (NULL, IDI_APPLICATION);
53     wc.hCursor = LoadCursor (NULL, IDC_ARROW);
54     wc.hbrBackground = GetStockObject (BLACK_BRUSH);
55     wc.lpszMenuName = "Threads_Menu";
56     wc.lpszClassName = "ThreadsWClass";
57
58     RegisterClass(&wc);
59     hWnd = CreateWindow ("ThreadsWClass",
60                 "Threads Example",
61                 WS_OVERLAPPEDWINDOW,
62                 CW_USEDEFAULT,
63                 CW_USEDEFAULT,
64                 CW_USEDEFAULT,
65                 CW_USEDEFAULT,
66                 NULL,
67                 NULL,
68                 hInstance,
69                 NULL);
70     ShowWindow(hWnd, nCmdShow);
71
72     while (GetMessage (&msg, NULL, 0, 0))
73       DispatchMessage (&msg);   // Dispatch message to window.
```

```
74
75    return (msg.wParam); // Returns value from PostQuitMessage.
76  }
```

The next function, MainWndProc, receives dispatched messages, processes them, and manipulates threads. For example, if the user selects Create-BlueThread from the menu, WinMain dispatches the message IDM_START_BLUE; MainWndProc processes this message and calls the CreateThread function on line 156. Other menu selections to suspend, resume, and terminate threads are handled similarly.

```
77   //////////////////////////////////////////////////////////////////////
78   // FUNCTION: MainWndProc()
79   // PURPOSE:  Process windows messages, create draw pens, create and
80   // terminate drawing threads.
81   //////////////////////////////////////////////////////////////////////
82
83   LONG APIENTRY MainWndProc (HWND hwnd,
84               UINT message,
85               UINT wParam,
86               LONG lParam)
87   {
88     PAINTSTRUCT ps;
89     DWORD  ThreadID1, ThreadID2, ThreadID3;
90     static HANDLE hThread1, hThread2, hThread3;
91     int i;
92
93     switch (message)
94     {
95     case WM_PAINT:
96       BeginPaint (hwnd, &ps);
97       EndPaint (hwnd, &ps);
98       return (0);
99
100    case WM_CREATE :
101      // create the color drawing pens
102      hBlackPen = CreatePen(PS_SOLID,1,(COLORREF) BLACK);
103      hRedPen = CreatePen(PS_SOLID,1,(COLORREF) RED);
104      hGreenPen = CreatePen(PS_SOLID,1,(COLORREF) GREEN);
105      hBluePen = CreatePen(PS_SOLID,1,(COLORREF) BLUE);
106
107      // create the event objects to later terminate threads
108      hTermRed = CreateEvent(NULL,
109            TRUE, // manual-reset event
110            FALSE, // initial state
111            "TerminateRed");
112      hTermGreen = CreateEvent(NULL,
113             TRUE, // manual-reset event
114             FALSE, // initial state
115             "TerminateGreen");
116      hTermBlue = CreateEvent(NULL,
117            TRUE, // manual-reset event
118            FALSE, // initial state
119            "TerminateBlue");
```

```
120
121     for (i=0;i<NUM_THREADS;i++){
122       nThreadState[i] = TERMINATED;
123     }
124
125     return(0);
126
127   case WM_COMMAND:
128     switch(LOWORD(wParam)){
129     case IDM_START_RED:        // start RED thread
130       // start only if it doesn't exist*/
131       if (nThreadState[THR_RED] == TERMINATED){
132         RedArgs.hPen = hRedPen;
133         RedArgs.hTermEvent = hTermRed;
134         hThread1 = CreateThread (NULL, 0,
135                 (LPTHREAD_START_ROUTINE)LineSweep,
136                 (LPVOID)&RedArgs, 0, (LPDWORD)&ThreadID1);
137         nThreadState[THR_RED] = ACTIVE;
138       }
139       return(0);
140
141     case IDM_START_GREEN:
142       if (nThreadState[THR_GREEN] == TERMINATED){
143         GreenArgs.hPen = hGreenPen;
144         GreenArgs.hTermEvent = hTermGreen;
145         hThread2 = CreateThread (NULL, 0,
146                 (LPTHREAD_START_ROUTINE)LineSweep,
147                 (LPVOID)&GreenArgs, 0, (LPDWORD)&ThreadID2);
148         nThreadState[THR_GREEN] = ACTIVE;
149       }
150       return(0);
151
152     case IDM_START_BLUE:
153       if (nThreadState[THR_BLUE] == TERMINATED){
154         BlueArgs.hPen = hBluePen;
155         BlueArgs.hTermEvent = hTermBlue;
156         hThread3 = CreateThread (NULL, 0,
157                 (LPTHREAD_START_ROUTINE)LineSweep,
158                 (LPVOID)&BlueArgs, 0, (LPDWORD)&ThreadID3);
159         nThreadState[THR_BLUE] = ACTIVE;
160       }
161       return (0);
162
163     // terminate threads
164     case IDM_TERMINATE_RED:
165       if (nThreadState[THR_RED] == ACTIVE) {
166         SetEvent(hTermRed);
167         hThread1 = NULL;
168         nThreadState[THR_RED] = TERMINATED;
169       }
170       return(0);
171
172     case IDM_TERMINATE_GREEN:
173       if (nThreadState[THR_GREEN] == ACTIVE) {
```

```
174        SetEvent(hTermGreen);
175        hThread2 = NULL;
176        nThreadState[THR_GREEN] = TERMINATED;
177        }
178      return(0);
179
180    case IDM_TERMINATE_BLUE:
181      if (nThreadState[THR_BLUE] == ACTIVE) {
182        SetEvent(hTermBlue);
183        hThread3 = NULL;
184        nThreadState[THR_BLUE] = TERMINATED;
185        }
186      return(0);
187
188    // suspending threads
189    case IDM_SUSPEND_RED:
190      if (nThreadState[THR_RED] != TERMINATED){
191        SuspendThread(hThread1);
192        nThreadState[THR_RED] = SUSPENDED;
193      }
194      return(0);
195
196    case IDM_SUSPEND_GREEN:
197      if (nThreadState[THR_GREEN] != TERMINATED){
198        SuspendThread(hThread2);
199        nThreadState[THR_GREEN] = SUSPENDED;
200      }
201      return(0);
202
203    case IDM_SUSPEND_BLUE:
204      if (nThreadState[THR_BLUE] != TERMINATED){
205        SuspendThread(hThread3);
206        nThreadState[THR_BLUE] = SUSPENDED;
207      }
208      return(0);
209
210    // resume threads
211    case IDM_RESUME_RED:
212      if (nThreadState[THR_RED] == SUSPENDED){
213        int count = ResumeThread(hThread1);
214        if (count <= 1){
215           nThreadState[THR_RED] = ACTIVE;
216        }
217      }
218      return(0);
219
220    case IDM_RESUME_GREEN:
221      if (nThreadState[THR_GREEN] == SUSPENDED){
222        int count = ResumeThread(hThread2);
223        if (count <= 1){
224           nThreadState[THR_GREEN] = ACTIVE;
225        }
226      }
227      return(0);
```

```
228
229        case IDM_RESUME_BLUE:
230          if (nThreadState[THR_BLUE] == SUSPENDED){
231            int count = ResumeThread(hThread3);
232            if (count <= 1){
233              nThreadState[THR_BLUE] = ACTIVE;
234            }
235          }
236          return(0);
237
238        default:
239          return(0);
240      }
241
242    case WM_DESTROY:
243      PostQuitMessage (0);
244      return (0);
245    }
246    return DefWindowProc (hwnd, message, wParam, lParam);
247 }
```

The first procedure that each new thread executes is LineSweep. It contains an infinite loop so that the thread, once started, continuously draws sweeping line paths across the screen until the thread is suspended or told to terminate by the main window thread.

As the reader may notice, in this example, we introduce yet another way to safely terminate a thread (by not using the TerminateThread function). When the program starts up, it creates three event objects (lines 108, 112, 116) that are polled by each of the LineSweep threads (line 291). When the user terminates a thread from the menu, the associated event object is set (lines 166, 174, 182), the associated thread sees the signaled event object and self-terminate (lines 291–295).

```
248 ////////////////////////////////////////////////////////////////////
249 // FUNCTION: LineSweep()
250 // PURPOSE:  Each draw thread begins here, has a different color pen.
251 // Each thread sweeps across the screen and draw lines using its pen.
252 ////////////////////////////////////////////////////////////////////
253
254 VOID LineSweep (ThrArgs *hArgs)
255 {
256    DWORD coords[SWEEPSIZE][4];
257    DWORD status;
258    int x1, y1, x2, y2;
259    int dx1, dy1, dx2, dy2;
260    int size = 0;
261    int current_pos = 0;
262    RECT rect;
263    HANDLE hDrawPen = hArgs->hPen;
264    HANDLE hTermEvent = hArgs->hTermEvent;
265
266    // first time: initialize
267    GetClientRect (hWnd, &rect);
268
```

```
269    // prefer to set these with random values
270    x1 = GetTickCount() % rect.right;
271    y1 = GetTickCount() % rect.bottom;
272    x2 = GetTickCount() % rect.right;
273    y2 = GetTickCount() % rect.bottom;
274
275    dx1 = 2;
276    dy1 = 3;
277    dx2 = -5;
278    dy2 = -4;
279
280    coords[current_pos][X1] = x1;
281    coords[current_pos][Y1] = y1;
282    coords[current_pos][X2] = x2;
283    coords[current_pos][Y2] = y2;
284
285    DrawLine(hWnd, hDrawPen, x1, y1, x2, y2);
286
287    size = 1;
288    current_pos = ((current_pos + 1) % SWEEPSIZE);
289    while (1){
290      // check to see if this thread has to self-terminate
291      status = WaitForSingleObject(hTermEvent,0);
292      if (status == WAIT_OBJECT_0){
293        // obj has been signaled, exit thread
294        ResetEvent(hTermEvent);
295        ExitThread(1);
296      }
297
298      GetClientRect (hWnd, &rect);
299
300      // compute new coords to draw
301      if (x1 >= rect.right){
302        x1 = rect.right -1;
303        dx1 = -dx1;
304      }
305      else if (x1 <= 0){
306        x1 = 1;
307        dx1 = -dx1;
308      }
309      if (x2 >= rect.right){
310        x2 = rect.right -1;
311        dx2 = -dx2;
312      }
313      else if (x2 <= 0){
314        x2 = 1;
315        dx2 = -dx2;
316      }
317      if (y1 >= rect.bottom){
318        y1 = rect.bottom -1;
319        dy1 = -dy1;
320      }
321      else if (y1 <= 0){
322        y1 = 1;
```

```
323          dy1 = -dy1;
324        }
325        if (y2 >= rect.bottom){
326          y2 = rect.bottom -1;
327          dy2 = -dy2;
328        }
329        else if (y2 <= 0){
330          y2 = 1;
331          dy2 = -dy2;
332        }
333
334        x1 += dx1;
335        y1 += dy1;
336        x2 += dx2;
337        y2 += dy2;
338
339        if (size == SWEEPSIZE){
340          // erase line at current position
341          DrawLine(hWnd, hBlackPen,
342              coords[current_pos][X1], coords[current_pos][Y1],
343              coords[current_pos][X2], coords[current_pos][Y2]);
344        }
345        else {
346          size++;
347        }
348
349        // draw line from x1,y1 to x2,y2
350        DrawLine(hWnd, hDrawPen, x1, y1, x2, y2);
351
352        coords[current_pos][X1] = x1;
353        coords[current_pos][Y1] = y1;
354        coords[current_pos][X2] = x2;
355        coords[current_pos][Y2] = y2;
356
357        current_pos = ((current_pos + 1) % SWEEPSIZE);
358
359        Sleep(10);  // optional, slow down to make things look good
360    }
361 }
362
363
364 ////////////////////////////////////////////////////////////////////
365 // FUNCTION: DrawLine
366 // PURPOSE:  draw a line between two coordinates using given pen
367 ////////////////////////////////////////////////////////////////////
368
369 VOID DrawLine(HWND hWnd, HANDLE hDrawPen,
370             DWORD x1, DWORD y1, DWORD x2, DWORD y2)
371
372 {
373   HDC hDC = GetDC(hWnd);
374
375   SelectObject(hDC, hDrawPen);
376   MoveToEx(hDC, x1, y1, NULL) ;
```

```
377    LineTo(hDC, x2, y2);
378    ReleaseDC (hWnd, hDC);
379 }
```

At this point we encourage you to think of writing this application as a single-threaded program; you will then realize some advantages of multithreaded programming. For example, in a single-threaded program, we have to explicitly schedule each different-colored line.

2.5 Thread Synchronization

One advantage of multithreaded programming is that you can speed up a program by dividing it into independent threads; the threads can execute concurrently. For example, suppose we have to program a server application that accepts requests from and provides services to client applications. Using multithreaded programming, we can implement this application with a dispatcher thread that listens to client requests, and then create a separate thread to handle each such request concurrently. The problem with this strategy, however, is that we must properly synchronize the several server threads if they access shared data, in order to ensure that updates do not interfere with one another. In other words, one thread may need to wait for another to finish before it can proceed.

To illustrate this problem, suppose we have a server that maintains a joint bank account and supports transactions like *open*, *deposit*, *withdraw*, and *close*. Suppose the server gets two simultaneous requests to perform $50 and $100 deposits. The server creates threads A and B to handle the requests. Obviously, each thread must increase the current account balance by its amount to be deposited. Since the two threads access the same account balance, it is possible that one thread (B) gets the account balance and computes the new amount, but before writing back the new balance, a context switch occurs and it is swapped out. Suppose the other thread (A) then has the processor and successfully completes its deposit transaction. When thread B is allowed to run again, it continues its work by updating the bank account balance with its own version of the balance. This problem is illustrated in Table 2–1.

What happened is that we just lost one deposit transaction because the account balance was overwritten. This type of error looms every time we have unsynchronized concurrent threads accessing common data.

Time	Thread A (Deposit $100)	Account Balance	Thread B (Deposit $50)
t_o		$200	i = balance
t_1	Context Switch		
t_2	i = balance		
t_3	balance = i + 100	$300	
t_4	Context Switch		
t_5		$250	balance = i + 50

Table 2–1. Problem Resulting from Lack of Thread Synchronization.

In order to make this work, we need to ensure that while a thread is reading or writing the account balance, no other thread can do the same. This can be done by using a *synchronization* object.

Before accessing the account balance, a thread has to *wait* to acquire ownership of a synchronization object. Once it does so, it can read and write on the account balance as it wishes. After it has finished accessing the balance, it must *release* the synchronization object, after which any other waiting thread can get a chance to access the account balance. Table 2–2 shows how this solves the problem shown in Table 2–1.

Time	Thread A (Deposit $100)	Account Balance	Thread B (Deposit $50)	Synchronization Object
t_0	Wait for Synchronization Object	$200	Wait for Synchronization Object	
t_1				With Thread B
t_2			i = balance;	With Thread B
t_3			balance = i + 50;	With Thread B
t_4		$250	Release Synchronization Object	Available
t_5	i = balance			With Thread A
t_6	balance = i + 100	$350		With Thread A
t_7	Release Synchronization Object			Available

Table 2–2. Thread Synchronization Using Synchronization Objects.

The Win32 API provides several kinds of synchronization objects: *mutexes*, *critical sections*, *semaphores*, and *events*. Objects such as *processes* and *threads* can also be used as synchronization objects. The next section introduces the thread synchronization objects and functions. Since synchronization is an important aspect of multithreaded programming, we will return to this topic in later chapters.

2.5.1 Wait Operations

A synchronization object can have one of two states: *signaled* (available) or *not-signaled* (owned). A thread wishing to synchronize using one of these objects must call `Wait-ForSingleObject`, or call `WaitForMultipleObjects` to use a set of them.

```
DWORD WaitForSingleObject(
            HANDLE hObject, // object to wait for
            DWORD dwTimeout // timeout duration in milliseconds
            );
```

`WaitForSingleObject` accepts a synchronization object handle plus a timeout argument. The timeout value can be 0, `INFINITE`, or some milliseconds. If the synchronization object's state is *signaled*, the function returns 0, indicating success, after updating the state. If the object's state is *not-signaled*, the function blocks until the object is available or the timeout interval expires. In the event of a timeout, the function returns the status word `WAIT_TIMEOUT`.

`WaitForSingleObject` can possibly return `WAIT_ABANDONED`. This occurs when the awaited object is a mutex owned by a thread that terminated without releasing ownership. The mutex is said to be "abandoned." Finally, if the call fails due to an error, the value -1 is returned and the user should call `GetLastError` to obtain more error information. Here is an example of using the `WaitForSingleObject` function:

```
DWORD Status;
HANDLE hMutex = CreateMutex(NULL,FALSE,NULL);
DWORD ErrorCode;
...
Status = WaitForSingleObject(hMutex,1000); // wait for Mutex,
                                    // 1 second timeout

if (Status != 0)
   switch(Status){
       case WAIT_TIMEOUT:
           // time out, recover operation
           ....
           break;
       case WAIT_ABANDONED:
           // abandoned mutex
           ....
           break;
       default:
           ErrorCode = GetLastError();
           // handle error
           ....
   }
```

A thread wishing to wait for one or all conditions in a set may call the `WaitForMultipleObjects` function, passing it a reference to an array of object handles. This function has the following interface:

```
DWORD WaitForMultipleObjects(
           DWORD nCount, // number of objects in array
           LPHANDLE lpHandles, // pointer to array of object
                               // handles to wait for
           BOOL bWaitAll, // wait for any or wait for all
           DWORD dwTimeout // timeout duration in milliseconds
           );
```

The first argument is the size of the array of object handles, which is passed as the second argument. The third argument is a boolean flag. If its value is `TRUE`, the function waits for all objects to be in the *signaled* state at the same time. If the flag value is `FALSE`, the function returns when any object in the array attains the *signaled* state. Because of this "wait for all" behavior, it is easy for this function to block indefinitely if it doesn't time out, possibly creating system deadlock.

A successful "wait-any" call returns the index of the object in signaled state, which is between 0 and nCount-1. An unsuccessful wait returns either WAIT_TIMEOUT or -1. In the event of an abandoned mutex, the status returned is WAIT_ABANDONED_0 plus the index of the abandoned mutex in the array of object handles.

The signaled or not-signaled property of synchronization objects provides a way to protect shared data from being inadvertently corrupted by concurrent accesses. The usual practice is to identify program regions where shared data might be modified by more than one thread. We can then associate each such critical region with a synchronization object to ensure that only a limited number of threads access the region at once. The kind of synchronization object that we use depends upon the program requirements that we'll discuss shortly. Let's now take a look at the synchronization objects provided by the Win32 API.

2.5.2 Mutex

The name "mutex" comes from the words "mutual exclusion." The state of a mutex object is strictly binary: *signaled* or *not-signaled* (owned or not owned). If each thread must acquire ownership of a mutex object before accessing shared data, we are guaranteed that the data accesses will be mutually exclusive because only one thread at a time is allowed to own a mutex.

To create a mutex object, a thread calls CreateMutex with three arguments: a security attribute pointer, an ownership flag, and a mutex name.

```
HANDLE CreateMutex(LPSECURITY_ATTRIBUTE lpsa, // pointer to security
                                      // attribute structure
           BOOL fInitialOwner, // initial ownership?
           LPTSTR lpszMutexName // mutex name string
           );
```

If the security descriptor is NULL, the mutex is created without a security attribute, and any process created by the caller will not inherit the mutex handle. The second argument, if TRUE, specifies that the creator of the mutex takes immediate ownership of it, otherwise, the mutex is available to the first caller of a wait operation on it. The third argument provides a name for the mutex, so other processes that know its name can open it. This argument can be NULL, in which case the mutex is created without a name.

To acquire ownership of the mutex object, a calling thread calls either of the two Wait functions described in the last section, which either block, time out, or eventually succeed. A thread that acquires ownership of the mutex may then execute code in the region "protected" by the mutex. When it leaves that region, the thread must call ReleaseMutex, which sets the mutex to the signaled state and lets another thread acquire ownership.

```
BOOL ReleaseMutex(HANDLE hMutex);
```

The region of code between the acquisition and release of a mutex is often called a *critical section*, in which access among threads is serialized to protect the integrity of shared data. The thread owning the mutex can repeatedly wait for the ownership of the same mutex object without deadlocking itself, but after each wait it must correspondingly call ReleaseMutex.

```
HANDLE hMutex;
char *szMutexName = "foo";
```

```
hMutex = CreateMutex(NULL, FALSE, szMutexName);
if (hMutex == NULL){
    // handle error
}
...
if (WaitForSingleObject(hMutex,INFINITE) != 0){
    // handle error
}
else { // begin critical section
    ...
    ReleaseMutex(hMutex); // release mutex, end critical section
}
```

If a named mutex already exists, we can obtain its handle by calling `OpenMutex` with an access flag, an inherit flag, and a name string:

```
HANDLE OpenMutex(
            DWORD fdwAccess, // access flag
            BOOL fInherit, // inheritable?
            LPTSTR lpszMutexName // mutex name string
            );
```

The first argument has two possible values: MUTEX_ALL_ACCESS or SYNCHRO-NIZE, and it is checked against the security descriptor of the mutex object. The second argument is a boolean, indicating whether the resulting handle is inheritable. The third argument is the name of the mutex.

```
HANDLE hMutex;
char *szMutexName = "foo";

hMutex = OpenMutex(MUTEX_ALL_ACCESS, FALSE, szMutexName);
if (hMutex == NULL)
    // handle error
...
```

2.5.3 Critical Section

Although a *critical section* synchronization object resembles a mutex, it can only be used between threads of the same process. Like a mutex object, only one thread at a time may gain ownership of a critical section object, and a thread can recursively lock this object without deadlocking itself. An attempt to lock such an object either succeeds or blocks until the object is available. There is no timeout option.

Before using a critical section object, a thread must initialize it by calling `InitializeCriticalSection`. A thread can then acquire a critical section by calling `EnterCriticalSection`, and release it by calling `LeaveCriticalSection`. Finally, a thread can destroy such an object by calling `DeleteCriticalSection`. The interfaces of these functions are:

```
InitializeCriticalSection(LPCRITICAL_SECTION lpcs);
EnterCriticalSection(LPCRITICAL_SECTION lpcs);
LeaveCriticalSection(LPCRITICAL_SECTION lpcs);
DeleteCriticalSection(LPCRITICAL_SECTION lpcs);
```

The next example shows how a critical section object is used. Keep in mind that the region of code between `EnterCriticalRegion` and `LeaveCriticalRegion` can only be executed by one thread at a time.

```
LPCRITICAl_SECTION Bar;
InitializeCriticalSection(&Bar); // initialize so all threads can
                                 // use from now on
...
EnterCriticalSection(&Bar); // block until obtain exclusive access
// critical section begins here
...
LeaveCriticalSection(&Bar); // end critical section
...
DeleteCriticalSection(&Bar); // when there is no need for it anymore
```

2.5.4 Semaphore

A *semaphore* object allows only a specified number of concurrent accesses among threads in a critical section. Each semaphore object has a count associated with it, specifying the maximum number of further accesses it can allow. If the count is greater than 0, a wait operation on the semaphore succeeds, and it is reduced by 1. When the count reaches 0, any threads waiting for the semaphore are blocked until some thread releases the semaphore, increasing the count.

A semaphore with a maximum count of 1 is called a *binary semaphore*. Like a mutex, its state can be either signaled or not-signaled to enforce mutual exclusion among threads.

A semaphore can be created by calling the `CreateSemaphore` function. Its arguments are a pointer to a security attribute, an initial count, a maximum count, and a semaphore name.

```
HANDLE CreateSemaphore(
          LPSECURITY_ATTRIBUTES lpsa, // pointer to
                                      // security attribute struct
          LONG cSemInitial, // initial count
          LONG cSemMax, // maximum count
          LPTSTR lpszSemName // optional semaphore name
          );
```

The first argument is a pointer specifying a security descriptor of the semaphore; if the argument is `NULL`, the semaphore will have none. The second argument is the semaphore's initial count, which can be initialized to 0 to prevent any thread from acquiring the semaphore during program initialization. The third argument is the maximum number of concurrent threads that can acquire the semaphore without being blocked. When the semaphore is ready to be used, it can be set to its maximum count by calling the `ReleaseSemaphore` function.

When a wait call using a semaphore succeeds, it decreases the semaphore count by one. When the count reaches 0, subsequent wait calls are blocked until some thread releases ownership of the semaphore by calling `ReleaseSemaphore`. Thus, unlike the mutex object, a thread owning a semaphore object can deadlock itself if it repeatedly calls the wait operation using the same semaphore object.

When a thread finishes executing in a critical section, it calls `ReleaseSemaphore` to increment the semaphore count, enabling another thread to gain ownership of the semaphore. In addition to the semaphore handle, this function takes an additional argument, a long integer, used to increment the semaphore count.

```
BOOL ReleaseSemaphore(HANDLE hSemaphore, // semaphore handle
        LONG cRelease, // count to add to current semaphore count
        LPLONG lplPrevious // (optional) point to a variable
                            //that receives semaphore's last count
        );
```

The following example shows how to use a semaphore object.

```
HANDLE hSemaA;
hSemaA = CreateSemaphore(NULL,0,3,NULL); // create a nameless semaphore
if (hSemA == NULL){
   // handle error
}
...
// more program initialization
 ...
ReleaseSemaphore(hSemaA,3,NULL); // up to 3 can own this, starting now
...
 ...
// need to gain access to semaphore
Status = WaitForSingleObject(hSemaA,INFINITE);
if (Status == -1){
   // handle error
}
// wait is successful, semaphore count just decreased by 1
// access shared resources
...
// release semaphore
ReleaseSemaphore(hSemaA,1,NULL); // increment semaphore count by 1
...
```

2.5.5   Event

Events are synchronization objects that may be used to notify waiting threads when a desired condition occurs. For example, in the manager-worker programming model (see Chapter 8), if there are several worker threads with no jobs, they may register themselves with an event object. When a job becomes available, the manager thread can place it in a job queue and change the state of the event object to wake up a waiting thread in order to perform the task. Using event objects, no thread spends unnecessary processor time in a polling loop looking for work to do.

To use an event object, one must create it, then set or reset its state. Like other synchronization objects, event objects can have one of two states: *signaled* or *not-signaled*. If a thread needs to know when a particular event occurs, it waits by calling either `WaitForSingleObject` or `WaitForMultipleObjects`. When the object is in the signaled state, the wait function returns and the thread may continue executing. If it is in the not-signaled state, the thread blocks until the event is signaled.

To create an event object, a thread calls the function `CreateEvent` with four arguments.

```
HANDLE CreateEvent(
        LPSECURITY_ATTRIBUTE lpsa,
        BOOL fManualReset, // type of create event
        BOOL fInitialState, // initial state
        LPTSTR lpszEventName // name of event object
        );
```

The first argument is a pointer specifying the security attribute of the event handle, indicating whether or not processes subsequently created by the caller will inherit the handle. The second argument is a boolean, indicating the type of event object to be created. The third argument specifies the initial state of the event object: *signaled* or *not-signaled*. The fourth argument is a string naming the event object that a different process can use to refer to the event object.

There are two kinds of event objects: *manual-reset* and *auto-reset*. To create a manual-reset event object, the second argument of `CreateEvent` (`fManualReset`) is set to `TRUE`; but to create an auto-reset event object, the argument is set to `FALSE`. Using a manual-reset event object, you must call `SetEvent` to explicitly set the object to signaled state and `ResetEvent` to reset to the not-signaled state. Between setting and resetting a manual-reset event object, all threads waiting for it are unblocked. When using an auto-reset event object, on the other hand, a call to `SetEvent` will set its state to signaled, let one waiting thread run, then automatically reset the object state to not-signaled. The functions `SetEvent` and `ResetEvent` have the following interface:

```
BOOL SetEvent(HANDLE hEvent);
BOOL ResetEvent(HANDLE hEvent);
```

In addition, there exists a function called `PulseEvent` that conveniently combines the effects of calling `SetEvent` and `ResetEvent`.

```
BOOL PulseEvent(HANDLE hEvent);
```

`PulseEvent` automatically sets, then resets, the state of an event object. Using a manual-reset event object, a call to `PulseEvent` sets the object to the signaled state, releases *all* waiting threads, then resets it to the not-signaled state. Using an auto-reset event object, a call to `PulseEvent` sets the object to signaled state, releases *one* waiting thread, then resets its state. If there are no waiting threads, `PulseEvent` sets and resets the event object, leaving it in a not-signaled state.

2.5.6 Other Synchronization Objects

The process and thread objects can also be synchronization objects. Handles to processes and threads can be passed as arguments to the `WaitForSingleObject` and `WaitForMultipleObjects` functions, and thus can be used for synchronization. When a thread or process terminates, its handle assumes a *signaled* state that satisfies any *wait* for it. This is useful when one thread must synchronize with another thread's exit or a process's termination. Here is an example.

```
HANDLE hThread1;
...
WaitForSingleObject(hThread1,INFINITE); // block until hThread1
                              // is signaled
// hThread1 is signaled (terminated)
// resume operation
...
```

A program may also wait for a file object that assumes the signaled state when file I/O is completed.

2.6 Thread Priorities

The operating system determines a thread's eligibility to run using a set of priority queues. When it is time for a context switch, the dispatcher examines the set of ready threads and selects the head of the highest-priority queue to run. The priority of a thread is determined using its process' priority class, and a thread's base and dynamic priorities. Within each priority level, threads are scheduled using a round-robin, first-come-first-served policy.

The most important component of a thread's priority is its process's priority class. There are four priority classes: *realtime*, *high, normal,* and *idle.* Normally, most processes are started with the NORMAL_PRIORITY_CLASS, which is the default. The next higher priority level, HIGH_PRIORITY_CLASS, is reserved for system processes or very important application processes, which take precedence over all normal processes.

The highest possible priority level is the REALTIME_PRIORITY_CLASS. This priority is reserved for important real-time activity that supersedes even the priority of system processes. Usage of this priority class should be extremely brief, since prolonged execution of threads in this class can halt the entire operating system.

At the other extreme is the IDLE_PRIORITY_CLASS. Processes at this level will only be active when all processes at other priorities are idle. Background processes, such as screen savers, are good candidates for this priority level.

To discover a process's priority class, we can use the GetPriorityClass function:

```
DWORD PriorityClass;
HANDLE hProcess;

hProcess = GetCurrentProcess();
PriorityClass = GetPriorityClass(hProcess);
```

GetPriorityClass accepts one argument, a process handle, and it returns the priority class of that process, or 0 in case of error. Possible return values of the priority class are IDLE_PRIORITY_CLASS, NORMAL_PRIORITY_CLASS, and HIGH_PRIORITY_CLASS.

To modify a process's priority class, the SetPriorityClass function accepts two arguments: a process handle and a process priority class. It returns TRUE if the operation is successful; otherwise, it returns FALSE. Possible values of the priority class argument are IDLE_PRIORITY_CLASS, NORMAL_PRIORITY_CLASS, and HIGH_PRIORITY_CLASS. One must be very careful in using this function, since it can drastically affect the performance of not only the current process, but all processes in the system. For example, raising the priority class of a process (and hence all its threads) to the HIGH_PRIORITY_CLASS could starve all processes in lower priority classes.

```
DWORD ErrorCode;
HANDLE hProcess;
BOOL Status;

hProcess = GetCurrentProcess();
Status = SetPriorityClass(hProcess,HIGH_PRIORITY_CLASS);
if (Status == 0)
   ErrorCode = GetLastError();
```

In order to improve responsiveness, the operating system automatically raises the priority class of a foreground process to the level of the highest-priority background process. By clicking and selecting a window on screen, we bring its process to the foreground. The operating system then assumes that the user is working with that application, and raises its process's priority class to make the application more responsive. When the user selects another foreground application, the first application returns to the background, and its priority class is restored to the original level.

Within each priority class is a thread's base priority level. There are five thread priority levels as follows:

- THREAD_PRIORITY_LOWEST
- THREAD_PRIORITY_BELOW_NORMAL
- THREAD_PRIORITY_NORMAL (default)
- THREAD_PRIORITY_ABOVE_NORMAL
- THREAD_PRIORITY_HIGHEST

A newly created thread has priority THREAD_PRIORITY_NORMAL by default. A program can determine a thread's priority by calling the GetThreadPriority function, which accepts a thread handle argument and returns that thread's priority. If the call fails, it returns a value represented by THREAD_PRIORITY_ERROR_RETURN.

```
int ThreadPriority;
DWORD ErrorCode;
HANDLE hThread;

hThread = GetCurrentThread();
ThreadPriority = GetThreadPriority(hThread);
if (ThreadPriority == THREAD_PRIORITY_ERROR_RETURN){
   ErrorCode = GetLastError();
   // handle error
}
```

A program can raise or lower a thread's base priority by calling the SetThread-Priority function, the interface of which is:

```
BOOL SetThreadPriority(HANDLE hThread, int nPriority);
```

This function accepts a thread handle and an integer priority level, and it returns a boolean value indicating whether the operation is successful. When setting the priority of a thread above the normal level, you must be careful so that lower-priority threads are not starved.

```
    int ThreadPriority = THREAD_PRIORITY_ABOVE_NORMAL;
    DWORD ErrorCode;
    HANDLE hThread;
    BOOL Status;

    hThread = GetCurrentThread();
    Status = SetThreadPriority(hThread,THREAD_PRIORITY_HIGHEST);
    if (Status == 0){
        ErrorCode = GetLastError();
        // handle the error
    }
    else {
        // run some job at high priority
        // return to normal priority
        Status = SetThreadPriority(hThread,THREAD_PRIORITY_NORMAL);
        if (Status == 0){
            ErrorCode = GetLastError();
            // handle the error
        }
    }
```

In addition to a base priority level, which a thread may itself modify, a thread also has a dynamic priority level that is raised or lowered by the operating system when it needs to raise a thread's priority level to make the thread more responsive to certain important events. The amount of priority boost depends upon what event the thread awaits. The scheduling algorithm is internal to the operating system, and this algorithm may and does change over time as Microsoft makes improvements to the system. Generally speaking, the dynamic scheduling policy is that threads awaiting keyboard input get the biggest boost so that they respond to user actions; those awaiting I/O events get a medium boost; and those that are compute-bound get the least boost. For example, when a user types on the keyboard or drags the mouse, the scheduler raises the dynamic priority of the thread handling this input so that the application can be more responsive. After the event has passed, the scheduler gradually lowers the dynamic priority (by one every time slice) until the thread priority returns to its base priority. Hence, the dynamic priority of a thread can never be lower than its base priority.

2.7 Thread Local Storage (TLS)

In conventional single-threaded programs, it is sometimes useful and convenient to use global variables. For example, a text editing program can maintain the text being edited and the position of an insertion point as global variables; functions for text insertion, deletion, modifications, search, and so on can then use those variables as needed. This is easier than passing the information as arguments to each function.

```
1    char *text_buffer;
2    int point;
3    #define BUF_SIZE 1024
4
5    Initialize_buffer()
6    {
7        int i ;
```

```
8      text_buffer = (char *) malloc(BUF_SIZE) ;
9      point = -1 ;
10     for (i = 0; i< BUF_SIZE; i++)
11        text_buffer[i] = '\0' ;
12   }
13
14   Insert(chr)
15   char chr ;
16   {
17     if ((point) > BUF_SIZE)
18        fprintf(stderr, "Cannot insert any more characters!\n") ;
19     else
20        text_buffer[++point] = chr ;
21   }
22
23   Delete()
24   {
25     if (point < 0)
26        fprintf(stderr, "No more characters\n") ;
27     else
28        text_buffer[point--] = '\0' ;
29   }
```

A global variable is a process resource, shared by all threads in that process. But sometimes it is useful to have a variable that is thread-specific—having different values for different thread contexts. For example, suppose we extend our simple example to multiple text buffers and multiple threads, using a thread to manage each buffer. In this case, we would still like to retain the simplicity of using global variables for the text buffer and the point of insertion. If we use them in a conventional way, then we must either use a fixed number of threads and assign independent global variables for each thread, or else maintain a dynamic list of global variables that is accessible to all the threads, where each thread uses the variables it needs. The first scheme is not generally applicable because it limits the number of threads that the application may have. The second is cumbersome to implement, and it unnecessarily exposes all global variables to all threads. A better alternative is variables that have different meanings to different threads.

In the Win32 API, such a mechanism is called Thread Local Storage (TLS). A multi-threaded application can declare a global variable that is a TLS index. Any thread can use a TLS index to store and retrieve data specific to that thread. But data that is stored by one thread in this "global" variable is invisible to other threads.

The TLS interface is provided by the following functions:

```
DWORD TlsAlloc(VOID);
BOOL TlsSetValue(DWORD dwTlsIndex, LPVOID lpTlsValue);
LPVOID TlsGetValue(DWORD dwTlsIndex);
BOOL TlsFree(DWORD dwTlsIndex);
```

The function TlsAlloc allocates a TLS index, which can be used to store and retrieve data in a TLS memory that is allocated for the thread during initialization. The minimum number of TLS indices available to each process are defined by the variable TLS_MINIMUM_AVAILABLE (defined as 64 in Windows NT). TlsAlloc returns TLS_OUT_OF_INDEXES if it fails, and returns a TLS index if it succeeds. When the thread no longer needs a TLS index, it can be freed by calling TlsFree, which returns a boolean indicating success or failure.

After a call to TlsAlloc succeeds, data can be stored in a thread's local storage by calling TlsSetValue. This function takes a TLS index (that was returned by TlsAlloc) and a pointer to the data. To retrieve the pointer, we can call TlsGetValue with the TLS index. The following example shows how TLS is used.

```
1    WORD dwTlsIndex;
2
3    Initialize_buffer()
4    {
5       int *point ;
6       char *text_buffer;
7       int i ;
8
9       point = (int *) malloc(sizeof(int) ;
10      *point = -1 ;
11
12      text_buffer = (char *) malloc(BUF_SIZE) ;
13      for (i=0; i<BUF_SIZE; i++)
14         text_buffer[i] = '\0' ;
15
16      TlsSetValue(dwIndex, point) ;
17      TlsSetValue(dwIndex+1, text_buffer) ;
18   }
19
20   Insert(chr)
21   char *chr ;
22   {
23      int *point;
24      char *text_buffer ;
25
26      point = TlsGetValue(dwIndex) ;
27      text_buffer = TlsGetValue(dwIndex+1) ;
28
29      if ((*point) > BUF_SIZE)
30         fprintf(stderr, "Cannot insert any more characters!\n") ;
31      else
32         text_buffer[++(*point)] = chr ;
33   }
34
35   Delete()
36   {
37      int *point;
38      char *text_buffer ;
39
40      point = TlsGetValue(dwIndex) ;
41      text_buffer = TlsGetValue(dwIndex+1) ;
42
43      if (*point < 0)
44         fprintf(stderr, "No more characters\n") ;
45      else
46         text_buffer[(*point)--] = '\0' ;
```

```
47  }
48
49  VOID main(VOID)
50  {
51      dwTlsIndex = TlsAlloc(); // create a TLS index
52
53      // create threads and do other processing
54
55      // clean up and end process here
56      TlsFree(dwTlsIndex); // free TLS index
57  }
```

The main function uses the TlsAlloc function to initialize a dwTlsIndex variable for several threads. The Initialize function allocates memory for the point and text_buffer variables, and it uses the TlsSetValue function to store them in a thread's local storage. The functions Insert and Delete can use TlsGetValue to manipulate these variables.

2.8 Summary

In this chapter we have introduced the thread programming interface. We discussed concepts of thread scheduling and synchronization and the programming interface for thread synchronization objects. Finally, we discussed the Thread Local Storage mechanism. Table 2–3 summarizes functions in the Win32 thread API.

Call	Description
_beginthreadex	Create a new thread in programs using the C runtime library
_beginthread	Create a new thread in programs using the C runtime library
CreateThread	Create a new thread
CreateRemoteThread	Create a new thread in a different process's address space
_endthreadex	Exit from a thread in programs using the C runtime libaray
_endthread	Exit from a thread in programs using the C runtime libaray
GetCurrentThread	Return a pseudo handle to the current thread
SuspendThread	Suspend a specified thread's execution
ResumeThread	Resume the execution of the specified thread

Table 2–3. Summary of the Win32 Thread API.

Call	Description
ExitThread	Kill the current thread
TerminateThread	Kill a specified thread (Avoid this function at all cost!)
DuplicateHandle	Obtain a handle to a thread object
CloseHandle	Relinquish a thread handle
WaitForSingleObject	Wait for the specified object to attain a signaled state
WaitForMultipleObjects	Wait for all or one of many objects to attain a signaled state
CreateMutex	Create a mutex synchronization object
ReleaseMutex	Signal a mutex object
OpenMutex	Obtain a handle to a mutex, given its name
InitializeCriticalSection	Initialize a critical section object
EnterCriticalSection	Acquire a critical section object
LeaveCriticalSection	Release a critical section object
DeleteCriticalSection	Remove a critical section object from the system
CreateSemaphore	Create a new semaphore synchronization object
ReleaseSemaphore	Signal a semaphore object
CreateEvent	Create an event synchronization object
SetEvent	Signal an event
ResetEvent	Set the state of an event object to not-signaled
PulseEvent	Set and reset an event
GetThreadPriority	Get the base priority of the specified thread
SetThreadPriority	Set the base priority of the specified thread
TlsAlloc	Allocate thread local storage

Table 2–3. Summary of the Win32 Thread API. (Continued)

Call	Description
TlsSetValue	Set the value of a thread local storage
TlsGetValue	Get the value of a thread local storage
TlsFree	De-allocate thread local storage

Table 2–3. Summary of the Win32 Thread API. (Continued)

Using these mechanisms, you can begin writing multithreaded programs and experimenting with them. You may encounter some difficulties, however, such as deciding how many threads an application will have, or how to ensure that they do not deadlock while waiting for each other to release resources. These and other problems will be addressed in the following chapters.

2.9 Exercises

1. What are the attributes of a thread that can be inherited by another thread?

2. What are the events that cause a thread context switch to occur?

3. What are all of the possible states of a thread, and how does a thread make a transition from one state to another?

4. What are the various thread priority levels? Describe a situation in which each thread priority is useful.

5. Describe the differences between mutex and semaphore objects, and between mutex and critical section objects.

6. The performance of multiprocessor systems usually increases as the number of processors is increased. The theoretical speedup of an n-processor system would be n times faster than a single-processor system. The actual speedup, however, is less than that. What are the reasons for such a phenomenon?

7. Calling WaitForSingleObject allows a thread to suspend itself while awaiting operations on various types of objects until the objects attain the signaled state. When do the following objects' states become signaled: (a) mutexes and semaphores, (b) threads, and (c) files?

8. Implement a program that displays three rectangular boxes horizontally. The color of the left box is blue, and it belongs to one thread. Another thread owns the right box, which is red. Each thread tries to put its color in the center box (i.e., if the "red" thread is drawing, the color of the center box is red). Protect the center box with a mutex object, and allow only the thread that has the mutex lock to draw its color.

9. Write a program with two threads that take turns writing a one-line message to a console. Threads should use an event object to communicate with each other. Then substitute other synchronization objects for the event object.

10. Implement a logging utility that allows different processes to append messages to the end of a log file. Synchronize the concurrent access by multiple processes to this file.

2.10 References

1. Custer, H. (1993). *Inside Windows NT.* Microsoft Press.
2. Microsoft (1992). *Windows NT Programmer's Reference: Application Programming Interface, Part 1 and 2.* Microsoft Corporation, Seattle, WA.

Thread Synchronization

*I*n the last chapter, we described several synchro-
nization objects for multithreaded programming. For correct concurrent programs, multiple
threads of execution must be synchronized to protect the integrity of shared data. In this chapter, we illustrate basic synchronization techniques using some classic concurrency problems
of *producer-consumer, bounded-buffer,* and *readers-writers.*

3.1 The Producer-Consumer Problem

In the last chapter, we saw the simplest form of mutual exclusion: before accessing
shared data, each thread acquires ownership of a synchronization object. Once the thread has
finished accessing the data, it relinquishes the ownership so that other threads can acquire the
synchronization object and access the same data. Therefore, when accessing shared data,
each thread excludes all others from accessing the same data.

This simple form of mutual exclusion, however, is not enough for certain classes of
applications where designated threads are *producers* and *consumers* of data. The producer
threads write new values, while consumer threads read them. An analogy of the producer-

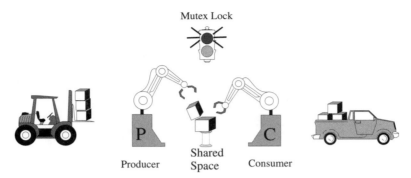

Figure 3-1. An Illustrative Analogy for the Producer-Consumer Problem.

consumer situation is illustrated in Figure 3-1, where each thread, *producer* and *consumer*, is represented by a robot arm. The producer picks up a box and puts it on a pedestal (shared buffer) from which the consumer can pick it up. The consumer robot picks up boxes from the pedestal for delivery. If we just use the simple synchronization technique of acquiring and relinquishing a synchronization object, we may get incorrect behavior. For example, the producer may try to put a block on the pedestal when there is already a block there. In such a case, the newly produced block will fall off the pedestal.

To illustrate this situation in a multithreaded program, we present an implementation of a producer-consumer situation with only mutual exclusion among threads.

```
1     #include <iostream.h>
2     #include <windows.h>
3
4     int SharedBuffer;
5     HANDLE hMutex;
6
7     void Producer()
8     {
9       int i;
10
11      for (i=20; i>=0; i--) {
12        if (WaitForSingleObject(hMutex,INFINITE) == WAIT_FAILED){
13          cerr << "ERROR: Producer()" << endl;
14          ExitThread(0);
15        }
16        // got Mutex, begin critical section
17        cout << "Produce: " << i << endl;
18        SharedBuffer = i;
19        ReleaseMutex(hMutex);  // end critical section
20      }
21    }
22
23
24    void Consumer()
25    {
26      int result;
```

```
27
28    while (1) {
29      if (WaitForSingleObject(hMutex,INFINITE) == WAIT_FAILED){
30        cerr << "ERROR: Producer" << endl;
31        ExitThread(0);
32      }
33      if (SharedBuffer == 0) {
34        cout << "Consumed " << SharedBuffer << ": end of data" << endl;
35        ReleaseMutex(hMutex); // end critical section
36        ExitThread(0);
37      }
38
39      // got Mutex, data in buffer, start consuming
40      if (SharedBuffer > 0){  // ignore negative values
41        result = SharedBuffer;
42        cout << "Consumed: " << result << endl;
43        ReleaseMutex(hMutex); // end critical section
44      }
45    }
46  }
47
48  void main()
49  {
50    HANDLE hThreadVector[2];
51    DWORD ThreadID;
52
53    SharedBuffer = -1;
54    hMutex = CreateMutex(NULL,FALSE,NULL);
55
56    hThreadVector[0]= CreateThread(NULL,0,
57      (LPTHREAD_START_ROUTINE)Producer,
58      NULL, 0, (LPDWORD)&ThreadID);
59    hThreadVector[1]=CreateThread(NULL,0,
60      (LPTHREAD_START_ROUTINE)Consumer,
61      NULL, 0, (LPDWORD)&ThreadID);
62    WaitForMultipleObjects(2,hThreadVector,TRUE,INFINITE);
63    // process ends here
64  }
65
```

This program creates two threads, *Producer* and *Consumer,* which exchange data using a shared variable, named SharedBuffer. All access to SharedBuffer must be from within a critical section. The program serializes access to the SharedBuffer, guaranteeing that concurrent accesses by producer and consumer threads will not corrupt the data in it. A sample output from a random run of the program is:

1. Produce: 20	16. Produce: 9
2. Consumed: 20	17. Produce: 8
3. Produce: 19	18. Produce: 7
4. Consumed: 19	19. Produce: 6
5. Produce: 18	20. Produce: 5
6. Produce: 17	21. Produce: 4
7. Produce: 16	22. Produce: 3

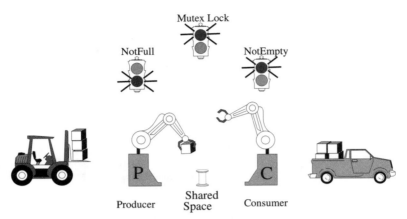

Figure 3-2. The Producer and Consumer Robots with Synchronization.

8. Produce: 15

9. Produce: 14

10. Produce: 13

11. Produce: 12

12. Produce: 11

13. Consumed: 11

14. Consumed: 11

15. Produce: 10

23. Produce: 2

24. Consumed: 2

25. Consumed: 2

26. Consumed: 2

27. Consumed: 2

28. Produce: 1

29. Consumed: 1

30. Consumed 0: end of data

As we can see, something is wrong: not every value produced by the producer is consumed, and sometimes the same value is consumed many times. The intended behavior is that the producer and consumer threads alternate in their access to the shared variable. We do not want the producer to overwrite the variable before its value is consumed; nor do we want the consumer thread to use the same value more than once.

The behavior occurs because mutual exclusion alone is not sufficient to solve the producer-consumer problem—we need both mutual exclusion and synchronization among the producer and consumer threads.

In order to achieve synchronization, we need a way for each thread to communicate with the others. When a producer produces a new value for the shared variable, it must inform the consumer threads of this event. Similarly, when a consumer has read a data value, it must trigger an event to notify possible producer threads about the empty buffer. Threads receiving such event signals can then gain access to the shared variable in order to produce or consume more data. Figure 3-2 shows our producer and consumer robots with added event signals.

The next program uses two event objects, named `hNotEmptyEvent` and `hNot-FullEvent`, to synchronize the producer and the consumer threads.

```
1    #include <iostream.h>
2    #include <windows.h>
3
4    #define FULL 1
5    #define EMPTY 0
```

```
6
7    int SharedBuffer;
8    int BufferState;
9    HANDLE hMutex;
10   HANDLE hNotFullEvent, hNotEmptyEvent;
11
12   void Producer()
13   {
14     int i;
15
16     for (i=20; i>=0; i--) {
17       while(1) {
18         if (WaitForSingleObject(hMutex,INFINITE) == WAIT_FAILED){
19           cerr << "ERROR: Producer()" << endl;
20           ExitThread(0);
21         }
22         if (BufferState == FULL) {
23           ReleaseMutex(hMutex);
24           // wait until buffer is not full
25           WaitForSingleObject(hNotFullEvent,INFINITE);
26           continue; // back to loop to test BufferState again
27         }
28         // got mutex and buffer is not FULL, break out of while loop
29         break;
30       }
31
32       // got Mutex, buffer is not full, producing data
33       cout << "Produce: " << i << endl;
34       SharedBuffer = i;
35       BufferState = FULL;
36       ReleaseMutex(hMutex);   // end critical section
37       PulseEvent(hNotEmptyEvent); // wake up consumer thread
38     }
39   }
40
41   void Consumer()
42   {
43     int result;
44
45     while (1) {
46       if (WaitForSingleObject(hMutex,INFINITE) == WAIT_FAILED){
47         cerr << "ERROR: Producer()" << endl;
48         ExitThread(0);
49       }
50       if (BufferState == EMPTY) { // nothing to consume
51         ReleaseMutex(hMutex); // release lock to wait
52         // wait until buffer is not empty
53         WaitForSingleObject(hNotEmptyEvent,INFINITE);
54         continue; // return to while loop to contend for Mutex again
55       }
56
57       if (SharedBuffer == 0) { // test for end of data token
58         cout << "Consumed " << SharedBuffer << ": end of data" << endl;
59         ReleaseMutex(hMutex); // end critical section
```

```
60          ExitThread(0);
61      }
62       else {  // got Mutex, data in buffer, start consuming
63          result = SharedBuffer;
64          cout << "Consumed: " << result << endl;
65          BufferState = EMPTY;
66          ReleaseMutex(hMutex); // end critical section
67          PulseEvent(hNotFullEvent); // wake up producer thread
68      }
69    }
70  }
71
72  void main()
73  {
74    HANDLE hThreadVector[2];
75    DWORD ThreadID;
76
77    BufferState = EMPTY;
78    hMutex = CreateMutex(NULL,FALSE,NULL);
79
80     // create manual event objects
81    hNotFullEvent  = CreateEvent(NULL,TRUE,FALSE,NULL);
82    hNotEmptyEvent = CreateEvent(NULL,TRUE,FALSE,NULL);
83
84     hThreadVector[0]=CreateThread(NULL,0,
85        (LPTHREAD_START_ROUTINE)Producer,
86       NULL, 0, (LPDWORD)&ThreadID);
87     hThreadVector[1]=CreateThread(NULL,0,
88        (LPTHREAD_START_ROUTINE)Consumer,
89       NULL, 0, (LPDWORD)&ThreadID);
90    WaitForMultipleObjects(2,hThreadVector,TRUE,INFINITE);
91     // process ends here
92  }
```

We add a state variable BufferState to indicate the state of the buffer (FULL or EMPTY) and initialize it to EMPTY. Like the SharedBuffer variable itself, the BufferState variable must be protected in a critical section to serialize access. Before producing a new value for the shared buffer, a producer thread must test BufferState (line 22). If the state of the buffer is FULL, the producer thread cannot produce data; it must release the mutex lock, and wait for the buffer to be empty on the event object hNotFullEvent. Similarly, before attempting to read data from the shared buffer, a consumer thread must check its state. If the state is EMPTY, there is no data to read. In such a situation, a consumer thread must release the mutex lock, and wait for a nonempty buffer using the event object hNotEmptyEvent. When a thread produces a new value, it triggers the event hNotEmptyEvent to wake up any consumer threads waiting for data. Similarly, when a thread consumes a value, it triggers the event hNotFullEvent to wake up any producer threads waiting for the buffer to empty.

Note that when a producer or consumer thread wakes up after waiting for an event object, it must retest the value of BufferState (lines 22 and 50) in order to handle the situation when there is more than one producer or consumer thread, since another thread may change the value of BufferState by the time a producer or consumer thread successfully regains access to the critical section. For example, suppose three consumer threads are awakened by an hNotEmptyEvent, and each of them immediately tries to get a mutex lock. The thread that gets the mutex lock will find data in the SharedBuffer, consume it, and set BufferState to EMPTY. Assuming that no new data is produced when the other two consumer threads get their respective mutex locks some time later, they will find that BufferState EMPTY; so they must wait on the hNotEmptyEvent again.

It is important that the producer and consumer threads each wait for the event objects outside their critical section; otherwise, the program can deadlock where each thread is waiting for the other to make progress. For example, suppose we do not release the mutex before waiting for the event object:

```
1    void Producer()
2    {
3      int i;
4
5      for (i=20; i>=0; i--) {
6        WaitForSingleObject(hMutex, INFINITE) ;
7        while(1) {
8            if (BufferState == FULL) {
9                WaitForSingleObject(hNotFullEvent,INFINITE);
10               continue; // back to loop to test BufferState again
11           }
12         break;
13       }
14       printf("Produce: %d\n", i);
15       SharedBuffer = i;
16       BufferState = FULL;
17       ReleaseMutex(hMutex);
18       PulseEvent(hNotEmptyEvent); // wake up consumer thread
19     }
20   }
```

In this program, a producer thread might enter its critical section and wait for the consumer to signal the event hNotFullEvent. The consumer thread, on the other hand, is waiting for the producer thread to leave its critical section before it can enter and make progress. Each thread is waiting for the other to make progress, so we have deadlock. Chapter 6 contains a more detailed discussion of deadlocks.

3.1.1 A Producer-Consumer Example—File Copy

To exemplify producers and consumers, we present a simple multithreaded file copy program (see Figure 3-3). The program spawns producer and consumer threads to perform the file copy; the threads share a common data buffer of SIZE bytes. The producer thread reads data from the original file up to SIZE bytes at a time into the shared buffer.

The consumer thread gets data from the shared buffer, and writes to a new file on disk.

```
1    #include <stdio.h>
2    #include <windows.h>
3
4    #define FULL 1
5    #define EMPTY 0
```

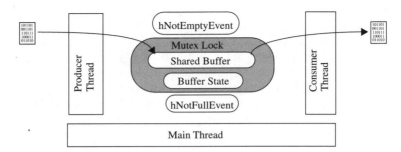

Figure 3-3. A File Copy Program Using Producer and Consumer Threads.

```
6    #define SIZE 10000
7
8    void *SharedBuffer[SIZE];
9    int BufferState;
10   HANDLE hMutex;
11   HANDLE hFullEvent, hEmptyEvent;
12   size_t nbyte = -1;
13
14   void Producer(FILE *infile)
15   {
16      size_t count;
17
18      do {
19         while(1){
20            WaitForSingleObject(hMutex,INFINITE);
21            if (BufferState == FULL) {
22               ReleaseMutex(hMutex);
23               // wait until buffer is not full
24               WaitForSingleObject(hEmptyEvent,INFINITE);
25               continue; // back to loop to test BufferState again
26            }
27            // got mutex and buffer is not FULL, break out of while loop
28            break;
29         }
30
31         // got Mutex, buffer is not full, producing data
32         nbyte = fread(SharedBuffer,1,SIZE,infile);
33         count = nbyte; // for use outside of critical section
34         printf("Produce %d bytes\n", nbyte);
35         BufferState = FULL;
36         ReleaseMutex(hMutex);   // end critical section
37         PulseEvent(hFullEvent); // wake up consumer thread
38      } while(count > 0);
39      printf("exit producer thread\n");
40   }
41
42   void Consumer(FILE *outfile)
43   {
44      while (1) {
```

```
45          WaitForSingleObject(hMutex,INFINITE);
46          if (nbyte == 0) {
47              printf("End of data, exit consumer thread\n");
48              ReleaseMutex(hMutex); // end critical section
49              ExitThread(0);
50          }
51
52          if (BufferState == EMPTY) { // nothing to consume
53              ReleaseMutex(hMutex); // release lock to wait
54              // wait until buffer is not empty
55              WaitForSingleObject(hFullEvent,INFINITE);
56          }
57          else {  // got Mutex, data in buffer, start consuming
58              fwrite(SharedBuffer,nbyte,1,outfile);
59              printf("Consumed: wrote %d bytes\n", nbyte);
60              BufferState = EMPTY;
61              ReleaseMutex(hMutex); // end critical section
62              PulseEvent(hEmptyEvent); // wake up producer thread
63          }
64      }
65  }
66
67  void main(int argc, char **argv)
68  {
69      HANDLE hThreadVector[2];
70      DWORD ThreadID;
71      FILE *infile, *outfile;
72
73      infile = fopen(argv[1],"rb");
74      outfile = fopen(argv[2],"wb");
75
76      BufferState = EMPTY;
77      hMutex = CreateMutex(NULL,FALSE,NULL);
78      hFullEvent  = CreateEvent(NULL,TRUE,FALSE,NULL);
79      hEmptyEvent = CreateEvent(NULL,TRUE,FALSE,NULL);
80
81      hThreadVector[0] = _beginthreadex (NULL, 0,
82          (LPTHREAD_START_ROUTINE)Producer,infile, 0,
83          (LPDWORD)&ThreadID);
84      hThreadVector[1] = _beginthreadex (NULL, 0,
85          (LPTHREAD_START_ROUTINE)Consumer, outfile, 0,
86          (LPDWORD)&ThreadID);
87      WaitForMultipleObjects(2,hThreadVector,TRUE,INFINITE);
88  }
```

3.2 The Bounded-Buffer Problem

The *bounded-buffer* problem is a natural extension of the producer-consumer problem, where producers and consumers share a set of buffers instead of just one. With multiple buffers, a producer does not necessarily have to wait for the last value to be consumed before producing another value. Similarly, a consumer is not forced to consume a single value each

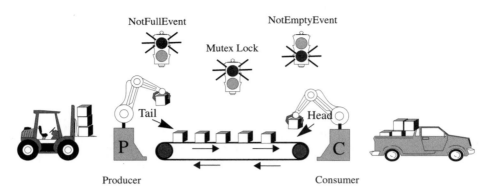

NotFullEvent   NotEmptyEvent

Mutex Lock

Tail   Head

P   C

Producer   Consumer

Figure 3-4. Producer and Consumer Robots with a Shared "Bounded Buffer."

time. This generalization enables producer and consumer threads to work much more efficiently by not having to wait for each other in lockstep.

Extending our analogy of producer and consumer robot arms, in the case of the
bounded-buffer problem the shared pedestal is replaced by a conveyer belt that can carry
more than one block at a time (Figure 3-4). The producer adds values at the **head** of the
buffer, while the consumer consumes values from the **tail**. Each production or consumption
moves the conveyor belt one step. The belt will lock when the buffer is full, and the conveyer
belt stops and waits for a consumer to pick-up a block from it. Each time a block is picked up
or a new block is produced, the belt moves forward one step. Therefore, consumers read values in the order in which they were produced.

A counter, named `count`, can be used to keep track of the number of buffers in use. As
in the producer-consumer situation, we use two events, `hNotEmptyEvent` and `hNot-`
`FullEvent`, to synchronize the producer and consumer threads. Whenever a producer finds
a full buffer space (`count == BUFSIZE`), it waits on the event `hNotFullEvent`. Similarly, when a consumer finds an empty buffer, it waits on the event `hNotEmptyEvent`.
Whenever a producer writes a new value, it signals the event `hNotEmptyEvent` to awaken
any waiting consumers. Likewise, when a consumer reads a value, it signals the event `hNot-`
`FullEvent` to wake any waiting producers. The following code illustrates this synchronization:

```
1     #include <iostream.h>
2     #include <windows.h>
3
4     #define BUFSIZE 5
5
6     int SharedBuffer[BUFSIZE];
7     int head,tail;
8     int count;
9
10    HANDLE hMutex;
11    HANDLE hNotFullEvent, hNotEmptyEvent;
12
13    void BB_Producer()
```

```
14  {
15     int i;
16
17     for (i=20; i>=0; i--) {
18        while(1) {
19           WaitForSingleObject(hMutex,INFINITE);
20           if (count == BUFSIZE) {  // buffer is full
21              ReleaseMutex(hMutex);
22              // wait until buffer is not full
23              WaitForSingleObject(hNotFullEvent,INFINITE);
24              continue; // back to loop to test buffer state again
25           }
26           // got mutex and buffer is not FULL, break out of while loop
27           break;
28        }
29
30        // got Mutex, buffer is not full, producing data
31        cout << "Produce: " << i << endl;
32        SharedBuffer[tail] = i;
33        tail = (tail+1) % BUFSIZE;
34        count++;
35        ReleaseMutex(hMutex);   // end critical section
36        PulseEvent(hNotEmptyEvent); // wake up consumer thread
37     }
38  }
39
40  void BB_Consumer()
41  {
42     int result;
43
44     while (1) {
45        WaitForSingleObject(hMutex,INFINITE);
46        if (count == 0) { // nothing to consume
47           ReleaseMutex(hMutex); // release lock to wait
48           // wait until buffer is not empty
49           WaitForSingleObject(hNotEmptyEvent,INFINITE);
50        }
51        else if (SharedBuffer[head] == 0) {// test for end of data token
52           cout << "Consumed 0: end of data" << endl;
53           ReleaseMutex(hMutex); // end critical section
54           ExitThread(0);
55        }
56        else {  // got Mutex, data in buffer, start consuming
57           result = SharedBuffer[head];
58           cout << "Consumed: " << result << endl;
59           head = (head+1) % BUFSIZE;
60           count--;
61           ReleaseMutex(hMutex); // end critical section
62           PulseEvent(hNotFullEvent); // wake up producer thread
63        }
64     }
65  }
66
67  void main()
```

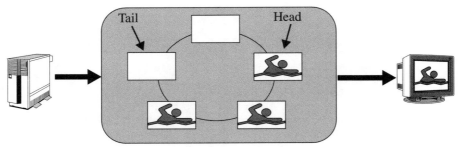

Figure 3-5. A Bounded-Buffer of Five Video Frames.

```
68   {
69       HANDLE hThreadVector[2];
70       DWORD ThreadID;
71
72       count = 0;
73       head = 0;
74       tail = 0;
75
76       hMutex = CreateMutex(NULL,FALSE,NULL);
77       hNotFullEvent  = CreateEvent(NULL,TRUE,FALSE,NULL);
78       hNotEmptyEvent = CreateEvent(NULL,TRUE,FALSE,NULL);
79
80       hThreadVector[0] = CreateThread (NULL, 0,
81              (LPTHREAD_START_ROUTINE) BB_Producer,
82              NULL, 0, (LPDWORD)&ThreadID);
83       hThreadVector[1] = CreateThread (NULL, 0,
84              (LPTHREAD_START_ROUTINE) BB_Consumer,
85              NULL, 0, (LPDWORD)&ThreadID);
86       WaitForMultipleObjects(2,hThreadVector,TRUE,INFINITE);
87   }
```

In general, this program resembles the producer-consumer example on page 56. The bounded-buffer program is, however, a more efficient way of sharing data when multiple values can be produced and consumed at the same time. In such cases, the producer-consumer program will force a thread context switch each time a new value is produced or consumed. In the bounded-buffer program, however, a producer thread can produce multiple values before it relinquishes processing to the consumer thread. Likewise, the consumer thread can consume multiple values during its time slice, when there is available data, before it is forced to context-switch.

An example of the bounded-buffer problem is a multimedia application that uncompresses and plays back video. Such an application might have two threads that manipulate a ring-buffer data structure, shown in Figure 3-5. One thread reads data from a disk, uncompresses, and fills each display buffer entry in memory, while another thread reads data from each buffer entry to display it. The two threads revolve around the ring supplying and getting data.

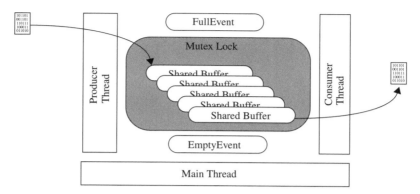

Figure 3-6. A File Copy Program Using Producer and Consumer Threads Sharing a Ring of Buffers.

3.2.1 Bounded-Buffer File Copy

With the bounded-buffer technique, we can now reimplement the multithreaded file copy program of Section 3.1.1 with several buffers instead of one (Figure 3-6).

```
1    #include <stdio.h>
2    #include <windows.h>
3    #include <stdlib.h>
4
5    #define SIZE 10000
6    #define BUFSIZE 5
7
8    typedef struct _Buffer {
9        void *Buf[SIZE];
10       size_t nbyte;
11   } Buffer;
12
13   Buffer *SharedBuffer[BUFSIZE];
14   int head, tail;
15   int count;
16
17   int TheEnd = FALSE;
18
19   HANDLE hMutex;
20   HANDLE hNotFullEvent, hNotEmptyEvent;
21   size_t nbyte;
22   void BB_Producer(FILE *infile)
23   {
24     size_t n;
25
26     do {
27       while(1){
28         WaitForSingleObject(hMutex,INFINITE);
29         if (count == BUFSIZE) {
30           ReleaseMutex(hMutex);
```

```
31              // wait until buffer is not full
32              WaitForSingleObject(hNotFullEvent,INFINITE);
33              continue; // back to loop to test buffer state again
34          }
35          // got mutex and buffer is not FULL, break out of while loop
36          break;
37      }
38
39      // got Mutex, buffer is not full, producing data
40      n = fread(SharedBuffer[tail]->Buf,1,SIZE,infile);
41      SharedBuffer[tail]->nbyte = n;
42      printf("Produce %d bytes\n",n);
43      tail = (tail+1) % BUFSIZE;
44      count++;
45      ReleaseMutex(hMutex);  // end critical section
46      PulseEvent(hNotEmptyEvent); // wake up consumer thread
47    } while(n > 0);
48    TheEnd = TRUE; // not thread safe here!
49    printf("exit producer thread\n");
50  }
51
52  void BB_Consumer(FILE *outfile)
53  {
54    While (1) {
55       WaitForSingleObject(hMutex,INFINITE);
56       if ((count == 0) && (TheEnd == TRUE)) {
57          printf("End of data, exit consumer thread\n");
58          ReleaseMutex(hMutex); // end critical section
59          ExitThread(0);
60       }
61
62       if (count == 0){ // nothing to consume
63          ReleaseMutex(hMutex); // release lock to wait
64          // wait until buffer is not empty
65          WaitForSingleObject(hNotEmptyEvent,INFINITE);
66          continue; // go back to while loop to try for mutex again
67       }
68
69       // got Mutex, data in buffer, start consuming
70       fwrite(SharedBuffer[head]->Buf,SharedBuffer[head]->nbyte,1,
71              outfile);
72       printf("Consumed: wrote %d bytes\n",SharedBuffer[head]->nbyte);
73       head = (head+1) % BUFSIZE;
74       count--;
75       ReleaseMutex(hMutex); // end critical section
76       PulseEvent(hNotFullEvent); // wake up producer thread
77    }
78  }
79
80  void main(int argc, char **argv)
81  {
82    HANDLE hThreadVector[2];
83    DWORD ThreadID;
84    FILE *infile, *outfile;
```

```
85    Buffer Buf0,Buf1,Buf2,Buf3,Buf4;
86
87    infile = fopen(argv[1],"rb");
88    outfile = fopen(argv[2],"wb");
89    count = 0;
90    head = 0;
91    tail = 0;
92    // create the bounded buffer
93    SharedBuffer[0] = &Buf0;
94    SharedBuffer[1] = &Buf1;
95    SharedBuffer[2] = &Buf2;
96    SharedBuffer[3] = &Buf3;
97    SharedBuffer[4] = &Buf4;
98    hMutex = CreateMutex(NULL,FALSE,NULL);
99    // create manual event objects
100   hNotFullEvent  = CreateEvent(NULL,TRUE,FALSE,NULL);
101   hNotEmptyEvent = CreateEvent(NULL,TRUE,FALSE,NULL);
102
103   hThreadVector[0] = _beginthreadex (NULL, 0,
104       (LPTHREAD_START_ROUTINE)BB_Producer, infile, 0,
105       (LPDWORD)&ThreadID);
106   hThreadVector[1] = _beginthreadex (NULL, 0,
107       (LPTHREAD_START_ROUTINE)BB_Consumer, outfile, 0,
108       (LPDWORD)&ThreadID);
109   WaitForMultipleObjects(2,hThreadVector,TRUE,INFINITE);
110 }
```

This example is more efficient than the producer-consumer file copy program with only one buffer, since producer and consumer threads don't necessarily proceed in lockstep. In this case, the granularity of locking is the entire set of buffers that is being shared among producer and consumer threads.

3.2.2 Bounded-Buffer with Finer Locking Granularity

To achieve even more concurrency, it is possible to implement a finer level of locking (Figure 3-7) where each buffer in the ring is locked individually. In this case, a producer can write data in one buffer while a consumer is reading from another. We get more concurrency at the expense of a little more complexity in managing the buffer locks. For this, we need two levels of mutex locks with one to protect the buffer state (i.e., a counter). In addition, there must be a mutex lock for each buffer in the ring. A producer or consumer thread must lock at the first level, then at the second level, increase the counter, and release the first-level lock so that other threads can proceed. Each thread produces or consumes data in the buffer it has locked, releases its lock, and then signals.

```
1    #include <stdio.h>
2    #include <windows.h>
3    #include <stdlib.h>
4
5    #define SIZE 10000
6    #define BUFSIZE 5
7
8    typedef struct _Buffer {
```

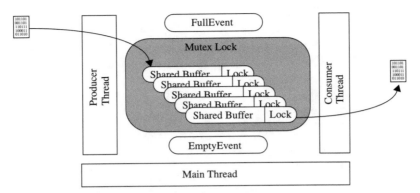

Figure 3-7. A File Copy Program with Individual Locks for Each Buffer in the Ring of Buffers.

```
9          void *Buf[SIZE];
10         HANDLE hBufferLock;
11         size_t nbyte;
12  } Buffer;
13
14  Buffer *SharedBuffer[BUFSIZE];
15  int head, tail;
16  int count;
17
18  int TheEnd;
19
20  HANDLE hMutex;
21  HANDLE hNotFullEvent, hNotEmptyEvent;
22  size_t nbyte;
23
24  void BB_Producer(FILE *infile)
25  {
26    size_t n;
27    int index;
28
29    do {
30      while(1){
31        // get lock for ring buffer
32        WaitForSingleObject(hMutex,INFINITE);
33        if (count == BUFSIZE) {
34          ReleaseMutex(hMutex);
35          // wait until buffer is not full
36          WaitForSingleObject(hNotFullEvent,INFINITE);
37          continue; // back to loop to test buffer state again
38        }
39        // got mutex and buffer is not FULL, break out of while loop
40        break;
41      }
42      // get lock for individual buffer, this is 2nd level lock
43      WaitForSingleObject(SharedBuffer[tail]->hBufferLock,INFINITE);
44      // got first and second level locks, update buffer state
```

```
45          //and release first level lock so other threads can access other
46          //parts of ring buffer
47          index = tail;
48          tail = (tail+1) % BUFSIZE;
49          count++;
50          ReleaseMutex(hMutex);  // release first level lock
51          // still have lock for this buffer, start producing data
52          n = fread(SharedBuffer[index]->Buf,1,SIZE,infile);
53          SharedBuffer[index]->nbyte = n;
54          printf("Produce %d bytes\n",n);
55          // release second level lock
56          ReleaseMutex(SharedBuffer[index]->hBufferLock);
57          PulseEvent(hNotEmptyEvent); // wake up consumer thread
58       } while(n > 0);
59       TheEnd = TRUE; // not thread safe here!
60       printf("exit producer thread\n");
61    }
62
63    void BB_Consumer(FILE *outfile)
64    {
65       int index;
66       while (1) {
67          WaitForSingleObject(hMutex,INFINITE);
68          if ((count == 0) && (TheEnd == TRUE)) {
69             printf("End of data, exit consumer thread\n");
70             ReleaseMutex(hMutex); // end critical section
71             ExitThread(0);
72          }
73          if (count == 0){ // nothing to consume
74             ReleaseMutex(hMutex); // release lock to wait
75             // wait until buffer is not empty
76             WaitForSingleObject(hNotEmptyEvent,INFINITE);
77             continue; // back to while loop and try for mutex again
78          }
79          // get lock for individual buffer, this is 2nd level lock
80          WaitForSingleObject(SharedBuffer[head]->hBufferLock,INFINITE);
81          // got first and second level locks, update buffer state
82          // and release first level lock so other threads can access
83          // other parts of ring buffer
84          index = head;
85          head = (head+1) % BUFSIZE;
86          count--;
87          ReleaseMutex(hMutex);  // release first level lock
88          // still have lock for this buffer, start consuming data
89          fwrite(SharedBuffer[index]->Buf, SharedBuffer[index]->nbyte,1,
90                  outfile);
91          printf("Consumed:wrote %d bytes\n",SharedBuffer[index]->nbyte);
92          // release second level lock
93          ReleaseMutex(SharedBuffer[index]->hBufferLock);
94          PulseEvent(hNotFullEvent); // wake up producer thread
95       }
96    }
97
98    void main(int argc, char **argv)
```

```
99    {
100       HANDLE hThreadVector[2];
101       DWORD ThreadID;
102       FILE *infile, *outfile;
103       Buffer Buf0,Buf1,Buf2,Buf3,Buf4;
104       int i;
105
106       infile = fopen(argv[1],"rb");
107       outfile = fopen(argv[2],"wb");
108
109       count = 0;
110       head = 0;
111       tail = 0;
112       // create the bounded buffer
113       SharedBuffer[0] = &Buf0;
114       SharedBuffer[1] = &Buf1;
115       SharedBuffer[2] = &Buf2;
116       SharedBuffer[3] = &Buf3;
117       SharedBuffer[4] = &Buf4;
118
119       // create mutex lock for each buffer in buffer ring
120       for (i=0;i<BUFSIZE;i++)
121           SharedBuffer[i]->hBufferLock = CreateMutex(NULL,FALSE,NULL);
122
123       // create mutex lock for buffer ring
124       hMutex = CreateMutex(NULL,FALSE,NULL);
125
126       // create manual event object for signaling
127       hNotFullEvent  = CreateEvent(NULL,TRUE,FALSE,NULL);
128       hNotEmptyEvent = CreateEvent(NULL,TRUE,FALSE,NULL);
129
130       // create producer and consumer threads
131       hThreadVector[0] = _beginthreadex (NULL, 0,
132           (LPTHREAD_START_ROUTINE)BB_Producer, infile, 0,
133           (LPDWORD)&ThreadID);
134       hThreadVector[1] = _beginthreadex (NULL, 0,
135           (LPTHREAD_START_ROUTINE)BB_Consumer, outfile, 0,
136           (LPDWORD)&ThreadID);
137
138       // wait for producer and consumer thread to finish before
139       // terminating process
140       WaitForMultipleObjects(2,hThreadVector,TRUE,INFINITE);
141   }
```

This implementation is more efficient than the previous version because we spend little time locking the first-level lock. The lengthy update or read operations are synchronized only by the second-level lock, so many threads can read or write concurrently to different parts of the ring buffer. They will not deadlock because we have ordered the lock acquisitions (see Section 6.6.3).

3.3 The Readers-Writers Problem

When multiple threads share data, sometimes strict mutual exclusion is not necessary. This happens when there are several threads that only read a data value, and once in a while a thread writes into it. Such programming situations are examples of the *readers-writers* problem. For these, an exclusive single read-write protocol is too restrictive. Such applications can be made more efficient by allowing multiple simultaneous reads and an exclusive write. For example, consider a server program that maintains information on the latest prices for a variety of stocks. Suppose that this server program gets requests from several clients to either read or change the price of a stock. It is quite likely that the server will get many more requests to read stock prices than to change them. In this case, it is more efficient to let multiple readers obtain stock prices concurrently, without requiring mutual exclusion for each reader. When a thread wants to update a stock price, however, we have to make sure that no other thread is reading or writing it.

We now describe the multiple-readers/single-writer locking protocol in which there are two mutually exclusive phases of operation: the read phase and the write phase. During a read phase, all reader threads read the shared data in parallel. During a write phase, only one writer thread updates the shared data.

If a read phase is in progress, and we continue to allow newly arrived reader threads to join those in progress, it is possible that no writer thread can ever have a chance to run. Similarly, during a write phase, if newly arrived writer threads succeed other writer threads (one at a time) in updating the data, it is also possible that no reader thread ever gets a chance to run. This problem is known as starvation.

To prevent starvation of either reader or writer threads, the locking protocol alternates the read and write phases when necessary. For example, suppose there are both reader and writer threads present, at the start of a read phase all existing reader threads at that time are allowed to proceed to read the shared data concurrently. All reader threads that arrive after this time, while there are pending writer threads, are forced to wait until the next read phase. When all the current reader threads finish, a write phase begins in which one writer thread is allowed access to the shared data. Likewise, to prevent starvation of reader threads, other writer threads must wait until another write phase begins. And when the writer thread finishes, another read phase begins, which allows all the waiting reader threads at this time to proceed. The switching of read and write phases continues as long as there are pending reader and writer threads.

Things are simpler when we only have reader threads or writer threads. If we only have reader threads, there would be no write phase, and all of them are allowed to read the shared data in parallel. Likewise, if we only have writer threads, there will only be one write phase where one writer thread is allowed to follow another in updating the shared data, sequentially.

In an active system where there are many active reader and writer threads, one will see that the read and write phases alternate, allowing one batch of reader threads to proceed, followed by one writer thread, followed by another batch of (newly arrived) reader threads, followed by a writer thread, and so on.

To further illustrate this multiple-readers/single-writer synchronization protocol, Table 3–1 lists the arrival time of five reader threads and two writer threads. Assuming that

Arrival Time (ms)	Thread
t = 0	R1
t = 50	R2
t = 70	W1
t = 80	R3
t = 100	W2
t = 110	R4
t = 170	R5

Table 3–1. Arriving Reader and Writer Threads to Access Shared Data.

each read operation takes 40 milliseconds and each write operations takes 50 milliseconds, Figure 3-8 shows their behavior through time.

As you can see, the reader thread R1 arrives first. The protocol allows R1 to read the shared data immediately. When the reader thread R2 arrives, it immediately gets to read the shared data because R1 has finished and there are no waiting writer threads. There is no need to alternate the read phase and the write phase at this point because there are no pending writer threads.

The third thread that arrives is the writer thread W1. Since W1 arrives while the read phase is in progress (with thread R2), it waits until R2 completes. Now that there is a pending writer thread, when the read phase completes, a write phase will be started.

Shortly after that, at time t=80, a reader thread R3 arrives. Since there is a pending writer thread, the protocol does not allow this reader thread to join the read phase in progress. It must instead wait for the next read phase. This policy ensures that there is no starvation of writer threads.

When R2 completes at time t=90, a write phase begins with thread W1. While thread W1 is in progress, threads W2 and R4 arrive at times t=100 and t=110, respectively. Both W2 and R4 must wait. Thread W2 cannot execute because we allow only one writer thread in a write phase. Thread R4 cannot proceed because it has to wait for the next read phase.

When thread W1 completes at time t=140, a read phase begins and we allow both reader threads R3 and R4 to proceed concurrently. It is important to note that although thread W2 arrived before thread R4, thread R4 is allowed to access the shared data before W2 because both R3 and R4 are present at the start of the read phase.

When threads R3 and R4 are in progress, another reader thread R5 arrives. Since R5 misses the start of the current read phase, it must now wait for the next read phase.

When threads R3 and R4 complete, a write phase begins with thread W2. Finally when W2 finishes, a read phase begins and we allow thread R5 to run.

We now demonstrate the use of mutexes and semaphores to implement this protocol. Before reading data, each reader thread will call a function `start_reading` to make sure that it is allowed to do so. After reading, it will call the function `stop_reading` to

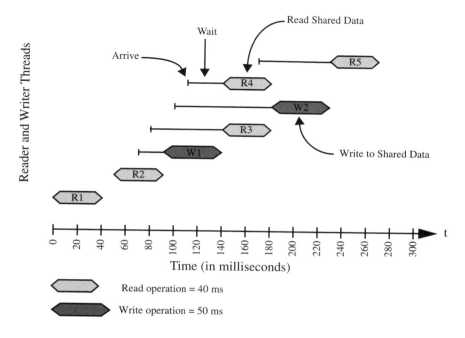

Figure 3-8. The Behavior of Reader and Writer Threads Operating Under the Multiple-Readers/ Single-Writer Synchronization Protocol.

announce that it has finished so that any waiting writer thread can be activated. Similarly, each writer thread will call functions start_writing and stop_writing before and after doing so. The following code implements this protocol:

```
1    #include <stdio.h>
2    #include <windows.h>
3    #include <stdlib.h>
4
5    #define MAX 9999
6    HANDLE mutex;            // init to count = 1, FALSE
7    HANDLE blockedReaders;  // init to count = 0, max = MAX
8    HANDLE blockedWriters;  // init to count = 0, max = MAX
9    int activeReaders = 0, waitingReader = 0;
10   int activeWriters = 0, waitingWriter = 0;
11   int sharedBuffer = 0;
12
13   VOID StartReading()
14   {
15       WaitForSingleObject(mutex, INFINITE);
16       // if there is active reader or waiting writer, wait for next
17       // read batch
18       if (activeWriters > 0 || waitingWriter > 0) {
19           waitingReader++;
20           ReleaseMutex(mutex);
```

```
21            WaitForSingleObject(blockedReaders, INFINITE);
22        }
23        else {
24            activeReaders++;
25            ReleaseMutex(mutex);
26        }
27    }
28
29    VOID StopReading()
30    {
31        WaitForSingleObject(mutex, INFINITE);
32        activeReaders--;
33        // last reader thread to finish reading needs to activate a
34        // waiting writer
35        if (activeReaders == 0 && waitingWriter > 0) {
36            activeWriters = 1;
37            waitingWriter--;
38            ReleaseSemaphore(blockedWriters, 1, NULL);
39        }
40        ReleaseMutex(mutex);
41    }
42
43    VOID StartWriting()
44    {
45        WaitForSingleObject(mutex, INFINITE);
46        if (activeReaders == 0 && activeWriters == 0) {
47            // there is no active reader or writer, OK to start writing
48            activeWriters = 1;
49            ReleaseMutex(mutex);
50        }
51        else {
52            // there is active readers or writer, put thread on write queue
53            waitingWriter++;
54            ReleaseMutex(mutex);
55            WaitForSingleObject(blockedWriters, INFINITE);
56        }
57    }
58
59    VOID StopWriting()
60    {
61        WaitForSingleObject(mutex, INFINITE);
62        activeWriters = 0;
63        if (waitingReader > 0) {
64        // if there are waiting readers, release them all from read queue
65            while (waitingReader > 0) {
66                waitingReader--;
67                activeReaders++;
68                ReleaseSemaphore(blockedReaders, 1, NULL);
69            }
70        }
71        else if (waitingWriter > 0) {
72            // no waiting reader and we have waiting writer,
73            // release 1 writer from write queue
74            waitingWriter--;
```

```
75              ReleaseSemaphore(blockedWriters, 1, NULL);
76      }
77      ReleaseMutex(mutex);
78  }
79
80  VOID Reader(LPVOID num)
81  {
82      int localVar, i;
83      for (i = 0; i<10;i++){
84          StartReading();
85          localVar = sharedBuffer;
86          cout << "Reader Thread " << num << " reads " << localVar << endl;
87          Sleep (1000);
88          StopReading();
89      }
90  }
91
92  VOID Writer(LPVOID num)
93  {
94      int i, j;
95
96      j = (int) num * 10;
97
98      for (i=j; i< j+5; i++){
99          StartWriting();
100         sharedBuffer = i;
101         cout << "\nWriter Thread " << num << " writes "
102             << sharedBuffer << endl;
103         Sleep (1000);
104         StopWriting();
105     }
106 }
107
108 main()
109 {
110     HANDLE hThreadVector[4];
111     DWORD ThreadID;
112     mutex = CreateMutex(NULL, FALSE, NULL);
113     blockedReaders = CreateSemaphore(NULL, 0, MAX, NULL);
114     blockedWriters = CreateSemaphore(NULL, 0, MAX, NULL);
115     hThreadVector[0] = CreateThread (NULL, 0,
116         (LPTHREAD_START_ROUTINE)Writer,(LPVOID) 1, 0,
117         (LPDWORD)&ThreadID);
118
119     hThreadVector[1] = CreateThread (NULL, 0,
120         (LPTHREAD_START_ROUTINE)Writer,(LPVOID) 2, 0,
121         (LPDWORD)&ThreadID);
122
123     hThreadVector[2] = CreateThread (NULL, 0,
124         (LPTHREAD_START_ROUTINE)Reader,(LPVOID) 3, 0,
125         (LPDWORD)&ThreadID);
126
127     hThreadVector[3] = CreateThread (NULL, 0,
128         (LPTHREAD_START_ROUTINE)Reader,(LPVOID) 4, 0,
```

```
129         (LPDWORD)&ThreadID);
130    WaitForMultipleObjects(4,hThreadVector,TRUE,INFINITE);
131 }
```

We maintain a count of the active readers and writers in the variables active-
Readers and activeWriters, and a count of readers and writers that are currently
blocked, waiting for a chance to read or write, in the variables waitingReaders and
waitingWriters. For synchronizing concurrent access to these variables, we use the
mutex mutex. Finally, we use two semaphore objects, blockedReaders and blocked-
Writers, to synchronize among reader and writer threads.

When a new reader wants access to start reading, it calls the function
start_reading. If currently there is a writer active or blocked (line 18), then the reader
will block on the semaphore blockedReaders after incrementing the count blocked-
Readers by 1. If there is no writer active or blocked, the reader increments the count for
activeReaders by 1 and proceeds to read. When a reader has finished, it calls the function stop_reading. Here it checks to see if all readers have finished and if there is any
waiting writer (line 35); if so, it wakes up the writer.

When a thread wants to write the shared variable, it calls the function
start_writing. The writer proceeds to write if there are no active readers and writers
(line 46). Otherwise, it increments the waitingWriters count by 1 and blocks on the
semaphore blockedWriters. Finally, when a writer thread finishes, it calls the function
stop_writing. Here it unblocks any readers waiting for the writer to finish. If there are
none, the writer checks to see if there are any waiting writers; if so, it unblocks one of them.

Using the above solution, we can improve certain programs' responsiveness by having
multiple concurrent readers, while preserving data integrity with exclusive writes.

3.4 Summary

In this chapter, we have demonstrated the use of synchronization objects to synchronize
the execution of multiple threads. Synchronization protects data that is shared among threads.
As we saw in the sample programs, failure to synchronize means we can get incorrect results
from one thread accidently overwriting the work of another. We illustrated the use of simple
mutual exclusion with critical sections, where only one thread is allowed to enter at a time.
We then extended this to a producer-consumer situation where, in addition to effecting mutually exclusive access to shared data, threads inform each other about the state of the data
using event objects. Finally, we introduced the situation where multiple readers can read from
data concurrently, but only one thread is allowed to write to them. In the next chapter, we will
see a more elegant solution to the synchronization problems using a concept called monitors.

3.5 Bibliography Notes

The mutual exclusion, producer-consumer, and bounded-buffer problems were all first
introduced and solved in [Dijkstra, 1968].

3.6 Exercises

1. The event objects in the file copy program are created as manual-reset objects (lines 82–83). What are the implications if these were auto-reset objects instead?

2. The sleeping barber problem is another classic synchronization problem [Dijkstra, 1968]: There are a barber, a barber chair, and n waiting chairs. The barber works on one customer at a time, and he sleeps when he has no customers. When a potential customer arrives and there are no other customers, the customer wakes up the barber. If the barber is working on someone else, the customer waits in one of the waiting chairs, or leaves the shop if all chairs are occupied. When the barber finishes giving a haircut to one customer, he selects the first waiting customer. Write a program that simulates the barber and his customers.

   Refer to Figure 3-8 to answer the following questions.

3. From looking at the picture, which are the read phases? Which are the write phases? How can you tell (from the picture) that the read and write phases are mutually exclusive?

4. How long does the writer thread W2 have to wait before it is allowed to update the shared data?

5. At time t=130, what phase is in progress (read or write)? How many threads are waiting? Which ones?

6. At time t=90, both reader thread R3 and writer thread W1 are waiting. Why was W1 chosen to run and not R3?

7. Thread W2 arrived before thread R4, but why does R4 access shared data before W2?

8. Thread R3 arrives during a read phase. Why isn't it allowed to join the readers in progress? What will happen if we change the protocol to allow R3 to join this read phase immediately?

3.7 References

1. Dijkstra, E. W. (1968). Cooperating sequential processes. In Genuys, F., ed., *Programming Languages*. Academic Press, Reading, MA.

C H A P T E R 4

Monitors

In this chapter, we describe *monitors*—a useful abstraction for concurrent programming. You can use monitors to simplify multithreaded programs by encapsulating shared data, and by centralizing low-level details of mutual exclusion and synchronization. In the next chapter, we will show you how to implement monitors using C++ classes and synchronization primitives.

The last chapter showed the use of synchronization objects (e.g., mutexes and semaphores) to establish critical sections when accessing shared data. To ensure correctness, each thread acquires ownership of a synchronization object before accessing the data; the thread then releases the synchronization object after accessing data.

The difficulty with this approach is that at each point in a program at which a thread accesses shared data, you must carefully remember to code these two extra steps explicitly. Since such accesses are often numerous, this becomes a fairly tedious programming task. Moreover, if by chance you forget even a single acquisition or release, the program might inadvertently corrupt shared data or deadlock.

This problem is solved by using monitors, which were originally invented for use in operating system [Hansen, 1973; Hoare, 1974]. A monitor abstraction combines data

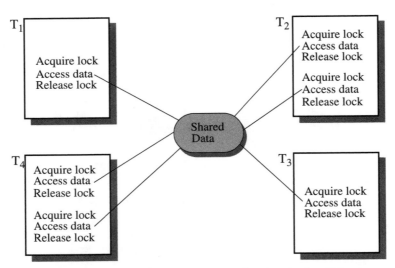

Figure 4-1. Multithreaded Access to Shared Data Using Synchronization Objects.

structures, subroutines, and a synchronization facility in a single module; the rest of a program can use a monitor without worrying about its internal details.[1] Using monitors, you can:

- Encapsulate data to be shared by multiple threads
- Gather synchronization operations into one place

Figures 4-1 and 4-2 illustrate the difference between using synchronization objects and using monitors for accessing shared data.

The use of monitors can greatly simplify a multithreaded program, reduce the likelihood of error, and facilitate future application enhancements. To demonstrate how monitors provide these advantages, we describe their structure and properties in the following sections.

4.1 Structure of a Monitor

A monitor is composed of three parts:

- *Declarations* that define a monitor's data and condition variables. Data variables are privately accessible to only one thread at a time when it executes within the monitor. Condition variables coordinate the passage of threads through the monitor.
- *Procedures* that access its encapsulated data and can be called from any part of the program which has the monitor in its lexical scope.
- *Initialization* code for a monitor's data and condition variables; this part is automatically executed when the monitor is created.

---

[1] The monitor abstraction provides multithreaded programmers with advantages similar to what objects provide in object-oriented programming.

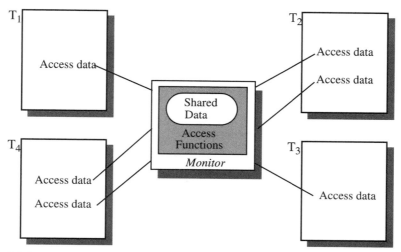

Figure 4-2. Multithreaded Access to Shared Data Using a Monitor.

The following skeletal code, similar to C++, illustrates these parts of a monitor named SharedBuffer.

```
1    monitor SharedBuffer {
2        // declarations
3        char *Buffer;    // encapsulated shared data buffer
4        condition notEmpty, notFull;  // condition variables
5
6    // Procedures
7    void read (char *result)
8    {
9    ... return the shared buffer ...
10   }
11
12   void write (char *data)
13   {
14   ... write data to the buffer ...
15   }
16
17   // initialization section
18       Buffer = NULL;
19   }
```

This monitor contains a string named Buffer that can be shared by calling the monitor procedures read and write. The condition variables, notEmpty and notFull, are used internally to coordinate threads' execution. Condition variables and their usage are explained later in Section 4.4.

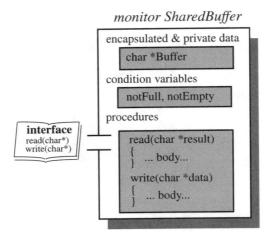

Figure 4-3. Data Encapsulation in a Monitor.

4.2 Data Encapsulation

An important benefit of monitors is data encapsulation, or information hiding: knowledge about how the data is represented and accessed is hidden from the rest of the program for simplicity and clarity. To access such data, you invoke procedures defined by the monitor. Figure 4-3 illustrates data encapsulation in the SharedBuffer monitor.

As long as the procedures interface presented by a monitor to surrounding application code remains unchanged, application code need not be modified when the monitor's procedures are modified. Moreover, a program accessing shared data using monitor procedures no longer needs to explicitly synchronize with other threads. The next section describes how a monitor controls and guarantees correct access to shared data that it protects.

4.3 Controlled Access to Data

Monitors guarantee that only one thread at a time can access shared data. This, combined with the fact that shared data can only be accessed by executing a monitor's procedures, serializes access to the shared data. Monitors, therefore, relieve programmers from the tedious task of using primitive synchronization objects like mutexes and semaphores to implement critical sections around all accesses to shared data. With monitors, the likelihood of a programming error is greatly reduced because you implement the monitor once, and the application program simply calls its data access subroutines. Synchronization is handled automatically inside the monitor.

We now complete the SharedBuffer monitor to illustrate synchronization between monitor procedures:

```
1    monitor SharedBuffer {
2       char *Buffer;   // encapsulated shared data buffer
```

```
3      condition notEmpty, notFull;  // condition variables
4
5    void read (char *result)
6    {
7      if (Buffer == NULL)
8         wait (notEmpty); // if buffer is empty, wait until not empty
9      // buffer is no longer empty
10     result = Buffer;
11     Buffer = NULL; // buffer consumed
12     signal (notFull);  // tell others it is not full (empty)
13     return; // exit monitor
14   }
15
16   void write (char *data)
17   {
18     if (Buffer)
19        wait (notFull); // if buffer is full, wait until not full
20     Buffer = strdup(data); // buffer is no longer full, put in data
21     signal (notEmpty); // tell others there is data in SharedBuffer
22     return; // exit monitor
23   }
24
25     // initialization section
26     Buffer = NULL;
27   }
```

In this example, the `SharedBuffer` monitor encapsulates a character buffer to be shared among different threads of execution. Two monitor procedures access the shared object: `read` and `write`. Since execution of monitor procedures is guaranteed to be mutually exclusive, threads can, without interfering with each other, access the data simply by calling `read` and `write`. The monitor automatically serializes access to the data. The following code illustrates the use of our `SharedBuffer` monitor: In order to use the monitor, you *instantiate* a monitor object and then call its interface functions.

```
1    // instantiate SharedBuffer monitor
2    SharedBuffer object;
3    void producer()
4    {
5      object.write("Hello World!");
6    }
7    void Consumer()
8    {
9      char *result ;
10     object.read(result) ;
11   }
```

4.4 Condition Variables

So far, we have seen a monitor's data encapsulation and mutual exclusion properties providing an effective way to manage shared data by serializing execution of threads that call its interface procedures. Data being updated by one thread is inaccessible to other threads, causing the latter to block. The `SharedBuffer` monitor above may not always have data to be read, so a thread calling `read` cannot make progress as long as the buffer is empty, and it must wait. But we do not want a thread to block inside the monitor, because that would cause deadlock: the blocked thread cannot make progress until the data is available, and since it is blocked in the monitor, which provides mutual exclusion, no other thread can enter the monitor to make data available.

A monitor provides a synchronization mechanism, called *condition variable*, to prevent this problem. This is a special data object that can suspend a thread and reactivate it when a particular condition is met. A condition variable supports two operations: *wait* and *signal*.

- *wait*: A thread calling *wait* while executing a monitor procedure is put to sleep on a queue associated with a condition variable.
- *signal*: When a thread causes a condition associated with a condition variable to become true, it notifies any waiting threads by calling *signal* using that condition variable. If there are no waiting threads, this call has no effect.

Using condition variables, monitor procedures synchronize the calling threads and achieve maximum parallelism without deadlock. We highlight code that uses condition variables in the following `SharedBuffer` example:

```
1    monitor SharedBuffer {
2       char *Buffer;   // encapsulated shared data buffer
3       condition notEmpty, notFull;  // condition variables
4
5    void read (char *result)
6    {
7       if (Buffer == NULL)
8          wait (notEmpty); // if buffer is empty, wait until not empty
9       // buffer is no longer empty
10      result = Buffer;
11      Buffer = NULL; // buffer consumed
12      signal (notFull);  // tell others it is not full (empty)
13      return; // exit monitor
14   }
15
16   void write (char *data)
17   {
18      if (Buffer)
19         wait (notFull); // if buffer is full, wait until not full
20      Buffer = strdup(data); // buffer is no longer full, put in data
21      signal (notEmpty); // tell others there is data in SharedBuffer
22      return; // exit monitor
23   }
24
25      // initialization section
26      Buffer = NULL;
27   }
```

This example illustrates a typical *producer-consumer* problem, like those in Chapter 3, in which several threads share data. Some threads "produce" the data, while other threads "consume" it. The `SharedBuffer` monitor encapsulates a shared buffer and two condition variables: `notFull` and `notEmpty`. To read or write the buffer, a thread must call monitor procedures `read` or `write`. Because our buffer has only room for one character string, we also want data in the buffer to be consumed before it can be updated. Thus, if the buffer is full, the monitor blocks all threads calling `write` using the condition `notFull` (line 19) until the buffer is no longer full. When a consumer thread reads the data and empties the buffer, it signals the condition `notFull` (line 12) to wake up a waiting producer thread. Likewise, all consumer threads calling `read` while the buffer is empty are blocked on the condition `notEmpty`. When a producer thread writes new data into the buffer, it signals the condition `notEmpty` (line 21) to awaken any such threads.

4.5 Benefits of Monitors

We have now examined the structure and several properties of monitors: data encapsulation, mutual exclusion, and condition variables; together these properties let us combine shared data and synchronization mechanisms into a single program module in order to build and maintain multithreaded programs more easily. Application programmers can simply call a monitor procedure to access shared data, knowing that the monitor will perform appropriate synchronization. Furthermore, if we wish to change the synchronization policy (say, from single-read/write to multiple-read/single-write), we only have to modify the monitor procedures in order to implement the new behavior. The code calling these remains unchanged. Without monitors, you have to rethink the interaction among *all* critical sections, and reimplement all of them—a tedious and error-prone task.

4.6 Using Monitors

To further demonstrate the usefulness of monitors, this section describes several classic concurrent-programming problems, and shows how to solve them using monitors. First, we introduce the bounded-buffer problem, which is a generalization of the producer–consumer problem illustrated by the `SharedBuffer` monitor example (Section 4.4). Next, we describe the credit account problem, followed by the readers–writers problem. We show how each of these can be solved elegantly using monitors.

4.6.1 Bounded-Buffer Problem

In the bounded-buffer problem, producer and consumer threads share a circular buffer pool capable of holding N data items, where $N > 1$. We summarize the problem as follows:

- A producer can fill the buffer until there are no more empty slots.
- A consumer cannot read the buffer until at least one slot is filled.
- Only one thread can access the buffer at any given time.

Assume that we have a monitor with two procedures, `put` and `get`, which control access to the buffer. Two or more *consumer* and *producer* threads can share data using these, as Figure 4-4 depicts. The following skeletal code describes this monitor.

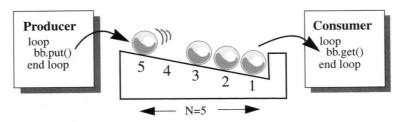

Figure 4-4. The Bounded-Buffer Problem.

```
1     #define N 24
2
3     monitor bounded_buffer {
4        int buffer[N];
5        int count;
6        int head, tail;
7        condition not_empty, not_full;
8
9     void put (int x)
10    {
11       if (count == N)
12          not_full.wait();
13       buffer[tail] = x;
14       tail = (tail + 1) % N;
15       count = count + 1;
16       not_empty.signal();
17    }
18
19    void get (int &x)
20    {
21       if (count == 0)
22          not_empty.wait();
23       x = buffer [head];
24       head = (head + 1) % N;
25       count = count - 1;
26       not_full.signal();
27    }
28
29       // initialization section
30       count = 0;
31       head = 0;
32       tail = 0;
33    }
```

The private data members, count, head, and tail, maintain the state of the buffer.
Count indicates the number of data items available in the buffer, while head and tail
index the first data slot and the first empty slot, respectively. Figure 4-5 illustrates the use of
the state variables.

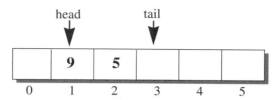

Figure 4-5. The Data Structure of the Bounded-Buffer Monitor.

The `put` procedure blocks a calling thread when the buffer is full (line 11). Otherwise, it writes the new data to the first empty slot (line 13), updates these state variables, and signals that the buffer is not empty (lines 14–16).

Likewise, if the buffer is empty, the `get` procedure suspends a consumer thread using `not_empty` until the buffer has at least one item (line 22). Otherwise, the procedure gets data from the head of the buffer, advances `head` to index the next slot, decrements `count`, and signals `not_full` to awaken any suspended producer thread.

4.6.2 Credit Account Example

As another example, we use monitors to manage a simple credit account, demonstrating their power and simplicity. Suppose a shoe manufacturer establishes credit accounts for various client firms. Using an account, authorized members of a client firm can independently and concurrently make purchases or payments up to the account's credit limit.

To protect each account balance from errors due to concurrent updates, the shoe manufacturer designs a credit account monitor. Figure 4-6 shows this monitor. It provides two access procedures `credit` and `debit`,[2] which application threads can concurrently invoke to execute credit transactions with guaranteed correctness.

For example, suppose that a manufacturer named Shoe-Mart creates a monitor named Bundy, as an account object for a client franchise, the Bundy shoe shop, with a credit limit of $10,000. When a Bundy store manager sends in shoe orders or payments, Shoe-Mart's state-of-the-art accounting system creates a thread to handle the transaction. Using the account monitor, Bundy, an application thread simply updates the account balance with a call to `Bundy.credit` for payment, or `Bundy.debit` for debit (Figure 4-6) without having to explicitly synchronize with any other thread. A skeletal implementation of this monitor is presented below.

```
1    monitor credit_account {
2       int balance;
3
4    void credit (int amount)
5    {
6       balance += amount;  // increase account balance
7    }
8
9    void debit (int amount)
```

[2.] We can make it more complicated by adding a password, etc. to the monitor.

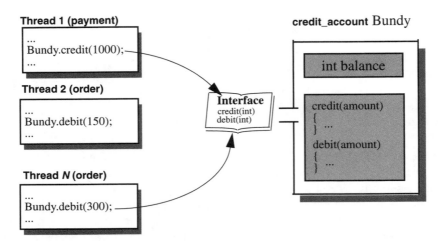

Figure 4-6. A Credit Account Monitor.

```
10   {
11      if (balance < amount)
12        printf("exceed credit limit, transaction denied\n");
13      // otherwise, adjust credit balance
14      else
15        balance -= amount;
16   }
17
18      // initialization
19      balance = 10000;  // initialize balance is $10000
20   }
```

Here a credit operation always increases the credit line because it is a payment made by the client. Conversely, a debit operation reduces the franchise's credit line unless it would exceed the credit limit, in which case it is rejected.

To illustrate the flexibility and extensibility of a monitor, let's extend this example so that in the event of an order over the limit, Shoe-Mart does not reject it, but instead suspends it, sends a note to the Bundy store, and then waits until there are sufficient funds in the account to resume shipping. This feature saves the client from having to resubmit an order if there is a temporary shortage of funds in the account.

To accommodate this change, Shoe-Mart's I.S. staff quickly extends the credit monitor implementation as shown below.

```
1    monitor credit_account {
2       int balance;
3       condition payment;
4
5    void credit (int amount)
6    {
7       balance += amount;  // increase account balance
8       payment.signal();  //signal other waiting threads that a payment
9                           //has been made
```

```
10  }
11
12  void debit (int amount)
13  {
14     while (balance < amount)
15        payment.wait();  // wait until a payment is made
16     // otherwise, adjust credit balance
17     balance -= amount;
18  }
19
20     // initialization
21     balance = 10000;  // initialize balance is $10000
22  }
```

These extensions are completely transparent to application code. Instead of rejecting a debit transaction that exceeds the credit limit, the monitor blocks the offending thread using a condition variable named payment. When a payment is made to the account, a signal operation (lines 8 and 9) awakens any suspended thread to compare its order amount against the credit limit (lines 14 and 15). If the thread passes the credit test, it debits the account and finishes the transaction; otherwise, it waits again for payment.

With this extension, the credit monitor has more ability to suspend and resume orders; but the solution is unfair. Consider a scenario in which an order from a Bundy branch is suspended because the account is short $1000. Soon thereafter, another branch sends a payment of $500, which is credited to the Bundy account and awakens the suspended thread. Upon resuming execution, this thread checks the credit limit and finds that it is still short $500, so it suspends itself again (on the condition variable payment) to await another payment. Now, if there are several suspended orders, this thread will be at the end of a queue, so it may not see the next payment signal[3] if the queue enforces a FIFO order.

To solve this problem, Shoe-Mart's crack team of MIS professionals quickly extends the monitor with an extra condition variable named the_rest (effectively another wait queue) to separate the next order to be processed from "the rest" of the orders, as shown below:

```
1   monitor credit_account {
2      int balance, rest_count;
3      condition payment, the_rest;
4
5   void credit (int amount)
6   {
7      balance += amount;  // increase account balance
8      payment.signal(); // signal other waiting threads that
9                        // a payment has been made
10  }
11
12  void debit (int amount)
13  {
14     if (rest_count > 0) {
```

---

[3]. This depends on how a monitor's condition variables are implemented. Some wake up all, in which case there will be a "race" condition. Other implementations wake up only the first thread in a wait queue.

```
15          rest_count++;
16          the_rest.wait(); // sleep at end of queue
17          rest_count--;   // signaled thread at head of queue wakes up
18                          // and run
19        }
20        // becomes the "next" order to be processed
21        rest_count++;
22        while (balance < amount)
23          payment.wait();  // wait until a payment is made
24        // the is enough credit, proceed with order and adjust credit
25        // balance
26        balance -= amount;
27        rest_count--;
28        the_rest.signal (); // finish transaction, signal others to
29                            // move up
30   }
31
32        // initialization
33        balance = 10000;  // initialize balance is $10000
34        rest_count = 0;
35   }
```

The first queue, associated with the condition variable `payment`, now contains at most one thread, representing the next order to be processed. If there is more than one pending order (due to insufficient credit), other threads wait on the queue associated with the condition variable `the_rest` in the order in which they are received by Shoe-Mart's system. When a payment is made that raises the spending limit above the amount required by a pending order on the payment queue, that thread resumes execution, processes the order, signals `the_rest`, and exits the monitor. When `the_rest` is signaled, the thread at the head of its queue wakes up and executes (line 16). If this thread again cannot process its order because of insufficient spending limit, it will block on the payment until another payment is made to the account.

Once again, the power of the monitor abstraction is demonstrated in that the application code remains oblivious to the monitor enhancements.

We have now shown several versions of this monitor with increasing levels of sophistication. The important thing is that all changes occur only in the monitor code module. All of the places in application code that use this monitor remain unchanged. With a facility for data encapsulation and synchronization, the monitor abstraction allows us to construct modular programs that are easy to understand and change.

4.6.3 Readers-Writers Problem

The readers-writers problem is another generalization of the producer–consumer problem, where strict mutual exclusion between all the threads is not needed. Since a reader thread does not change the value of shared data, we can improve performance by allowing many threads to read shared data simultaneously. The characteristics of this problem are:

*   Many readers can simultaneously read shared data.
*   Only one writer can update the shared data at a time.

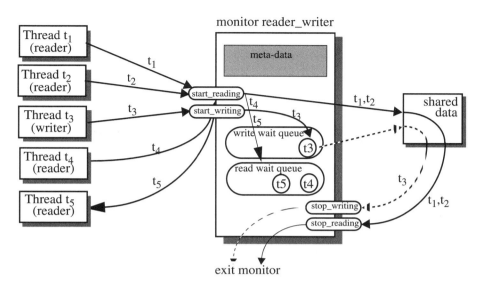

Figure 4-7. A Multiple-Readers/Single-Writer Monitor.

Under these conditions, it appears that we cannot use a monitor to encapsulate shared data and still perform concurrent read operations, since a monitor allows only one thread to execute inside it at a time.

A monitor *can* be used to solve this problem, however, if it encapsulates not the shared data itself but some associated "meta-data." Conceptually, by pairing a monitor with the shared data object, the monitor behaves like a "gatekeeper" controlling access to the associated data. Before accessing actual data, each thread must go through a monitor. Based on the meta-data, the monitor decides to either block a calling thread or let it perform its task. After a thread exits the monitor, the monitor again examines the meta-data to resume any blocked threads.

Figure 4-7 illustrates this idea using an example with five threads t_1 through t_5. Suppose that while thread t_1 reads shared data, thread t_2 calls the monitor, also wanting to read. t_2 is allowed to proceed, since concurrent reading is allowed. Another thread, t_3, comes along and wants to update the data. The monitor blocks t_3 until both t_1 and t_2 indicate that they have finished reading. At that point, the monitor unblocks t_3 and allows it to write data in the buffer. When t_3 finishes writing it informs the monitor so that the monitor can allow other threads (t_4 and t_5) to proceed.

Below is a skeletal implementation of a readers-writers monitor incorporating a multiple-readers, single-writer synchronization protocol. Once again, it guarantees that read and write operations are mutually exclusive, while allowing read operations to execute in parallel.

```
1    monitor reader_writer {
2       condition ok_to_read;
3       condition ok_to_write;
4       int ar_cnt, aw_cnt;
5       int wait_to_write;
6
7    void start_reading ()
8    {
9       if ((aw_cnt != 0) || (wait_to_write != 0))
10        ok_to_read.wait (); // if there are active or pending writer,
11                             // then wait
12      ar_cnt++; // OK to read now
13      ok_to_read.signal (); // signal other processes waiting on read
14      // exit monitor and proceed (to read)
15   }
16
17   void stop_reading ()
18   {
19      ar_cnt--;  // done reading, one less active reader thread
20      if (ar_cnt == 0) ok_to_write.signal (); // if no more
21                                      // active reader, let writer proceed
22   }
23
24   void start_writing ()
25   {
26      wait_to_write++;
27      if ((aw_cnt != 0) || (ar_cnt != 0))
28        ok_to_write.wait (); // if there are active readers or writer,
29                             // then wait
30      aw_cnt = 1; // OK to write now
31      wait_to_write--;
32      // exit monitor and proceed (to write)
33   }
34
35   void stop_writing ()
36   {
37      aw_cnt = 0; // done writing, indicate no active writer thread
38      ok_to_read.signal (); // tell pending readers to proceed
39      if ((aw_cnt == 0) && (ar_cnt == 0))
40        ok_to_write.signal (); // if there are no pending reader,
41                                      // next writer proceed
42   }
43
44      // initialization
45      ar_cnt = 0;
46      aw_cnt = 0;
47      wait_to_write = 0;
48   }
```

This monitor has four procedures: start_reading, stop_reading, start_writing, and stop_writing. It encapsulates three meta-data variables: ar_cnt (number of active readers), aw_cnt (number of active writers), and wait_to_write (number of threads waiting to write). To read data, a thread must first execute the start_reading operation in order to request a read lock. If there are no active or waiting writers, the monitor registers that thread as an active reader, allowing it to proceed. On the other hand, if there are threads actively writing or waiting to write to the shared data (line 9), the monitor blocks the thread using the condition variable ok_to_read.

Similarly, a thread must call start_writing before updating shared data. If there are active reader or writer threads, the thread is blocked inside the monitor on ok_to_write until these earlier operations are completed.

When a thread finishes reading, it calls the stop_reading procedure to notify the monitor that it no longer needs the data. When all readers have finished, the monitor releases one writer thread from the ok_to_write queue (line 19). Similarly, when a writer thread finishes, it calls stop_writing to notify the monitor so that all waiting readers may proceed. If there are none, the next writer is allowed to execute (lines 36 and 37).

This shows how we can solve a readers-writers problem by using a monitor to encapsulate meta-data that controls how shared data may be accessed. This is another way monitors can be used: to define and control access policies to shared data.

4.7 Summary

As we have seen, a monitor is a simple and powerful tool to encapsulate data and synchronize concurrent access by multiple threads. There are some drawbacks to using monitors. The fact that a monitor provides more than simple synchronization, additionally controlling access to data with mutual exclusion, means that the entire monitor behaves like a critical section; this may unnecessarily serialize threads' access. Another drawback is that if a thread calls a monitor procedure, it may block inside the monitor if requested resources are not available. Within certain programs such as real-time systems, however, we may prefer to let the thread do something else until the resources become available, then resubmit its request later.

Overall, monitors are an excellent tool for implementing concurrent programs. We can implement them in application code using C++ classes and synchronization primitives, as we will show in the next chapter.

4.8 Bibliographic Notes

Monitors were first suggested by Per Brinch-Hansen [1973]. They were then extended and formalized by C. A. R. Hoare [1974], who also showed how to solve the producer-consumer and readers-writers problems.

4.9 Exercises

1. Show that semaphores and monitors are equivalent (i.e., one can be used to implement the other).

2. Compare and contrast a semaphore's acquire and release operations and a monitor's wait and signal operations.

3. A restaurant has twenty seats for nonsmokers and ten for smokers. Write pseudo code for a monitor allowing the right number of nonsmokers and smokers to enter and leave the restaurant.

Hint: The monitor should have four procedures: `nonsmoker_enter`, `nonsmoker_leave`, `smoker_enter`, `smoker_leave`.

4. Implement the above problem using mutexes, and show that mutexes are just as powerful.

5. Give a solution to the readers-writers problem that favors: (a) readers, (b) writers.

6. Show that the solution to Exercise 5 can result in starvation.

4.10 References

1. Hansen, P. B. (1973). *Operating System Principles*. Prentice-Hall, Englewood Cliffs, NJ.
2. Hoare, C. A. R. (1974). Monitors: An Operating System Structuring Concept. *Communications of the ACM*, 17(10):549–557.

Simulating Monitors

*I*n the last chapter, we introduced monitors and presented several examples to illustrate their usefulness. In this chapter, we will show you how to build monitors using the data encapsulation facilities of C++ and the Win32 synchronization primitives. We will explore several ways in which a monitor can synchronize threads internally, and we will show how to implement monitors for several synchronization problems described in the previous chapter: bounded-buffer, credit account, and readers-writers.

For this chapter, a cursory knowledge of C++ is necessary to understand the simulations and examples.

5.1 Simulation of Monitor Constructs

Recall from Chapter 4 that a monitor, like a mutex, semaphore, or any other synchronization object, is a tool to control sharing of data in a multithreaded program. Monitors have the same synchronization capabilities as mutexes and semaphores, with the addition of data encapsulation. A monitor encapsulates data shared by many threads, and it specifies functions that must be used to access the data.

```
monitor Buffer                          class Buffer
{                                       {
    int data;                               int data;
                                        public:
    procedure put(int value)                void put(int value)
    {                                        {
        data = value;                            data = value;
    }                                        }
    procedure get(int &value)                void get(int &value)
    {                                        {
        value = data;                            value = data;
    }                                        }
    data = 0 ;                               Buffer()
}                                            {
                                                 data = 0 ;
                                             }
                                        };
```

Figure 5–1. Simulating a Monitor with the C++ Class Construct.

From a broader viewpoint, a monitor is a point of temporal synchronization in a multi-threaded program. All access to the data that it encapsulates is automatically serialized, because a monitor only allows one of its procedures to be executed at a time.

Some programming languages, such as Mesa [Lampson and Redell, 1980], Modula2 [Wirth, 1985], and Concurrent C [Gehani and Roome, 1989], include a monitor data type so that enforcement of mutual exclusion by compiler-generated code is automatic. C and C++ do not; but we can easily simulate one using C++ classes (for data encapsulation) together with synchronization objects (for mutual exclusion and condition variables), as the following subsections demonstrate.

5.1.1   Data Encapsulation

Suppose we want to simulate a monitor named `Buffer` that protects a shared integer variable with operations `get` and `put`. In Figure 5–1, comparing the pseudocode on the left with the C++ program on the right, we can see that a C++ class provides data encapsulation similar to that of a monitor.

5.1.2   Access Synchronization

A monitor synchronizes access to shared data by allowing only one function to execute inside it at a time; C++ classes by themselves do not have this capability. We can, however, easily implement this policy by augmenting each class instance with a mutex object and forcing all methods of a class to synchronize with each other so that only one can run at a time.

First, we must declare the mutex object as private data of the class. Then, we must force each method-function in the class to lock the mutex before execution and release it afterward. Because we have only one mutex object per class instance, only one method can lock it and execute at a time. Until the mutex is unlocked, other threads calling methods in the same class instance will block. This provides the mutual exclusion of a monitor.

```
1    class Buffer
2    {
3      HANDLE hMutex;
4      int data;
5    public:
6    void put(int value)
7    {
8      WaitForSingleObject(hMutex, INFINITE);
9      data = value;
10     ReleaseMutex(hMutex);
11   }
12
13   void get(int &value)
14   {
15     WaitForSingleObject(hMutex, INFINITE);
16     value = data;
17     ReleaseMutex(hMutex);
18   }
19
20   Buffer()
21   {
22     hMutex = CreateMutex(NULL, FALSE NULL) ;
23     data = 0 ;
24   };
```

The above code extends that of Figure 5–1 to include simulation of our sample monitor's synchronization mechanism. By making `put` and `get` call `WaitForSingleObject` as their first statement and `ReleaseMutex` as their last, we ensure that only one calling thread can run at a time. Access to the shared data is thus serialized.

5.1.3 Condition Variables

Condition variables facilitate communication and synchronization among a monitor's procedures, in addition to the mutual exclusion provided by its mutex. Two operations are possible on condition variables: *wait* and *signal*. A thread calling *wait* blocks until a condition associated with the variable becomes true. Calling *signal* releases a thread waiting for that condition. If there is no waiting thread, a *signal* call has no effect.

Building on our `Buffer` monitor example, we use two condition variables: `notEmpty` and `notFull`. If a thread calls `get` when there is no data available, it waits for a condition represented by the variable `notEmpty`. When another thread makes data available (by calling `put`), it will signal the condition `notEmpty` so that the thread awaiting `notEmpty` will awaken to consume the data.

Similarly, a producing thread that calls `put` when the buffer is full must wait for the condition represented by the variable `notFull`. When another thread subsequently calls `get` in order to consume buffered data, it will signal the condition `notFull`, causing the producer thread to awaken and put new data in the buffer. The following code shows how our example in Figure 5–1 can be enhanced with condition variables.

```
1    class Buffer
2    {
3       HANDLE lock;
4       Condition notEmpty, notFull;
5       int data;
6       bool empty;
7    public:
8    void put(int value)
9    {
10      WaitForSingleObject(lock, INFINITE) ;
11      while (!empty)
12         notFull.wait();
13      data = value;
14      empty = FALSE;
15      notEmpty.signal();
16      releaseMutex(lock);
17   }
18   void get(int &value)
19   {
20      WaitForSingleObject(lock, INFINITE) ;
21      while (empty)
22         notEmpty.wait();
23      value = data;
24      empty = TRUE;
25      notFull.signal();
26      ReleaseMutex(lock);
27   }
28   };
```

We can simulate a condition variable using two things: a binary semaphore and a reference count. The semaphore is used to block threads waiting for a particular event and to release them when the event occurs. The reference count is used to keep track of the number of waiting threads. Blocking and waiting for events within a monitor is risky, as it can lead to deadlock. We discuss this more fully in the next section.

5.1.4 A Shared Buffer Monitor

We will now show a complete simulation of a shared buffer monitor. The basic building blocks of our simulation consist of three C++ classes, Monitor, Semaphore, and Condition, as defined below:

```
1    class Monitor
2    {
3    protected:
4       HANDLE hMutex;
5       virtual void lock(){WaitForSingleObject(hMutex,INFINITE); };
6       virtual void release() { ReleaseMutex(hMutex); };
7       friend class Condition;
8
9    public:
10      Monitor() { hMutex = CreateMutex(NULL,FALSE,NULL); };
11      ~Monitor() { CloseHandle(hMutex); } ;
12   };
```

```
13   class Semaphore
14   {
15   protected:
16      HANDLE hSemaphore; //semaphore to be used by condition variable
17   public:
18      Semaphore() { hSemaphore = CreateSemaphore(NULL,0,1,NULL); };
19      ~Semaphore() { CloseHandle(hSemaphore); } ;
20      void P() { WaitForSingleObject(hSemaphore,INFINITE); };
21      void V() { ReleaseSemaphore(hSemaphore,1,NULL); };
22   };
23   class Condition
24   {
25   protected:
26      Semaphore semaphore;// semaphore object
27      int semaCount;// number of waiting thread on semaphore
28      Monitor *monitor;
29
30   public:
31   Condition(Monitor *mon) {
32      monitor = mon;
33      semaCount = 0;
34   };
35   ~Condition() {};
36
37   void wait() {
38      semaCount++; // one more thread waiting for this
39      monitor->release();// release monitor's lock
40      semaphore.P();// block until we are signaled
41      // signaled and unblocked, re-acquire monitor's lock
42      monitor->lock();
43      semaCount--;// got monitor lock, no longer in wait state
44   };
45
46   void signal() {
47      // release a thread blocked on the semaphore, if any
48      if (semaCount > 0)semaphore.V();
49   };
50   };
```

The class Semaphore (line 13) provides a constructor and two operations: P and V. When a Semaphore class object is created, the constructor function creates a semaphore object, and assigns its handle to the variable hSemaphore. The semaphore object has an initial count of zero and a maximum count of one (binary semaphore). Method P tries to acquire the semaphore object and blocks the calling thread if the object is owned by another thread. Conversely, method V releases semaphore ownership.

The Condition class (line 23) simulates a condition variable using a Semaphore class instance and a reference count. It defines methods named wait and signal that simulate a condition variable's *wait* and *signal* operations, respectively.

Since only one thread may enter a monitor at a given time, if a thread holding the mutex lock waits for a condition variable, no other thread can enter the monitor to make the condition true, and we have a deadlocked program. To avoid this, the *wait* operation on a condition variable must release the mutex lock before going to sleep (line 39). In order to maintain the mutual exclusion property of monitors, *wait* must then reacquire the monitor lock upon resumption, before returning control to the calling program.

Similarly, we cannot use the `ReleaseSemaphore` operation by itself in order to simulate the condition *signal*. If no thread waits for the condition represented by a condition variable, calling `ReleaseSemaphore` would increment the semaphore's counter preventing a subsequent *wait* from blocking even if the condition were false; so a correct implementation must check the reference count to see if there is a waiting thread. Only if the reference count is greater than 0 should it call `ReleaseSemaphore` to wake up that thread. Otherwise, if the reference count is zero, the *signal* operation simply returns, leaving the binary semaphore in the not-signaled state.

Using all four of the preceding building blocks, we can now implement our simple buffer monitor example:

```
1     class BufMon : public Monitor
2     {
3     protected:
4        Condition *notEmpty, *notFull;// condition variables
5        int empty;
6        int data; // shared data being protected by monitor
7
8     public:
9        BufMon();
10       ~BufMon();
11       void put(int value);
12       void get(int *value);
13    };
14
15    BufMon::BufMon()
16    {
17       // create condition variables
18       notEmpty = new Condition(this);
19       notFull = new Condition(this);
20       // there is no data initially
21       empty = TRUE;
22    }
23
24    BufMon::~BufMon()
25    {
26       delete notEmpty;
27       delete notFull;
28    }
29
30    void BufMon::put(int value)
31    {
32       // begin each method of monitor with lock and end with release
33       lock();
34       // wait until buffer is not empty
35       while(!empty) notFull->wait();
36       // buffer is empty, can put new value in now
37       data = value;
38       empty = FALSE;
39       notEmpty->signal();// signal so consumer threads can read data
```

```
40      release();
41   }
42
43   void BufMon::get(int *value)
44   {
45      lock();
46      // wait until buffer is not empty
47      while(empty)notEmpty->wait();
48      // there is stuff in buffer to consume now
49      *value = data;
50      empty = TRUE;
51      notFull->signal();//signal so producer threads can put in new data
52      release();
53   }
```

With this implementation, threads sharing data no longer need to synchronize with each other explicitly by manipulating mutexes and semaphores in every critical section. Instead, they can simply call the monitor put and get methods, which automatically synchronize access. For example, a producer-consumer solution can be simply programmed as follows:

```
 1   void Producer(BufMon *buffer)
 2   {
 3      int i;
 4      for (i=0; i<10; i++){
 5         buffer->put(i);
 6         cout << "produced: " << i << endl;
 7      }
 8      buffer->put(FINISHED);
 9   }
10
11   void Consumer(BufMon *buffer)
12   {
13      int value;
14      while(1){
15         buffer->get(&value);
16         if (value == FINISHED)
17            break;
18         cout << "consumed: " << value << endl;
19      }
20   }
21
22   void main()
23   {
24      HANDLE hThreadVector[2];
25      DWORD ThreadID;
26      BufMon buffer;
27      hThreadVector[0] = CreateThread (NULL, 0,
28            (LPTHREAD_START_ROUTINE)Producer,
29            (LPVOID) &buffer, 0, (LPDWORD)&ThreadID);
30
31      hThreadVector[1] = CreateThread (NULL, 0,
32            (LPTHREAD_START_ROUTINE)Consumer,
33            (LPVOID) &buffer, 0, (LPDWORD)&ThreadID);
34
```

```
35      WaitForMultipleObjects(2,hThreadVector,TRUE,INFINITE);
36   }
```

As we can see by comparing this to the code in Section 3.1, the sequence of operations needed to synchronize threads sharing buffered data is reduced to two simple lines of monitor invocation: lines 5 and 15 are all we need. By simulating and using a monitor, we have abstracted the synchronization mechanism and greatly simplified the application. This technique can significantly reduce subtle synchronization errors in large and complex multithreaded programs. In addition, by consolidating the synchronization mechanism in a monitor module, both the monitor and the application program become simpler to understand and easier to change. In order to change synchronization behavior, for example, we can simply modify the monitor instead of changing many critical sections throughout the application program.

5.2 Using Monitors

We have shown several solutions to the producer-consumer problem in previous sections, and we will now extend these to the bounded-buffer problem. Then we will use monitors to solve the shared bank account problem and the readers-writers problem.

5.2.1 Bounded-Buffer Problem

Like the producer-consumer example discussed in previous sections, bounded-buffer code manages a buffer of shared data. Although a set of buffers can be very large, compared to the one-slot variant used in our producer-consumer example, the two are identical in function. The following code implements a bounded-buffer monitor with BUFSIZE data elements.

```
1    class BoundedBuffer : public Monitor
2    {
3    protected:
4      Condition *notEmpty, *notFull;// condition variables
5      int data[BUFSIZE]; // shared data being protected by monitor
6      int count;
7      int head,tail;
8
9    public:
10     BoundedBuffer();
11     ~BoundedBuffer();
12     void put(int value);
13     void get(int *value);
14   };
15
16   BoundedBuffer::BoundedBuffer()
17   {
18     // create condition variables
19     notEmpty = new Condition(this);
20     notFull = new Condition(this);
21     // there is no data initially
22     count = head = tail = 0;
23   }
```

```
24
25   BoundedBuffer::~BoundedBuffer()
26   {
27     delete notEmpty;
28     delete notFull;
29   }
30
31   void BoundedBuffer::put(int value)
32   {
33     // begin each method of monitor with lock and end with release
34     cout << "BoundedBuffer::put()" << endl;
35     lock();
36     // wait until buffer is not empty
37     if (count == BUFSIZE)notFull->wait();
38     // buffer is not full, can put new value in now
39     data[tail] = value;
40     tail = (tail + 1) % BUFSIZE;
41     count++;
42     // signal so consumer threads can read data
43     // possibly blocked here if some thread waits for notEmpty
44     notEmpty->signal();
45     // resume execution here ... exit monitor
46     release();
47   }
48
49   void BoundedBuffer::get(int *value)
50   {
51     cout << "BoundedBuffer::get()" << endl;
52     lock();
53     // wait until buffer is not empty
54     if (count == 0) notEmpty->wait();
55     // there is stuff in buffer to consume now
56     *value = data[head];
57     head = (head + 1) % BUFSIZE;
58     count--;
59     // signal so producer threads can put in new data
60     // possibly blocked here if some thread waits for notFull
61     notFull->signal();
62     // resume execution here ... exit monitor
63     release();
64   }
```

5.2.2 Shared Credit Account Problem

The next program implements a monitor to control credit accounts in order to solve the problem introduced in Section 4.6.2. This monitor provides two main access functions: credit and debit. It maintains a credit balance that is increased by a credit (payment) and decreased by a debit (charge). A thread attempting to debit is blocked while the account balance is less than the debit amount.

```
1    const int CREDIT_LIMIT = 10000;
2
3    class CreditAccount : public Monitor
```

```
4   {
5   protected:
6       int balance; // credit balance of account
7       int wait_count; // number of pending/waiting transactions
8       Condition *payment, *the_rest; // condition variables
9
10  public:
11      CreditAccount();
12      ~CreditAccount();
13      void credit(int amount);
14      void debit(int amount);
15  };
16
17  CreditAccount::CreditAccount()
18  {
19      // create condition variables
20      payment = new Condition(this);
21      the_rest = new Condition(this);
22      // initial data state
23      balance = CREDIT_LIMIT;
24      wait_count = 0;// no one is waiting initially
25  }
26
27  CreditAccount::~CreditAccount()
28  {
29      delete payment;
30      delete the_rest;
31  }
32
33  void CreditAccount::credit(int amount)
34  {
35      // begin each method of monitor with lock and end with release
36      lock();
37      balance += amount;// increase account balance
38      // signal other threads that payment has just been made
39      payment->signal();
40      // resume execution here, ... exit monitor
41      release();
42  }
43
44  void CreditAccount::debit(int amount)
45  {
46      lock();
47      if (wait_count) {
48          // there are others on wait queue, so we get in line and wait...
49          wait_count++;
50          the_rest->wait();
51          // signaled and wake up here, resume execution
52          wait_count--;
53      }
54      wait_count++;
55      // wait for sufficient fund if necessary
56      while(balance < amount)
57          payment->wait();
```

```
58     // there is now enough credit for our transaction, proceed...
59     balance -= amount;
60     wait_count--;
61     // finish transaction, signal other threads
62     the_rest->signal();
63     release(); // exit monitor
64   }
```

And here is a sample use of this monitor to manage the account of Bundy shoe shop.

```
1    void Charge(CreditAccount *account)
2    {
3      int i;
4      for (i=0; i<10; i++)
5        account->debit(i*500);
6    }
7
8    void Payment(CreditAccount *account)
9    {
10     int value, i;
11     for (i =0; i<10; i++)
12       account->credit(i*500);
13   }
14
15   void main()
16   {
17     HANDLE hThreadVector[2];
18     DWORD ThreadID;
19     CreditAccount Bundy;
20
21     hThreadVector[0] = CreateThread (NULL, 0,
22                 (LPTHREAD_START_ROUTINE)Charge,
23                 (LPVOID) &Bundy, 0, (LPDWORD)&ThreadID);
24
25     hThreadVector[1] = CreateThread (NULL, 0,
26                 (LPTHREAD_START_ROUTINE)Payment,
27                 (LPVOID) &Bundy, 0, (LPDWORD)&ThreadID);
28
29     WaitForMultipleObjects(2,hThreadVector,TRUE,INFINITE);
30   }
```

To use a charge account, each store debits and credits the account as it orders and pays for merchandise.

5.2.3 Readers-Writers Problem

We can use monitors to solve the multiple readers and writers problem described in Chapter 4. Recall that many threads want to read from and write to a data repository (e.g., a file or a region of memory), and several threads may read, but only a single thread may write, at any given time. Clearly, we cannot use a monitor to encapsulate the shared data because it does not allow more than one thread to access data simultaneously. As the implementation below shows, however, a monitor can provide synchronization between the threads by encapsulating not the data, but *meta-data* describing the shared data.

In our solution to the readers-writers problem, the meta-data consists of two counters named `readerCount` and `writerCount`. `readerCount` is the number of threads reading the shared data, and `writerCount` is the number of threads writing to it. Before reading, a thread calls the `start_reading` method, which blocks on the condition `readWaitQueue` if a thread is currently writing data or other threads are waiting to write.

When a thread finishes reading shared data, it calls the `stop_reading` method. When the last reader thread exits, any waiting writer threads are signaled.

Similarly, a thread calls `start_writing` before updating shared data, and `stop_writing` afterward. The `stop_writing` method releases all threads waiting to read shared data. In this way, the monitor serializes read/write access to the data. Below, we show the implementation of a readers-writers monitor named `RW_Monitor`.

```
1     class RW_Monitor : public Monitor
2     {
3     protected:
4        int readerCount; // number of active readers
5        int writerCount; // number of active writers
6        int waitingReaders; // number of threads waiting to read
7        int waitingWriters; // number of threads waiting to write
8
9        Condition *readWaitQueue, *writeWaitQueue; // condition variables
10
11    public:
12        RW_Monitor();
13        ~RW_Monitor();
14        void StartReading();
15        void StopReading();
16        void StartWriting();
17        void StopWriting();
18    };
19
20    RW_Monitor::RW_Monitor()
21    {
22        // create condition variables
23        readWaitQueue = new Condition(this);
24        writeWaitQueue = new Condition(this);
25        // initial data state
26        readerCount = writerCount = 0; // no one is active initially
27        waitingReaders = waitingWriters = 0; // no one is waiting to read
28                           // or write yet
29    }
30
31    RW_Monitor::~RW_Monitor()
32    {
33        delete readWaitQueue;
34        delete writeWaitQueue;
35    }
36
37    void RW_Monitor::StartReading()
38    {
39        // begin each method of monitor with lock and end with release
40        lock();
```

```
41      // if there are threads waiting to read or write,
42      // this thread waits on queue
43      if (readerCount || waitingWriters){
44        waitingReaders++;
45        readWaitQueue->wait();
46        waitingReaders--;
47      }
48      // Ok_to_read got signaled, wake up thread....
49      readerCount++;
50      readWaitQueue->signal();
51      release();
52   }
53
54   void RW_Monitor::StopReading()
55   {
56      // begin each method of monitor with lock and end with release
57      lock();
58      readerCount--;
59      // if no more reader, tell writer thread to go ahead.
60      if ((readerCount == 0) && waitingWriters)
61        writeWaitQueue->signal();
62      else
63        readWaitQueue->signal();
64      release();
65   }
66
67   void RW_Monitor::StartWriting()
68   {
69      lock();
70      // if there are waiting writers or readers, need to wait on
71      // the queue
72      if (writerCount || readerCount){
73        waitingWriters++;
74        writeWaitQueue->wait();
75        waitingWriters--;
76      }
77      // ok_to_write got signaled, resume execution...
78      writerCount++;
79      // exit monitor
80      release();
81   }
82   void RW_Monitor::StopWriting()
83   {
84      lock();
85      writerCount--;
86      // if there are waiting readers, signal them to read
87      if (waitingReaders)
88        readWaitQueue->signal();
89      // otherwise signal to let the next writer proceed
90      else
91        writeWaitQueue->signal();
92      release();
93   }
```

And here is a sample use of a RW_Monitor.

```
1    int activeWriters; // indicate number of active writers
2    int buffer; // shared buffer
3    RW_Monitor *rwMonitor;
4
5    void Reader(int Id)
6    {
7       for (;;){
8          rwMonitor->StartReading();
9          if (activeWriters <= 0) { // all writers have terminated,
10                         // nothing more to read
11            rwMonitor->StopReading();
12            return;
13         }
14         cout << "Reader #" << Id << ": reading from shared space: "
15              << buffer << endl;
16         rwMonitor->StopReading();
17      }
18   }
19
20   void Writer(int Id)
21   {
22      int i,j = Id*10;
23      for (i=j; i<j+5; i++){
24         rwMonitor->StartWriting();
25         cout << "\nWriter #" << Id <<
26              " writing to shared space: " << i << endl;
27         buffer = i;
28         rwMonitor->StopWriting();
29      }
30      // indicate that this writer thread finishes.
31      rwMonitor->StartWriting();
32      activeWriters--;
33      rwMonitor->StopWriting();
34   }
35
36   void main()
37   {
38      HANDLE hThreadVector[5];
39      DWORD ThreadID;
40      rwMonitor = new RW_Monitor;
41      activeWriters = 2;
42      hThreadVector[2] = CreateThread (NULL, 0,
43               (LPTHREAD_START_ROUTINE)Reader,
44               (LPVOID) 1, 0, (LPDWORD)&ThreadID);
45      hThreadVector[3] = CreateThread (NULL, 0,
46               (LPTHREAD_START_ROUTINE)Reader,
47               (LPVOID) 2, 0, (LPDWORD)&ThreadID);
48      hThreadVector[4] = CreateThread (NULL, 0,
49               (LPTHREAD_START_ROUTINE)Reader,
50               (LPVOID) 3, 0, (LPDWORD)&ThreadID);
51      hThreadVector[0] = CreateThread (NULL, 0,
52               (LPTHREAD_START_ROUTINE)Writer,
```

```
53                    (LPVOID) 1, 0, (LPDWORD)&ThreadID);
54        hThreadVector[1] = CreateThread (NULL, 0,
55                    (LPTHREAD_START_ROUTINE)Writer,
56                    (LPVOID) 2, 0, (LPDWORD)&ThreadID);
57        WaitForMultipleObjects(5,hThreadVector,TRUE,INFINITE);
58    }
```

5.3 Summary

This chapter concludes our discussion of monitors. We described how to simulate them using the data encapsulation of C++ classes and the Win32 synchronization objects. As our examples have illustrated, using monitors considerably eases the burden of synchronization in multithreaded applications. Once a monitor and its condition variable classes have been implemented, all synchronization is confined to those classes. Many threads can then use a monitor without having to explicitly synchronize among themselves.

In the next chapter, we turn our attention to another important problem of multithreaded programming—how to ensure that multiple threads in an application do not deadlock.

5.4 Bibliographic Notes

Ben-Ari [1990] discusses an implementation of monitors, and he also gives a wonderful correctness proof for the *readers-writers* example. Andrews [1991] simulates *signal-continue* monitors, while Lampson and Redell [1980] describe an implementation of *signal-urgent* monitors in the Mesa system.

5.5 Exercises

1. What is the effect of using a FIFO list instead of LIFO stack to simulate a monitor?

2. What is the difference between "relinquishing ownership" and "exiting" a monitor?

3. In our solution to the readers-writers problem, reader threads suspend on an `ok_to_read` condition variable until an active writer calls the `stop_writing` procedure. As each reader thread goes through the `start_reading` procedure, it releases another reader thread with the *signal* call. The second reader releases another reader, and so forth, until the queue of waiting readers is empty. Implement a broadcast operation that replaces the *signal* operation in the `start_reading` procedure. When called by the first reader thread that enters the critical section, it should awaken all reader threads on the wait queue.

5.6 References

1. Andrews, G. (1991). *Concurrent Programming: Principles and Practice.* The Benjamin-Cimmungs Publishing Company, Inc., Redwood City, CA.
2. Ben-Ari (1990). *Principles of Concurrent and Distributed Programming.* Prentice Hall, New York, NY.
3. Gehani, N. H. and Roome, W. D. (1989). *Concurrent C.* Silicon Press.

Deadlock Analysis

*D*eadlock among a group of processes or threads is a situation in which each of them waits for a condition that can only be satisfied by the others. This situation usually arises when threads exhaust a finite pool of shared system resources, and the unmet condition is the release of some resources back into the pool. Since the deadlocked threads all wait for the others to release the needed resources, none of them makes any forward progress. In this chapter, we theoretically examine resource requirements and conditions that create deadlock. Using Dijkstra's dining philosophers example, we discuss the strategies and techniques commonly used to detect, prevent, and avoid system deadlocks.

6.1 Examples of Deadlock

Deadlock comes in many forms, but it can always be described in terms of a resource *requirement, acquisition,* and *release.* All of us have encountered and possibly been frustrated by deadlocks in one form or another. Let us examine a few:

- The working of the U.S. Congress. We can view each political party as a subsystem that requires the resources held by the other subsystems: power, concessions, or

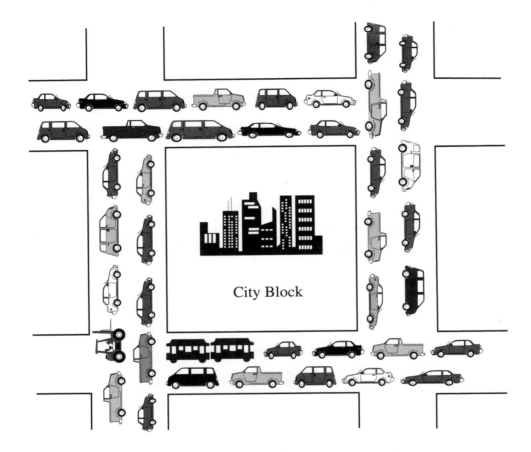

Figure 6–1. Traffic Gridlock.

compromises. With every subsystem tightly holding onto its own while resources waiting for the others to give up theirs, it is clear why there is a perpetual deadlock on Cap-
itol Hill.

- Another example is an automobile traffic deadlock (also known as gridlock). Figure 6–1
  illustrates such a situation where drivers enter an already congested intersection, blocking the flow of traffic around a block. In this example, the individual automobiles are
  the consuming processes and the resources are the spaces they occupy.

- In a multithreaded program, a deadlock could result from two threads requesting file
  descriptors, usually a limited resource. Suppose a system has ten file descriptors, where
  thread T_1 was granted five and thread T_2 was granted four. If each thread makes an
  additional request for two file descriptors in order to finish their respective tasks, the
  system cannot satisfy either request with the one remaining file descriptor. We thus

have a deadlock, even though each thread individually made a reasonable request and did not require more file descriptors than the system's total resources.

In the following sections, we will explore the requirements and conditions for deadlock, and what we can do to detect, prevent, or avoid it.

6.2 System Resources

Our definition of "resources" is not limited to hardware devices (printers, terminals, etc.), processors (CPU, FPU), or storage media (memory, disks, tapes). It also includes stored information such as programs, subroutines, files, and data. A resource can exist alone or as a collection of several similar instances. For example, in a single-processor machine, the CPU is the only resource of its type; but in a multiprocessor computer, a CPU is one resource unit among several of the same kind.

Computer programs need these resources to complete their tasks. When a resource is needed, a thread asks for it, uses it, and returns it back to the system when done. When a resource request is issued, the system may grant the resource if available, or deny the request when it cannot be satisfied.

Since each resource unit can only be used by one thread at a time, and threads may execute in parallel, access to resources must be carefully managed, and the potential for deadlock must be considered when determining the sequence in which requests are granted.

6.3 Conditions for Deadlock

The early work of Coffman et al. [1971] showed that in order for deadlock to occur, four conditions must exist:

1. **Mutual Exclusion**: A thread can seize exclusive control of an object, and no other thread can have access to it.
2. **Hold and Wait**: A thread can hold locked resources while waiting to acquire more.
3. **No Preemption**: Once a certain resource is held by a thread, it cannot be involuntarily reassigned to another thread.
4. **Circular Wait**: Two or more threads can hold some resources and await some held by other threads. If this dependency is circular, the threads will all be waiting for others to release needed resources, and none will make progress.

The following example shows three threads in a potential deadlock:

*   Thread T_1 wants resources R_1, R_2
*   Thread T_2 wants resources R_2, R_3
*   Thread T_3 wants resources R_3, R_1

Each thread wants to acquire the resources it needs, perform some computation, and then return the resources to the system when finished (Figure 6-2).

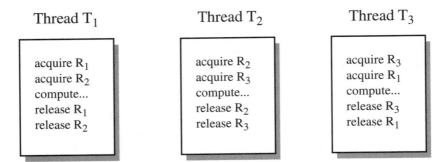

Figure 6-2. Individual Threads and their Resource Requirements.

Most of the time, threads T_1, T_2, and T_3 will each be able to seize all of their required resources in some order and proceed with their computations. Then there is no deadlock. For example:

T_1 gets R_1 & R_2, starts to compute

T_2 wants $R2 \Rightarrow$ blocks on R_2

T_3 wants R_3 & $R_1 \Rightarrow$ gets $R_3 \Rightarrow$ blocks on R_1

T_1 finishes and releases R_1 & R_2

T_2 gets R_2, wants $R_3 \Rightarrow$ blocks on R_3

T_3 gets R_1 and starts to compute

T_3 finishes and releases R_3, R_1

T_2 gets R_3 and starts to compute

T_2 finishes and releases R_2, R_3

This order of execution is just one possible permutation of the scheduling order, but as long as one thread is able to obtain its required resources there is no deadlock. Other threads might have to wait, but eventually they will finish.

However, deadlock occurs if the scheduler happens to interleave them like this:

T_1 gets R_1

T_2 gets R_2

T_3 gets R_3

T_1 wants $R_2 \Rightarrow$ block (T_2 has it)

T_2 wants $R_3 \Rightarrow$ block (T_3 has it)

T_3 wants $R_1 \Rightarrow$ block (T_1 has it)

Deadlock!

Since we usually cannot control the order of thread execution, we must be prepared for the worst and handle this case if we want to avoid deadlock unconditionally. This deadlock example satisfies all four deadlock requirements discussed earlier:

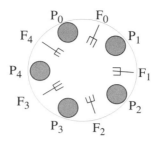

Figure 6-3. The Dining Philosophers' Table.

Mutual exclusion: Threads T_1, T_2, and T_3 lock and hold exclusive access to resources R_1, R_2, and R_3, respectively.

Hold and wait: T_1, T_2, and T_3 individually hold R_1, R_2, and R_3, while waiting for R_2, R_3, and R_1, respectively.

No preemption: Neither the system nor the thread themselves voluntarily reassign resources held by the other threads. Once each thread waits for the others in a deadlock, there is no mechanism for the system to automatically seize a resource from one thread and give it to another thread in order to break the deadlock.

Circular wait: Each thread depends on resources held by other threads to make progress. In this case, the dependency is circular. Since T_1 depends on T_2 to release R_2, T_2 depends on T_3 to release R_3, and T_3 depends on T_1 to release R_1, all threads wait and none makes progress.

6.4 The Dining Philosophers Problem

A classic example of deadlock was first described by E. Dijkstra [1968]. In this problem, there are five philosophers sitting around a round table eating a meal of spaghetti. The table has been arranged such that each philosopher has one plate and between each pair of plates is a fork to be used for eating spaghetti. Each philosopher alternately eats spaghetti and thinks. The constraint is that each philosopher needs both a left and a right fork to eat the spaghetti. As each philosopher picks up the forks, eats, then sets them down to think, there is a possibility that none of them can eat again because of deadlock. This situation occurs when all five philosophers simultaneously pick up their left forks, and forever wait for the others to release another fork needed to begin eating. The same situation will also happen when all five philosophers simultaneously pick up their right forks. Figure 6-3 shows the table arrangement for the five philosophers. The philosophers are represented by P_0 to P_4, and the forks are represented by F_0 to F_4.

The following naive implementation of this problem demonstrates the occurrence of deadlock:

```
1    #include <iostream.h>
2    #include <windows.h>
3
```

```
4    #define PCOUNT 5
5
6    HANDLE hForkMutex[PCOUNT]; // array of mutex representing forks
7
8    VOID Philosopher(LPVOID id)
9    {
10     int left = (int) id;
11     int right = (left + 1) % PCOUNT;
12
13     while(1){
14       // pick up left fork
15       WaitForSingleObject(hForkMutex[left],INFINITE);
16       cout <<"Philosopher #" << id << ": picked up left fork" << endl;
17       // pick up right fork
18       WaitForSingleObject(hForkMutex[right],INFINITE);
19       cout <<"Philosopher #" << id << ": picked right fork & eat" << endl;
20       ReleaseMutex(hForkMutex[left]);
21       ReleaseMutex(hForkMutex[right]);
22       cout <<"Philosopher #" << id ": released forks & think" << endl;
23     }
24   }
25
26   void main()
27   {
28     HANDLE hThreadVector[PCOUNT];
29     DWORD ThreadID;
30     int i;
31
32     for (i=0; i<PCOUNT; i++)
33       hForkMutex[i] = CreateMutex(NULL, FALSE, NULL);
34
35     for (i=0; i<PCOUNT; i++)
36       hThreadVector[i] = CreateThread (NULL, 0,
37                 (LPTHREAD_START_ROUTINE)Philosopher,
38                 (LPVOID) i, 0, (LPDWORD)&ThreadID);
39
40     WaitForMultipleObjects(PCOUNT,hThreadVector,TRUE,INFINITE);
41   }
```

We will revise this example in the next few sections to demonstrate several deadlock prevention strategies.

6.5 Handling Deadlocks

In general, there are several ways to deal with deadlocks:

- **Ignoration**: Handling deadlock is costly, and sometimes it is not practical to spend much computing resource to handle it, particularly in systems and situations where deadlock possibility is small. Since deadlock is a benign and easily detectable problem, in some cases one may choose not to handle deadlock in a program, and then manually break the cycle (usually by terminating one or several deadlocked threads or processes) when a deadlock is detected.

- **Detection**: There are algorithms to search for cycles of deadlocked threads and processes. When such cycles are detected, we can sometimes preempt some threads to release their resources, roll back their execution state, or simply terminate them.

- **Prevention**: Through a set of rigid rules and restrictive resource allocation requirements, we can prevent deadlock from occurring by precluding any one of the four conditions for deadlock at every point in a program.

- **Avoidance**: We can implement algorithms and services to carefully manage resource allocation in order to avoid getting into a potential deadlock situation. For efficiency, this solution does not rule out all possibility of deadlock like the *deadlock prevention* strategy; it simply monitors the state of the system's resource allocation and circumvents deadlock when imminent by being very conservative about resource allocation. Djikstra's *banker's algorithm* is a classic example of this approach.

Although these strategies provide the desired result, they have associated costs. If we decide to ignore the deadlock problem, we may eventually have to face a deadlock situation, and the cost will be the loss of work due to terminating some of the deadlocked threads. Using the deadlock detection, prevention, and avoidance strategies, the cost involves lengthy algorithms to detect deadlock, inefficient resource usage, or an elaborate resource allocation scheme, respectively. Furthermore, each strategy has other limitations. In all cases, implementing these strategies will no doubt result in programs that are more complex and slower. We now examine each strategy and its weaknesses in more detail.

6.6 Deadlock Prevention

Prevention is the most conservative and costly strategy for eliminating deadlock. Of the four conditions that must be present for deadlock to occur, we try to preclude at least one at each point in a program.

Removing the first condition, mutual exclusion, is not desirable or feasible since we need it in order to run threads without corrupting shared resources. That leaves three remaining conditions. Havender [1968] proposed the following strategies, each aimed at precluding one of them:

- **Prevent hold-and-wait**: Each thread must request all resources at once, and it cannot proceed until all resources are granted.

- **Allow preemption**: If a thread holding a resource is denied further resource requests, it must release all resources that it holds and request them later with the additional resource.

- **Prevent circular wait**: Impose a linear ordering on all resources R_j such that the order of resource request and allocation follows this ordering. For example, if a task has been allocated resources of type R_j, it can subsequently request only resource R_{j+1} or, later in the ordering, R_1 to R_n.

Although it is theoretically possible to eliminate deadlock with these strategies, implementing any of these in practice can involve cost and inefficiency. In the following sections, we examine these strategies in more detail.

6.6.1   Preventing the Hold-and-Wait Condition

The first strategy proposed by Havender, aimed at denying the hold-and-wait condition, requires that a process requests all resources at once, and that the system grants either all resources or none. Using this strategy, threads no longer hold resources while trying to acquire other resources, and the possibility of deadlock is eliminated.

In the following example, we modify the program of Section 6.4 to prevent a hold-and-wait condition. Note that in lines 12–14, we try to get both forks at once. Since the Win32 API does not provide any function that can guarantee an all-or-nothing lock on multiple resources, we simulate it with our GetBothForks function, which either successfully locks both resources or indicates its failure to do so.

```
1     #include <iostream.h>
2     #include <windows.h>
3
4     #define PCOUNT 5
5
6     HANDLE hForkMutex[PCOUNT]; // array of mutex representing forks
7
8     int GetForks(HANDLE fork1, HANDLE fork2)
9     {
10       DWORD status;
11
12       status = WaitForSingleObject(fork1,0);
13       if (status)   return 0;
14       // got first resource, try for the second
15       status = WaitForSingleObject(fork2,0);
16       if (status){
17         // failed to get second resource, release all held resources
18         // and abort
19         ReleaseMutex(fork1);
20         return 0;
21       }
22       //else we have successfully gotten both resources,announce success
23       return 1;
24    }
25
26    VOID Philosopher(LPVOID id)
27    {
28       int left = (int) id;
29       int right = (left + 1) % PCOUNT;
30       int status = 0;
31
32       while(1){
33         // pick up both forks at once, or nothing at all
34         status = GetForks(hForkMutex[left],hForkMutex[right]);
35         if (status == 0){
36           cout << "Philosopher #" << id <<
```

```
37               ": couldn't get forks, try again..." << endl;
38            continue; // did not get both forks, try again
39         }
40         cout << "Philosopher #" << id <<
41            ": picked up forks & eat" << endl;
42         ReleaseMutex(hForkMutex[left]);
43         ReleaseMutex(hForkMutex[right]);
44         cout << "Philosopher #" << id <<
45            ": released forks & think" << endl;
46      }
47 }
48 void main()
49 {
50      HANDLE hThreadVector[PCOUNT];
51      DWORD ThreadID;
52      int i;
53
54      for (i=0; i<PCOUNT; i++)
55         hForkMutex[i] = CreateMutex(NULL, FALSE, NULL);
56      for (i=0; i<PCOUNT; i++)
57         hThreadVector[i] = CreateThread (NULL, 0,
58               (LPTHREAD_START_ROUTINE)Philosopher,
59               (LPVOID) i, 0, (LPDWORD)&ThreadID);
60      WaitForMultipleObjects(PCOUNT,hThreadVector,TRUE,INFINITE);
61 }
```

In practice, this solution can lead to inefficient resource usage. For example, suppose a batch job requires a plotter and a printer, but it only needs to use the printer after it has plotted data, which takes several hours. During this time, other threads that want the printer cannot be started because the printer is unavailable. Starvation can also occur with this solution, since each thread must be granted all requested resources in order to start, but it is possible that not all are available at once, so a thread might never run.

6.6.2 Allowing the Preemption Condition

In allowing preemption, Havender's strategy requires each thread to release all resources held upon denial of an additional resource request. This strategy introduces (voluntary) preemption and eliminates deadlock. Below, we modify the dining philosophers program to demonstrate this strategy:

```
1    #include <iostream.h>
2    #include <windows.h>
3
4    #define PCOUNT 5
5
6    HANDLE hForkMutex[PCOUNT]; // array of mutex representing forks
7
8    VOID Philosopher(LPVOID id)
9    {
10     int left = (int) id;
11     int right = (left + 1) % PCOUNT;
12     DWORD status;
13
```

```
14      while(1){
15          status = WaitForSingleObject(hForkMutex[left],0);
16          if (status)   continue;
17          cout << "Philosopher #" << id <<
18              "picked up left fork" << endl;
19          // got first resource, try for the second
20          status = WaitForSingleObject(hForkMutex[right],0);
21          if (status){
22              // failed to get second resource, release all held resources
23              // and retry
24              ReleaseMutex(hForkMutex[left]);
25              cout << "Philosopher #" << id <<
26                  ": gave up left fork" << endl;
27              continue;
28          }
29          // else we successfully got the resources
30          cout << "Philosopher #" << id <<
31              ": picked up forks & started eating" << endl;
32          ReleaseMutex(hForkMutex[left]);
33          ReleaseMutex(hForkMutex[right]);
34          cout << "Philosopher #" << id <<
35              ": released forks and now thinking" << endl;
36      }
37  }
38
39  void main()
40  {
41      HANDLE hThreadVector[PCOUNT];
42      DWORD ThreadID;
43      int i;
44
45      for (i=0; i<PCOUNT; i++)
46          hForkMutex[i] = CreateMutex(NULL, FALSE, NULL);
47
48      for (i=0; i<PCOUNT; i++)
49          hThreadVector[i] = CreateThread (NULL, 0,
50                  (LPTHREAD_START_ROUTINE)Philosopher,
51                  (LPVOID) i, 0, (LPDWORD)&ThreadID);
52      WaitForMultipleObjects(PCOUNT,hThreadVector,TRUE,INFINITE);
53  }
```

Here, we try to get each of the two forks (lines 9 and 13), and if we fail to get either one (lines 11 and 15), we back off (lines 12 and 17), release all previously held resources (line 16), and start over again.

This technique can lead to wasted work because threads may have to roll back their execution state when releasing held resources. This may be tolerated if it happens infrequently, but it can be very disruptive otherwise. Furthermore, starvation and livelocks are possible, since several threads can simultaneously request resources held by others, have their requests denied, release their resources, acquire resources again, be denied other resources, release their resources... again and again, running but making no progress.

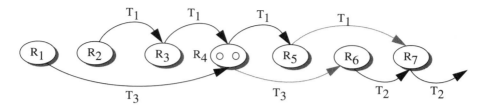

Figure 6-4. Deadlock Prevention by Resource Ordering.

6.6.3 Precluding Circular Waiting

To prevent circular waiting, Havender's third strategy requires that resources be ordered linearly, according to which they are requested, granted, and released. For example, threads holding resource R_i can only make subsequent requests for resource R_{i+1} or later in the ordering scheme. It can be proven that this strategy is deadlock-free, and we can intuitively see from Figure 6-4 that because the resource dependency arrows only flow one way, a closed circuit of dependency leading to deadlock is not possible.

In Figure 6-4, thread T_1 acquires resources R_2, R_3, R_4, and R_5, and is blocked on R_7 because T_2 has it. T_3 has R_1 and R_4, but blocks on R_6, also because of T_2. Eventually, T_2 finishes and releases its resources, allowing T_1 and T_3 to finish.

The following implementation of the dining philosophers program is deadlock-free because we use resource ordering:

```
1     #include <iostream.h>
2     #include <windows.h>
3
4     #define PCOUNT 5
5
6     HANDLE hForkMutex[PCOUNT]; // array of mutex representing forks
7     VOID Philosopher(LPVOID id)
8     {
9        int i = (int) id;
10       int j = (i + 1) % PCOUNT;
11       int smaller = (i<j)? i : j;
12       int bigger = (i>j)? i : j;
13
14       while(1){
15          // pick up left fork
16          WaitForSingleObject(hForkMutex[smaller],INFINITE);
17          cout << "Philosopher #" << id <<
18             ": picked up first fork" << endl;
19          // pick up right fork
20          WaitForSingleObject(hForkMutex[bigger],INFINITE);
21          cout << "Philosopher #" << id <<
22             ": picked up forks & start eating" << endl;
23          ReleaseMutex(hForkMutex[smaller]);
24          ReleaseMutex(hForkMutex[bigger]);
25          cout << "Philosopher #" << id <<
```

```
26              ": released forks and now thinking" << endl;
27      }
28  }
29
30  void main()
31  {
32      HANDLE hThreadVector[PCOUNT];
33      DWORD ThreadID;
34      int i;
35
36      for (i=0; i<PCOUNT; i++)
37          hForkMutex[i] = CreateMutex(NULL, FALSE, NULL);
38
39      for (i=0; i<PCOUNT; i++)
40          hThreadVector[i] = CreateThread (NULL, 0,
41                      (LPTHREAD_START_ROUTINE)Philosopher,
42                      (LPVOID) i, 0, (LPDWORD)&ThreadID);
43
44      WaitForMultipleObjects(PCOUNT,hThreadVector,TRUE,INFINITE);
45  }
```

In this code, we assign each fork a unique sequence number and force each philosopher thread to take a lower number fork first. Following this fork acquisition order, the philosophers will never deadlock.

Like the two earlier deadlock prevention strategies, this one also suffers from the undesirable characteristics similar to the other two strategies: inflexibility and inefficiency. Not every thread needs resources in the same order, and forcing each to obtain resources in order means that some are allocated well before use, possibly causing other threads to wait for arbitrarily long periods. Furthermore, ordering works well only for a fixed set of resources, and poorly for a changing or dynamic set.

6.7 Deadlock Detection and Recovery

One way of handling deadlock is to let it occur, then detect and break it. When there is a circular dependency, early research on deadlock Holt [1972] showed that we can use directed graphs to model and reveal it more clearly.

6.7.1 Resource Allocation Graph

Let's define a directed graph in which each node represents a thread or a resource to be acquired. Furthermore, let's define an arc from node T_i to node R_j to denote that *thread T_i is waiting for resource R_j*, and an arc from R_j to T_i to denote that *thread T_i is holding resource R_j*. Using this definition to model our running example, we have the **resource allocation graph** in Figure 6-5.

This graph has a closed circuit (a circular path), which means that a condition for deadlock is possible among this set of threads and their resource demands. With a single resource of each type, this closed circuit of resource dependency is a necessary and sufficient condition for deadlock. Note, however, that having the closed circuit does not mean that deadlock

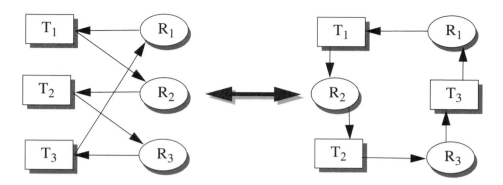

Figure 6-5. Two Views of the Same *Resource Allocation Graph.*

will occur every time, but rather that the potential for deadlock exists. The three-thread system in our example clearly shows that despite a cycle in its resource allocation graph, deadlock only happens when the threads' instructions are perfectly interleaved.

With multiple resources of each type, having a closed circuit is still a necessary condition for deadlock, but we need to extend our graph model to account for this property. In our extended graph, the resource node R_j represents a group of one or more resources of the same type. In this case, our graphical depiction of the resource node contains a number or several small circles to indicate the quantity of resources. Naturally, with more than one resource of a type, there can be more than one outgoing arc from the resource R_i to the threads T_i. To be exact, if R_j contains n resources, then there can be from 1 to n outgoing arcs from node R_j

Using the same example, let's change R_1 to be a set of two resource units. We now have a slightly different resource allocation graph, as illustrated in Figure 6-6. Even with the same scheduling sequence that led to deadlock earlier, no deadlock is possible here since there is no closed circuit in this resource allocation graph. This time, T_3 will be able to have all of its required resources (R_3, R_1) and finish its computation. The release of R_3 and R_1 upon the completion of T_3 enables T_2 to complete and release R_2, which let T_1 finish.

6.7.2 Graph Reduction

This analysis can be done with a technique called **graph reduction**, consisting of two phases: *resource allocation* (see Figure 6-7) and arc/node *reduction*. Given a set of threads and their required resources, we can allocate resources to threads in different ways, and for each allocation we can run a reduction algorithm to see if there is a deadlock. Given a system of N threads, the computation cost to determine if it is deadlock free is $O(N^2)$, which is not cheap.

6.7.3 Deadlock Recovery

If deadlock occurs, there are a few recovery techniques we can use. Which to choose depends upon the relative cost and benefits. The common options are:

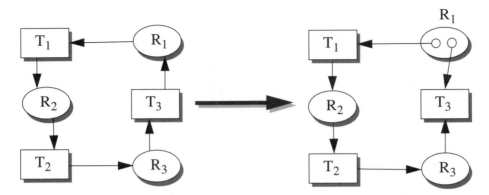

Figure 6-6. A Resource Allocation with Multiple Resource Units of R_1.

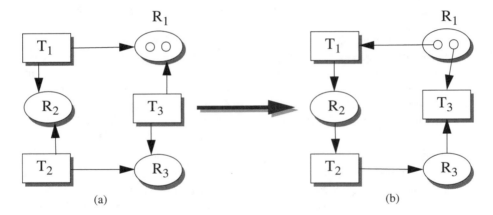

Figure 6-7. Resource Allocation: Granting Resources to Threads, (a) request, (b) allocated.

1. **Termination**. The simplest method of recovery is to terminate one or more threads in the deadlock cycle and allow others to proceed using the freed resources. But how do we decide which threads to terminate? One strategy is to terminate one thread at a time until the deadlock is broken. At the other extreme, we can simply terminate all threads in the resource-dependency cycle. It may also be possible to construct an analysis algorithm that suggests which thread to kill (such as the one holding the most needed resources), but this would add complexity and running time to the program. In general, terminating threads is an effective technique if they can be restarted without much inconvenience (e.g., a print job). In terminating a thread and restarting threads, however, we lose the time and work already done to that point.

2. **Preemption**. In a few cases, we may be able to preempt certain deadlocked threads and give their resources to others. For example, in a particular system we ported to the multithreaded environment [Pham and Garg, 1992], there was a thread that held a

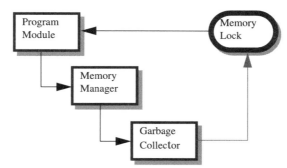

Figure 6-8. Deadlock from Nested Procedure Calls.

mutex lock on heap space to write shared data, and allocated heap memory in the writing process. Sometimes memory was low and needed to be garbage-collected. The garbage collector (GC), however, needed to lock the heap so that it could move the data safely. So the writing thread held a lock on heap space and waited for the GC, while the GC couldn't go on because it waited for the mutex lock on heap to be released by our thread. We had a deadlock. Knowing this behavior pattern, we preempted the writing thread by making it release the heap mutex, call the garbage collector, and terminate by calling itself with its own argument. This sequence of actions effectively preempted the execution of the writing thread in favor of the garbage collector (Figure 6-8).

3.   **Roll back from log**: This is the most expensive technique, since it requires threads to have a log of *checkpoints*. When deadlock is detected, we roll back the system state to the checkpoint where the resource causing the deadlock was allocated, in order to try a different allocation of resources. This requires rolling back the state of all threads in the system to that point, often difficult and costly. If we insist upon preventing deadlock at all cost, we are better off attacking this problem using the deadlock prevention technique, eliminating any possibility of deadlock from the onset.

6.8 Deadlock Avoidance

A less extreme practice than deadlock prevention is deadlock avoidance. Here, the possibility of deadlock still looms but when it is imminent we sidestep it with careful resource allocation, paying the full cost of thread serialization if necessary. By being less insistent about complete deadlock elimination, this technique allows resources to be allocated more flexibly, leading to improved utilization and performance.

Deadlock avoidance techniques are based on the idea that if we know how resource and processing units remain available in the system, we can determine whether granting a particular request will bring us to a state where deadlock is imminent. If so, we deny the request at that time. In effect, we implement an algorithm that can help us to carefully allocate resources and make the right choice every time about whether to grant or deny a resource request.

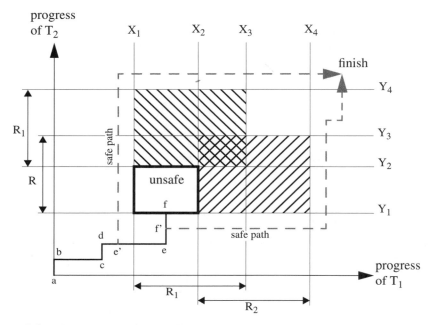

Figure 6-9. Safe and Unsafe States of System Progress.

6.8.1   Safe and Unsafe States

Before exploring deadlock avoidance techniques in greater detail, we must discuss the concept of *safe* and *unsafe* system states. A *safe state* is a state of computation in which there can be no deadlock resulting from the execution of threads and from granting them the requested resources. In other words, with the resources available in the system, there is a way to allocate resources to requesting threads so that they will all be satisfied, eventually complete their execution, and return resources to the system. An *unsafe state*, on the other hand, is one that eventually leads to deadlock.

This concept of safety can be illustrated in graphical form. In Figure 6-9, we model the progress of two threads, T_1 and T_2, sharing two resources, R_1 and R_2. The X and Y axes indicate the progress of threads T_1 and T_2, respectively. The shaded regions indicate resource requirements of the two threads. The step-like trajectory denotes their joint progress. In uniprocessor systems, only one thread at a time actually runs on the processor, so the progress trajectory is in either the X or Y direction. In multiprocessor machines, parts of the trajectory can be diagonal if the threads make progress in parallel across several processors.

In this diagram, every point in the trajectory indicates the joint progress of the two threads. In our example, progress can be made in either the positive X or Y direction, depending on the scheduling. When the trajectory crosses the X_1 line, resource R_1 is granted to T_1. At X_2, T_1 gets R_2. At X_3 and X_4, T_1 releases R_1 and R_2, respectively. Similarly, one can describe the progress of thread T_2 in the vertical direction at lines Y_1 to Y_4.

In our example, the progress trajectory first indicates progress made by T_2 (a–b), then T_1 (b–c), and so on, up to point f, where we find ourselves at the border of an unsafe state. At this point, if we allow progress to be made in the Y direction, we'll face imminent deadlock (at the shaded region). The reason for deadlock is obvious: thread T_1 has the resource R_1 and will need R_2 in the future. If we allow T_2 to own R_2 by crossing the line Y_1 at point f, the two threads will eventually deadlock with T_1 waiting for T_2 to release R_2 and T_2 waiting for T_1 to release R_1. This is exactly what happens at the X_2 and Y_2 borders of the unsafe regions. Note that it is impossible for a progress trajectory to enter the shaded regions, since that denotes resources needed by both threads. Our mutual exclusion rules ensure that two threads cannot own the same resources at the same time.

So, graphically and intuitively, if we can monitor the progress of thread execution and force progress in either the X or Y direction to avoid the unsafe region, we can avoid deadlock. One way to force progress in a particular direction is by denying resources to a particular thread, thereby making it wait while progress is made in the other direction past the unsafe region.

Using the two-threaded system in Figure 6-9 as an example, at points a, b, c, and d, we have complete freedom in granting resources R_1 and R_2 to either thread. As we give R_1 to T_1 moving from d to e, however, our options become limited because of potential deadlock. At point e, our safe choice is to move forward in the X direction past the unsafe region. At e, we can still allow T_2 to make progress, but only as far as point f without crossing line Y_1 into the unsafe region. At f, our safe resource allocation option is limited to denying R_2 to T_2 in favor of T_1, even if it means forcing R_2 to block when T_1 may not need R_2 just yet. In general, a deadlock avoidance algorithm uses its knowledge of resource availability in a system to direct allocation among threads and steer the system's progress away from unsafe states in order to avoid deadlocks.

6.8.2 Banker's Algorithm

Among various deadlock avoidance techniques, Dijkstra's *banker algorithm* is perhaps the most famous. The algorithm is known by this name because it mimics the way in which a banker would grant lines of credit to a group of clients, whose combined financial need is often larger than the banker's liquid assets. The banker must therefore manage his resources so that he can satisfy his customers' borrowing needs. If he is not careful in lending, he may eventually run into a situation where he runs out of money and still has unsatisfied loan applications. The customers then cannot repay their loans since they were not able to borrow enough to finish their investment tasks. Thus, we have a deadlock in which borrowers cannot borrow and the lender cannot lend.

For example, in Figure 6-10 the banker has three customers, Robert, Susan, and Terry, who are granted lines of credit of 5, 8, and 7 units, respectively. (A unit can be a certain number of dollars, but this is not important in our discussion.) The total needed is 20 units, but suppose our banker only has 12 units available to lend. Let us assume that if the banker can grant a customer the full loan requested, the customer is satisfied, uses the money, and repays it at some future time. (In our ideal world, there is no default or interest.) The initial state of this situation is described in Figure 6-10a.

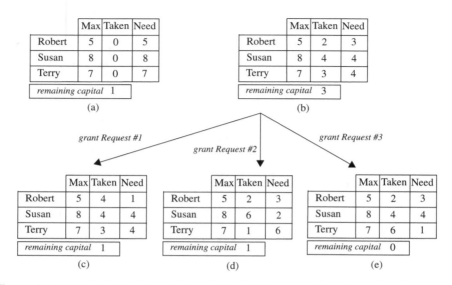

Figure 6-10. Banker's Algorithm: Safe and Unsafe Resource Allocations, (a) safe, (b) safe, (c) safe, (d) unsafe, (e) unsafe.

Over time, the customers take out their loans, and this could eventually produce a situation where Robert, Susan, and Terry took out loans of 2, 4, and 3 credit units, respectively, and the banker has only 3 units of capital left to lend (Figure 6-10b). He must carefully examine each incoming loan request to avoid running out of money and being unable to satisfy the borrowing need of at least one customer.

Suppose the banker now receives three loan requests from his customers: Robert asks for 2 units (Request #1), Susan asks for 2 (Request #2), and Terry asks for 3 (Request #3). Our banker must examine each request and check to see if granting it will cause him to be in an unsafe state. The banker knows he is currently in a safe state, since he has 3 units left in his vault, which could be used to satisfy Robert's total need, after which he will repay all 5 resources units when finished. Granting Robert's request will leave our banker with 1 resource unit, still able to satisfy the minimum borrowing need of 1 (from Robert) in the future (Figure 6-10c). This is a safe state. On the other hand, granting 2 units to Susan will leave our banker with 1 resource unit, unable to complete any one loan in the future because the minimum need is 2 units (Figure 6-10d). Similarly, granting 3 units to Terry will deplete the resources available, but there will still be three unsatisfied customers (Figure 6-10e). Thus, the only safe move is to grant Robert's loan request.

This strategy applies directly to computer resources, where customers correspond to threads and credit lines correspond to the resource requirements of each thread, such as disks, shared data, I/O devices, and so on. The banker becomes an algorithm and resource allocation process that we must implement to avoid deadlock.

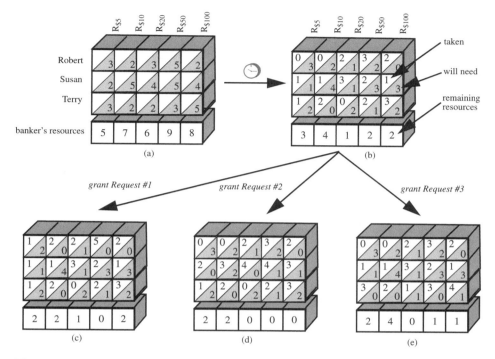

Figure 6-11. Banker's Algorithm for Multiple Resources, (a) initial state, (b) safe, (c) safe, (d) unsafe, (e) unsafe.

6.8.3 Banker's Algorithm for Multiple Resources

The banker's algorithm can easily be generalized to handle several kinds of resources. Let us extend our example to illustrate this by allowing the lender and borrowers to handle loan units of several currency denominations: $5, $10, $20, $50, and $100. Again, a unit can be a fixed number of bills, say 100, but this does not affect our discussion.

Using Figure 6-11a as an illustration, suppose the banker has [5,7,6,9,8] units of the respective currency denominations, and the customers qualify for the lines of credit Robert [3,2,3,5,2], Susan [2,5,4,5,4], and Terry [3,2,2,3,5]. Again, total customer need exceeds the banker's resources, so he must manage the transactions carefully to avoid deadlock.

Over time, Robert, Susan, and Terry take out the loans [0,0,2,3,2], [1,1,3,2,1], and [1,2,0,2,3], respectively. The system comes to a state described by Figure 6-11b.

Suppose the banker now receives three loan requests: (#1) Robert asks for [1,2,0,2,0], (#2) Susan asks for [1,2,1,2,2], and (#3) Terry wants [2,0,1,1,1]. To be safe from deadlock, the banker must compute the state he will be in if he grants each request, and he must approve it only if he will be in a safe state. Granting Robert's request will leave the banker with [2,2,1,0,2] resource units, enough to satisfy at least one customer (Figure 6-11c). Similarly, granting Susan's request will put the banker in a safe state, because his remaining resources will be large enough to fulfill the minimum need of at least customer, namely Robert

(Figure 6-11d). On the other hand, granting Terry's request will eventually cause deadlock because the banker's remaining resources will not be enough for any of his customer's needs (Figure 6-11e). Thus, the banker can safely grant either Robert's or Susan's loan request. Again, the strategy applies directly to multiple types of computer resources, such as file descriptors, disk arrays, and so forth.

6.8.4   Limitations of Bankers' Algorithm

The *banker's algorithm* is simple and elegant, but there are some serious weaknesses that prevent its use in practice. As you might have observed in our running example, the algorithm requires that we know a priori:

- The number of resources

- The number of resource users

- The maximum resource need of each user

In a modern computing system, users and resources change dynamically, so these requirements are restrictive and impractical. It is also very hard to require each thread or process to specify in advance the resources it will need. Finally, there is no simple way to determine how long a thread must wait until the system can safely grant its request. This may be unacceptable for real-time systems.

Despite its weaknesses, the algorithm remains theoretically interesting and important because it is occasionally practical and provides a standard against which to compare other algorithms.

6.9 Summary

This chapter illustrated several examples of deadlock, listed the conditions under which deadlock occurs, and discussed various deadlock handling techniques. Deadlock is a situation in which two or more threads wait for conditions that can only be established by the others. Four conditions must be present for deadlock to occur: mutual exclusion, hold and wait, no preemption, and circular wait.

There are several ways to handle deadlock. One is to ignore it altogether. For deadlock detection there are algorithms to search for deadlocked threads, allowing us to preempt, roll back, or simply terminate the deadlocked threads. Resource allocation graphs and the graph reduction technique are useful to identify a potential deadlock situation among a group of processes or threads. Deadlock prevention can be achieved by precluding the conditions for deadlock at every point in the program. The deadlock avoidance technique seeks to improve resource utilization by not ruling out all possibilities of deadlock, but rather monitor and control a system's resource allocation to steer it away from a potentially deadlocked (unsafe) state. Finally, the concept of state safety and Dijkstra's banker's algorithm for single and multiple resources were illustrated by two examples.

6.10 Bibliographic Notes

The concept of system deadlock was studied actively during the late 1960s and throughout the 1970s to early 1980s. The four conditions for deadlock were defined by Coffman et al. [1971]. The techniques for deadlock prevention originated from the pioneering work of Havender [1968]. The concept of state safety and the banker's algorithm were introduced by Dijkstra [1968]. Haberman [1969] provided proofs on state safety and state transitions for deadlock avoidance. Modeling of resource requests and allocations using graphs was done by Holt [1972]. Much work was done on deadlock detection techniques by Murphy [1968], Newton [1979], and others. The two operating system textbooks, [Deitel, 1990] and [Tanenbaum, 1992], have excellent chapters and references on deadlock. The presentation of Dijkstra's *banker's algorithm* for a single resource was modeled after a very clear explanation in [Tanenbaum, 1992].

6.11 Exercises

1. What are the four conditions for deadlock? Describe them.
2. What are the four ways in which we can handle a system deadlock?
3. Trace the program steps of the five philosophers in Section 6.4 simultaneously picking up forks and show how they can deadlock.
4. In the example of Section 6.6.1, why can't we use the function `WaitForMultipleObject` to get all the resources at once? What can happen if you use this function?
5. As in question 3, trace the program steps of the five philosophers in Section 6.6.3. Show why they cannot possibly deadlock.
6. Deadlock prevention strategies can effectively eliminate the possibility of system deadlock. But at what price? Describe the inefficiencies that result from implementing each of the three deadlock prevention strategies.
7. In Figure 6-9, what does the "unsafe" area signify? Why don't we want the execution path to reach point f?
8. What is the Banker's algorithm? How does it work? And, what are its strengths and weaknesses?

6.12 References

1. Coffman, Jr., E. G., Elphick, M. J., and Shoshani, A. (1971). System Deadlocks. *Computing Surveys*, 3(2):67–78.
2. Deitel, H. M. (1990). *An Introduction to Operating Systems.* Addison-Wesley, Reading, MA.
3. Dijkstra, E. W. (1968). Cooperating sequential processes. In Genuys, F., editor, *Programming Languages.* Academic Press, New York.
4. Haberman, A. N. (1969). Prevention of System Deadlocks. *Communications of the ACM*, 12(7):373–377.
5. Havender, J. W. (1968). Avoiding Deadlock in Multitasking Systems. *IBM Systems Journal*, 7(2):74–84.
6. Holt, R. C. (1972). Some Deadlock Properties of Computer Systems. *ACM Computing Surveys*, 4(3):179–196.
7. Murphy, J. E. (1968). Resource Allocation with Interlock Detection in a Multitask System. In *Proceedings of the AFIPS Fall Joint Computer Conference*, vol. 33, pp. 1169–1176.

Thread-Package Architectures

*M*odern computing systems increasingly support multiple threads of execution in a single address space in order to let application programs take advantage of hardware-supported concurrency while maintaining modularity. Two important factors affect the performance and modularity of multithreaded applications: (1) the *implementation architecture* of an underlying thread package, and (2) the *programming model* used by the application. In this chapter, we survey the most common thread-package architectures, and in the next chapter we will discuss programming models for multithreaded applications.

To appreciate how a thread package is implemented in relation to the operating system, we begin with an overview of a typical operating system structure. We then describe the implementation of *user-level threads, kernel-level threads, multiplexed threads,* and *kernel-supported user-level threads* (also called *scheduler activations*). We discuss the strengths and weaknesses of each implementation, and the implications for application program design. Since the architecture and performance characteristics of a thread package can sometimes influence the performance, concurrency, and modularity of a multithreaded application, knowledge of the underlying thread package will help you when porting or designing such applications.

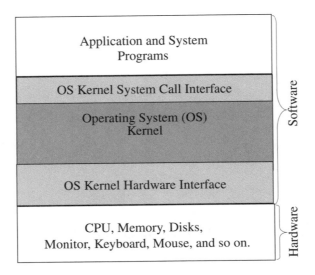

Figure 7-1. The Structure of a Typical Computer System.

7.1 Operating System Structure

Thread packages are intimately related to operating systems. A thread package is built either as a part of an operating system, as a library on top of it, or a combination of both. In order to understand its behavior, we must therefore review some basic operating system concepts. Figure 7-1 illustrates the structure of a typical application running on a computer. The foundation is computer hardware, including a central processing unit (CPU), memory, disks, monitors, keyboards, and so forth. Executing on this is an operating system, a special program that manages the machine's resources. It provides an environment in which application programs can more easily use hardware to carry out their computations.

The central component of an operating system is a *kernel* (or *supervisor*), which provides such services as memory, process, and I/O management, networking, and so forth, through a set of subroutine-like *system calls*. Applications use the *system call interface* to perform operations like reading from a file (on disk), writing to a file or a terminal, sending data to another computer, and so on.

Applications are rarely allowed to access shareable hardware resources directly, only to request that the kernel provide equivalent services. This is necessary in multiuser and multi-programmed computing systems, in order to prevent one application from inadvertently or maliciously destroying data belonging to another. The hardware and operating system usually cooperate to establish a memory-access barrier. On one side of the barrier is a kernel process that runs in a special, privileged execution mode (*kernel mode*). On the other side is a user's application program, which runs in nonprivileged execution mode (*user mode*). When an application program thread makes a system call, the operating system *traps* the call, suspends the calling thread, invokes the kernel to perform the requested service, places the result on the

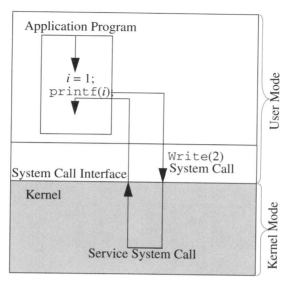

Figure 7-2. User and Kernel Modes in a Typical Operating System Call.

calling thread's stack, and then resumes the thread's execution. This sequence of actions involves two context switches in order to transfer control of the CPU from a user program to the kernel and back.

For example, Figure 7-2 shows how an application program writes an integer, i, to a terminal. An executing thread calls a function named printf, which invokes a write system call. At this point, a context switch passes control of the CPU to the kernel, which services the call by sending appropriate commands to a device driver software module for the terminal, which in turn causes hardware to display information on screen. Once output is done, the system call terminates, and another context switch resumes the application program. Because of these context switches, making a system call is much more expensive than calling a local application program subroutine.

Until recently, most operating systems were large monolithic programs in which a kernel could not easily be distinguished from other subsystems. Because the entire operating system runs in a privileged mode, an expensive system call is required in order to switch from user code to operating system code and back. Furthermore, such a large complex program is hard to implement and maintain as it evolves, since a bug can create widespread damage. Thus, operating systems, like application programs, are evolving towards more modular designs. Modern operating systems often have a small kernel (called a *microkernel*) that provides only essential services, like memory management, process scheduling, and I/O device access. All other services are provided by nonprivileged processes. Examples of these microkernel-based operating systems are Mach, Chorus, Amoeba, and, to an extent, Windows NT.

In the following, we will see how various thread packages coordinate with an operating system kernel in order to cope with the high cost of kernel context switching.

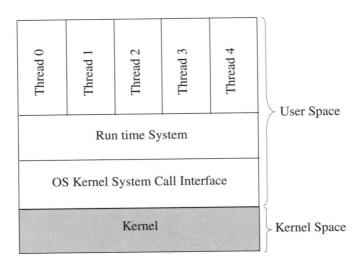

Figure 7-3. Implementation Architecture of a User-Level Thread Package (adapted from [Tanenbaum, 1992]).

7.2 Thread Package Implementations

The most important factor affecting the performance of a thread implementation is whether, and how much, operating system intervention is required in order to create, schedule, synchronize, and switch context among threads. Some thread packages are part of the operating system, which directly manipulates and schedules the threads, but not all. Other thread packages avoid expensive operating system calls and provide greater speed by managing threads in an application program's address space; still others combine both of these strategies.

We now describe several implementation architectures: *user-level threads, kernel-level threads, multiplexed threads*, and *scheduler activations*. We discuss their strengths, weaknesses, and implications for application programming.

7.2.1 User-Level Threads

A *user-level thread package* is implemented as a subroutine library that is linked and loaded with an application program (Figure 7-3). It includes all of the thread management and synchronization functions that an application program normally expects to call. As the name for this kind of package suggests, it resides entirely in an application program's memory address space at runtime. In this implementation, the operating system is not aware of multiple threads in the application program, and it views each user process as a single "kernel thread." Within such a program, the thread management code is responsible for multiplexing various threads of control on the process's CPU. In a time-sharing operating system, a process's time slice is thus shared among its user-level threads.

Some examples of user-level thread packages are Digital Equipment Corporation's (DEC) CMA threads [DEC, 1990], which is the basis for the Distributed Computing

Environment's (DCE) threads [OSF, 1993]; the thread package of the Portable Common Runtime (PCR) system developed at Xerox's Palo Alto Research Center [Weiser et al., 1989]; and the FastThreads package developed for DEC's Firefly multiprocessor at DEC's System's Research Center [McJones and Swart, 1987].

7.2.1.1 Advantages of User-Level Threads

User-level thread packages can be implemented on operating systems that do not by themselves support multithreaded processes. Using a runtime library, multiple threads can run in a single process, sharing its memory space and other system resources. Even though the operating system kernel treats an application as if it had only a single thread of execution, from an application programmer's point of view the code behaves as if it had multiple threads; so user-level thread packages allow the two models to coexist in the same environment.

User-level threads are fast and efficient. Because a runtime library manages threads without operating system intervention, creating threads and context switching among them is very fast. For example, when a thread makes a blocking call (e.g., blocking on a mutex), yields control of the CPU, or exhausts its time quantum, the runtime library saves the thread's context, selects the next thread to run, and installs its context. By managing scheduling of all the threads in a process, a user thread library can maximally utilize the CPU time slice allocated to that process. The speed of the user-level threads comes from the fact that everything happens in the user space, without any need for a time-consuming system call.

User-level threads are flexible. Since each application program has its own copy of the runtime library, each can, for example, choose its own thread scheduling policy. In a system of two programs you could set the scheduling policy of one program to SCHED_FIFO (First In, First Out), while threads in the other process use SCHED_RR (Round Robin, priority time sliced).

7.2.1.2 Drawbacks of User-Level Threads

Blocking System Calls

Despite their advantages, user-level thread packages are hard to implement. One difficulty is the proper handling of blocking system calls. Since an operating system only sees a single thread of control in each process, if one thread makes a system call that blocks, the kernel blocks the entire process even though other threads in it may be ready to run. In other words, a user thread making a blocking call effectively suspends all other threads in that process. Examples of UNIX© system calls that may block are *read*(2), *select*(2), *wait*(2), *pause*(2), and so on. A typical operating system might have several dozen such calls.

A good user threads library cannot allow such behavior since it defeats the purpose of having multiple threads and concurrent execution. If the operating system provides nonblocking versions of a system calls, the library can use these to perform its own thread scheduling. For example, some UNIX operating systems have a select system call that has both a blocking version and a nonblocking version. If a thread wants to read from a socket that does not have data available yet, the library could first use the nonblocking select to check for data and, if there is none, block the thread, save its execution context, then run another thread.

When the library's scheduler runs again, it polls the socket using another non-blocking `select`, and, if data is available, schedules the blocked thread.

To avoid blocking in the kernel, a user-threads library mush re-implement all blocking system calls by first checking for possible blocks using the nonblocking version. Although this is laborious and inelegant, it is necessary because the only other alternative is to modify all operating system calls to make them nonblocking. Such an approach is undesirable because it is intrusive (and the operating system source code is rarely available!), and it would affect other application programs.

Shared System Resources

Another problem with user-level thread packages is the inadvertent sharing of data that is hidden in libraries without proper locking and synchronization. For example, UNIX defines a variable, named `errno`, in each process which stores error information, if any, resulting from a system call. Suppose that there are two user-level threads in a process, T_1 and T_2, where T_1 makes a system call that results in an error. But before it reads the `errno` variable, it gets suspended by the thread package, then T_2 executes and makes a system call that also results in an error. At this point, the `errno` variable contains the error code for T_2's system call, overwriting that of thread T_1. To remedy this problem, the thread runtime library must provide each thread with its own copy of such a variable.

Library subroutines exhibiting this kind of problem are not *re-entrant* (or *thread-safe*). This means that if two user threads make the same library call concurrently, the execution of one might interfere with the other, leading to an incorrect result. One way to solve this problem is to provide re-entrant libraries for multithreaded applications. For example, all thread packages that conform to the IEEE P1003.4A specification provide a re-entrant C library, called *libc_r*, which is used in place of the standard *libc* library.

But not all popular subroutine libraries are re-entrant. In this case, a programmer must ensure safety by serializing thread execution in those modules in order to eliminate concurrent updates to unintentionally shared resources. For example, the X Windows library for UNIX is currently not re-entrant. Thus, when several threads send events to an X server to update various windows, they overwrite each other in the server's event queue, resulting in a loss of data. As a result, a user sees erratic, missing, and inconsistent window updates. The easiest way to solve this problem is to serialize all calls into the X library. This requires the main thread (which executes the windows main loop) to first lock a mutex guarding the X library before processing each X event, then release it when done. Other threads wanting to call X Windows functions must do so from inside a critical section using the same mutex. This is not elegant or efficient because it virtually eliminates concurrency when using X Windows. Even worse, we have created a potential deadlock situation, since any thread using the X library's callback mechanism may deadlock. All of these problems result from simulating a multithreaded runtime environment using a single-threaded operating system.

Signal Handling

Perhaps the most difficult problem confronting a user-thread implementation is the per-thread signal handling required by such application programs interface standards as the P1003.4A proposal. Since the operating system only knows about underlying processes, it can only send a signal to a process at large. Within the process, the runtime library must somehow deliver a signal to the appropriate thread.

Roughly speaking, when a thread indicates that it is willing to receive a signal, the thread runtime library stores this information in a per-thread data structure in user space, and then registers the signal-handling subroutine with the operating system. When the operating system signals the process, the thread's runtime library receives control in order to check which thread wants this signal. If the recipient is the current thread, the runtime library immediately invokes the thread's signal-handling routine; otherwise, the runtime library performs a context switch to install the appropriate thread. This mechanism is very hard to implement, as it involves complicated bookkeeping and thread scheduling.

Thread Scheduling

Another difficult issue in user-thread packages is thread scheduling, because the threads library does not normally receive hardware clock interrupts to manage timeslices. To offer preemptive scheduling, the library must therefore, register to receive timer signals from the kernel. If your application also registers handles for such signals, there will be a conflict. When the operating system delivers such a signal to process, the library receives it and performs a thread context switch if necessary. Handling a timer alarm signal is as difficult as any other signals, making preemptive user-thread scheduling hard to implement.

Multiprocessor Utilization

A major drawback of multiple user-level threads within the same process is that they cannot simultaneously use more than one CPU because they are invisible to the kernel. Therefore, the thread package must time-share one processor between all threads in a program.

Summary

All of these problems with user-level threads are artifacts of simulating a multithreaded runtime environment on operating systems that support only single-threaded processes. But despite the complexity and difficulty of implementation, user-level thread packages offer the advantages of concurrency and efficiency on computing systems that ordinarily would not.

7.2.2 Kernel-Level Threads

An operating system directly manages threads and synchronization objects in a *kernel-level thread package*. Figure 7-4 depicts this architecture. Windows NT, Mach, Solaris, Chorus, and OS/2 are examples of such operating systems. In these and similar operating systems, a process contains at least one and possibly many threads of execution; the operating system knows about each thread and can schedule them individually.

7.2.2.1 Advantages of Kernel-Level Threads

Most of the problems exhibited by user-level threads, discussed in the last section, do not exist with kernel-level thread. For example, an application can use blocking system calls without blocking an entire process. Since each kernel thread is scheduled independently,

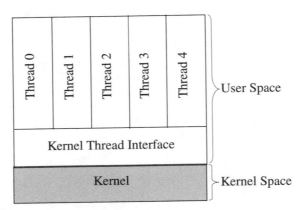

Figure 7-4 Implementation Architecture of Kernel-Level Threads (adapted from [Tanenbaum, 1992]).

other threads in the same process can still execute. Moreover, the kernel can schedule these threads on different processors and deliver signals to each individual thread.

7.2.2.2 Drawbacks of Kernel-Level Threads

Kernel-level threads have no significant disadvantage except that they are slower than user-level threads, due to thread context switching. When a thread blocks, or its time-slice runs out, a user-level thread package performs very fast context switching because it all happens in the user space, without a system call. On the other hand, the operating system manages kernel-level threads, so context switching of kernel-level threads is slow simply because control is passed from user mode to kernel mode and back. In a particular example, context switches of kernel-level threads were about ten times slower than those of user-level threads [Marovich, 1990].

In addition, the problem of re-entrant libraries is usually less troublesome in systems with kernel threads because the operating system's developers have probably also done the work of making most standard libraries thread-safe. But in the event that some libraries are not reentrant (such as the X Windows system), you have to enforce serialization as previously described.

7.2.3 Multiplexed Threads

Our description suggests that there might be a benefit to combining kernel- and user-level threads in the same package, in order to obtain the performance of user-level threads and the generality of kernel-level threads. The SunOS operating system provides an example of such an architecture, called multiplexed threads.

In SunOS, kernel-level threads are called Lightweight Processes (LWP) and user-level threads are simply called "threads." A process can have many LWPs, and an LWP can have many threads. The kernel knows about LWPs and can schedule each of them independently. Since several threads can be multiplexed onto one or more LWPs, a thread can execute in one LWP for a period of time, then execute in another LWP. A programmer can use either LWPs,

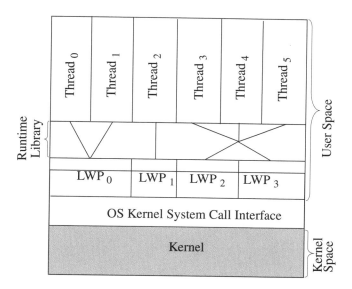

Figure 7-5. Multiplexed Threads.

threads, or both. Figure 7-5 shows the different ways of combining threads with lightweight processes. Threads 0 and 1 run on LWP 0; Thread 2 runs solely on LWP1; Threads 3, 4, and 5 share LWP 2 and 3.

7.2.3.1 Programming with Multiplexed Threads

Powell et al. [1991] discuss the design criteria that an application programmer may use to select LWPs or threads. The important considerations are:

1. Hardware parallelism
2. Thread creation and switching expense
3. Need for kernel-level scheduling

Since the kernel knows about LWPs and can schedule them independently on multiple CPUs, an application can effectively exploit hardware parallelism by using LWPs. But multiple LWP's must be created with care, since multiple threads can increase concurrency without improving performance. For example, suppose we wish to sort an array of n numbers using two processors. We can productively use two LWPs in a WorkCrew model (see Chapter 8), where one LWP executes at each CPU, but we cannot productively use more than two LWPs due to the overhead of multiplexing each CPU among multiple LWPs.

In SunOS, an application programmer can make trade-offs between user and kernel-level threads. For example, when a program requires many threads (as in a large multiwindow application with one thread per window) a programmer might choose user-level threads because switching them is inexpensive. But if some threads of the application are expected to block (e.g., for disk I/O), one can use LWPs for those.

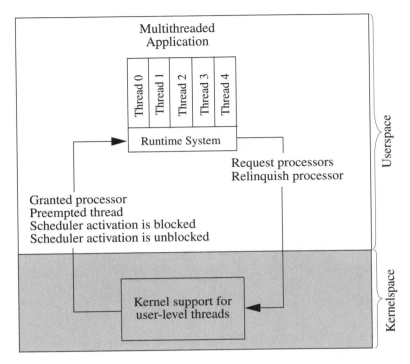

Figure 7-6. The Architecture of Scheduler Activations Thread Package.

So far, we've seen advantages and disadvantages of both user- and kernel-level threads. Multiplexed thread packages allow a programmer more flexibility for a particular application. For example, the programmer can use LWPs to exploit hardware parallelism and to make blocking calls, while using threads for program modularity in the same process.

Multiplexed threads, however, exhibit some undesirable characteristics of both user and kernel threads. When an LWP is blocked, all of its threads are suspended, and LWPs are as expensive to context-switch as kernel threads. User threads that want to use multiple CPUs must be in different LWPs, and a programmer can degrade performance by creating too many LWPs. These problems exist because kernel and user threads do not communicate with each other. Ideally, we want an implementation to be as general as kernel-level threads, with context switching as fast as user-level threads. In the next section, we introduce an architecture called *Scheduler Activations*, in which the operating system kernel and user-threads library collaborate to provide a fast, robust thread package.

7.2.4 Scheduler Activations

Recently invented at the University of Washington [Anderson et al., 1991], this system employs user-level threads; but instead of multiplexing them among kernel-level threads, a kernel exchanges information with a thread library using a data structure called a *scheduler activation* (Figure 7-6). For example, the threads library can tell the kernel when it relinquishes a processor, or the kernel can notify the library of a blocked thread. A scheduler activation represents a virtual processor allocated to an address space (a process) by the kernel. At application start-up, the kernel provides the process with a number of these virtual processors (or scheduler activations). During program execution this number may fluctuate. Within an application program, library code schedules a thread for execution in the context of a scheduler activation. At this point, the scheduler activation resembles a kernel thread because the kernel can schedule a thread on a physical processor independent of other threads in other scheduler activations. When a thread blocks in the kernel or is preempted, the kernel sends a scheduler activation containing the thread context to the runtime library, saves the thread's execution state, then installs another runnable thread in the scheduler activation.

The efficiency of scheduler activations arises from the fact that the kernel does not reschedule threads when it is not necessary. For example, when a thread blocks while waiting to acquire ownership of an application-program object, such as a mutex or a condition variable, the thread library simply switches to another runnable thread. But scheduler activations have as much generality as kernel-level threads. They can be scheduled directly by the kernel, even across multiple processors, and they can block in the kernel without suspending other threads in the same process.

Scheduler activations provide efficiency and transparency because the kernel and thread library can communicate and collaborate with each other. Each subsystem makes decisions about thread scheduling in its own domain, and it only communicates essential information to the other layer when necessary. On one hand, the library decides which threads to run on the virtual processors, on the other hand, the kernel schedules threads to execute on particular processors. The kernel does not interfere with the runtime library unless a thread is blocked or preempted in the kernel. Similarly, the library does not need to communicate with the kernel unless it wants to give up scheduler activations or to ask for more.

One drawback of this scheme is insecurity. In order to efficiently communicate activations across address spaces, the kernel and library code must be exceptionally trustworthy and bug-free. In the presence of bugs or maliciousness, the scheme may not be very robust.

Scheduler activation is a recent invention and has not yet made its way into commercial operating systems. The system was originally implemented on the experimental Firefly multiprocessor workstation [Thacker et al., 1988] at DEC SRC, using the FastThreads user-level thread package and kernel threads of the Topaz operating system. Recently, this system was ported to the Mach operating system [Barton-Davis et al., 1993].

7.3 Summary

Thread packages have been implemented in a variety of ways. We surveyed four major approaches: user-level threads, kernel-level threads, multiplexed threads, and scheduler activations. A runtime library manages user-level threads within a process; individual user-level threads are not all visible to the operating system. An operating system manages kernel-level threads. With multiplexed threads, you can choose among user- and kernel-level threads. Finally, scheduler activations facilitate cooperation between an operating system kernel and a user-level threads runtime library, providing fast user-level threads that are known to, and schedulable by, the operating system's kernel. Table 7–1 summarizes the thread architectures for various operating systems.

System	Thread package architecture
Digital Equipment Corporation, CMA threads	User-level
Distributed Computing Environment (DCE)	User-level
Xerox's Portable Common Runtime (PCR)	User-level
FastThreads	User-level
Windows NT	Kernel-level
MACH	Kernel-level
Chorus	Kernel-level
OS/2	Kernel-level
Sun Microsystems' SunOS	Multiplexed
University of Washington's FastThreads	Scheduler activations

Table 7–1. Thread Package Architectures for Various Systems.

Each implementation technique has advantages and disadvantages that may affect the performance of a multithreaded application. To effectively port or implement a multithreaded application, you have to understand the thread package architecture of your operating system.

7.4 Bibliographic Notes

Andrew Tanenbaum describes user-level and kernel-level threads in Chapter 12 of his book [Tanenbaum, 1992]. Powell et al. [1991] and Stein and Shah [1992] discuss SunOS's multiplexed threads. Weiser et al. [1989] and Anderson et al. [1989] discuss user-level threads. Tevanian et al. [1987], Thacker et al. [1988], and Cheriton [1988] discuss kernel-level threads. Anderson et al. [1991] describe scheduler activations, a kernel-supported user-level thread package. They also discuss several limitations of user-level, kernel-level, and multiplexed threads. Our section on problems of programming with user-level threads is based on an excellent technical report describing an implementation of user-level threads on the HP-UX operating system by Marovich [1990].

7.5 Exercises

1. You are the main developer of an operating systems company. Your customers would like to use different scheduling algorithms for different applications. Which thread architecture would you implement for them? Why?

2. Which thread architecture would be most appropriate for an application needing to spawn a large number of threads. Hint: Consider user-level and kernel-level thread packages.

3. Some systems provide a user-level thread package with an operating system that does not support threads. A problem with this is that not all system libraries are re-entrant. How would you design multithreaded programs that use these libraries to work correctly?

4. Your computer system provides a multiplexed thread package (i.e., both user- and kernel-level threads). Which type of threads would you choose for an application that often blocks for I/O?

5. Describe scheduler activations, and explain how they communicate between the user space and kernel space to improve thread scheduling.

6. Discuss the advantages and disadvantages of scheduler activations compared to multiplexed thread architectures.

7.6 References

1. Anderson, T. E., Bershad, B. N., Lazowska, E. D., and Levy, H. M. (1991). Scheduler Activations: Effective Kernel Support for User-level Management of Parallelism. In *Proceedings of the Thirteenth Symposium on Operating System Principles*, pp. 95–109.

2. Anderson, T. E., Lazowska, E., and Levy, H. (1989). The Performance Implications of Thread Management Alternatives for Shared Memory Multiprocessors. *IEEE Transactions on Computers*, 38(12):1631–1644.

3. Barton-Davis, P., McNamee, D., Vaswani, R., and Lazowska, E. (1993). Adding Scheduler Activations to Mach 3.0. In *Proceedings of the 3rd Mach Symposium*, pp. 119–136. USENIX Association.

4. Cheriton, D. (1988). The V Distributed System. *Communications of the ACM*, 31(3):314–333.

5. DEC (1990). *Concert Multithread Architecture*. Digital Equipment Corporation.

6. Marovich, S. B. (1990). Interprocess Concurrency under UNIX. Technical Report HPL-90-02, Hewlett-Packard Labs, Palo Alto, CA 94304.

7. McJones, P. R. and Swart, G. F. (1987). Evolving the UNIX System Interface to Support Multithreaded Programs. Technical Report 27, Digital Equipment Corporation, Systems Research Center, 130 Lytton Avenue, Palo Alto, CA 94301.

8. OSF (1993). *OSF DCE Application Development Guide*. Prentice Hall, Englewood Cliffs, NJ.

9. Powell, M. L., Kleiman, S. R., Barton, S., Shah, D., and Weeks, M. (1991). SunOS Multithread Architecture. In *Proceedings of the 1991 USENIX Winter Conference*, pp. 65–79, Dallas, TX.

10. Stein, D. and Shah, D. (1992). Implementing Lightweight Threads. In *Proceedings of the 1992 USENIX Summer Conference*, pp. 1–9, San Antonio, TX.

11. Tanenbaum, A. (1992). *Modern Operating Systems*. Prentice Hall, Englewood Cliffs, NJ.

12. Tevanian, A., Rashid, R. F., Golub, D. B., Black, D. L., Cooper, E., and Young, M. W. (1987). MACH Threads and the UNIX Kernel: The Battle for Control. Technical Report CMU-CS-87-149, Carnegie Mellon University.

13. Thacker, C., Stewart, L., and Satterthwaite, Jr., E. (1988). Firefly: A Multiprocessor Workstation. *IEEE Transactions on Computers*, 37(8):909–920.

14. Weiser, M., Demers, A., and Hauser, C. (1989). The Portable Common Runtime Approach to Interoperability. In *Proceedings of the Twelfth ACM Symposium on Operating System Principles*, pp. 114–122.

Programming Models

*I*n this chapter, we present some *programming models* that can help you organize a multithreaded application. There are many different ways to divide an application among multiple threads of control, and some questions that you may consider are: *How many threads should the application have? Should it always create a new thread for each transaction? Is there a performance problem with having too many threads? How should the threads interact with each other?*

The answers to these questions usually depend on: (1) the implementation architecture of your threads package, and (2) the nature of the problem to be solved. In Chapter 7, we described several types of thread packages, and discussed their advantages and limitations. Using this information and one of the programming models discussed in this chapter, you can decide how best to solve a problem.

Choosing a programming model for a multithreaded application is analogous to organizing a group of people to do a job: depending on the job, some forms of organization may be more effective than others. If the task is to prepare a dinner, for example, one person can make the main dish, one person can make the salad, another can arrange the table, and so forth. Each person can work independently and concurrently, perhaps with a master chef coordinating the activities. To be very effective, one must usually assign subtasks according to the skills and number of people involved. If the number of subtasks exceeds the number of people, then the group must decide who will do which subtasks (and how many). If the assignments are inappropriate, then using more people may actually result in loss of time. For example, if two people are assigned to cut meat and there is only one knife, deciding who will use it may take more time than if one person were assigned.

Analogously, if one frivolously creates many threads without a clear purpose, a program may deadlock, produce unpredictable results, or perform poorly because so much computer time is spent managing the extra threads.

This chapter describes several basic programming models. We first describe the *workgroup model* in which several threads work on separate parts of an application. Next, we describe the *manager-worker model* in which a single manager thread controls various worker threads. We then describe the *deferred-computation model*, which resembles the manager-worker model in that new worker threads are created when there are new subtasks to perform, but work is scheduled to be done later rather than immediately. After that, we describe the *pipeline model* in which overlapping pairs of threads cooperate as producers and consumers to work on a sequence of tasks, like a factory assembly line. Finally, we describe the *WorkCrew model* in which the number of threads spawned by the application can be varied to match the number of processors available in a system. An implementation of the WorkCrew model is presented in Appendix A.

8.1   Workgroup Model

In the workgroup model, each application thread is an equal partner, and all collaborate to perform a large task. Typically, each thread performs a distinct well-defined subtask. If an application naturally has independent subtasks that can be executed concurrently, it could apply the workgroup model by mapping each subtask to an independent thread of control.

As an example, we show how to build a multithreaded game program called *Frogger*. In this game, there is a busy street on which cars are traveling at different speeds in both direction. A user tries to safely direct a frog across the street without it being run over by a car. The frog can move forward, backward, left, or right. Figure 8-1 shows a screen image of this game. This game program may be cumbersome to write using only a single thread of control, because it must keep track of the state of all objects in play (frog and cars) and, for each cycle of a clock, it must update this information and reposition all objects that move about the screen, checking for possible collisions between the frog and cars.

Using multiple threads, the program logic becomes much simpler to understand—create one thread for each game object (cars and one frog, in our case) and let them run (Figure 8-2). In our sample program, each car thread executes a `RunCar` procedure, independently managing the car's speed, direction, and bitmap display. After the main thread creates the car threads, it assumes the role of the frog, changing the frog's position in response to user input. In this way, all threads of the application become part of a workgroup. The data shared among them is the frog's position and liveliness. When a car moves, its thread checks to see whether the frog is hit. If so, then that thread sets the frog's state to "dead," and the game is over.

The Frogger workgroup shares the following variables:

```
1    LONG frogX, frogY, frogWidth, frogHeight ;
2    BOOL frogExists = FALSE ;
```

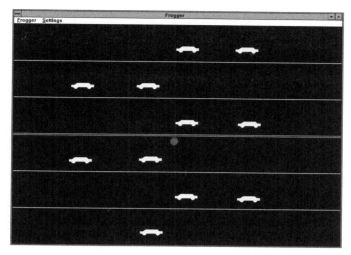

Figure 8-1. Screen Image of the *Frogger* Game.

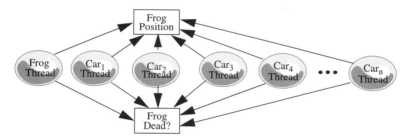

Figure 8-2. Workgroup of Car and Frog Threads.

The shared variables are protected by a critical section object named `protectFrog`. In addition, the initial thread (which eventually represents the frog) maintains a list of all the threads created in the workgroup, so it can control their behavior if necessary (e.g., to terminate them).

```
1    int nCars = 6 ;
2    struct ThreadArg {
3        HWND hwnd ;
4        LONG carX, carY ;
5        RECT rect ;
6        HANDLE hThread ;
7        DWORD dwThreadId ;
8        BOOL hitFrog ;
9        BOOL endReached ;
10       int speed, direction ;
11       HANDLE hMutex ;
12   } threadArg[MAXCARS] ;
```

The initial thread runs the main window procedure, which takes action upon receiving the messages.

```
1    LRESULT CALLBACK MainWndProc(HWND hwnd, UINT message,
2                        WPARAM wParam, LPARAM lParam)
3    {
4        int i ;
5        static HWND hInst1 ;
6
7        switch (message) {
8          case WM_CREATE:
9              hPenMiddle = CreatePen(PS_SOLID, 2, (COLORREF) 0x0100000f);
10             hPenLane=CreatePen(PS_DASH,2,(COLORREF)RGB(255, 255, 255)) ;
11             hBlackPen=CreatePen(PS_SOLID, 2, (COLORREF) RGB(0, 0, 0)) ;
12             hGrayPen=CreatePen(PS_SOLID,40,(COLORREF)RGB(100,100,100)) ;
13             for (i=0; i<MAXCARS; i++)
14                 threadArg[i].hMutex = CreateMutex(NULL, FALSE, NULL) ;
15             hFrogMutex = CreateMutex(NULL, FALSE, "FrogMutex");
16             hCarMutex = CreateMutex(NULL, FALSE, NULL) ;
17             hInst1 = ((LPCREATESTRUCT) lParam) -> hInstance ;
18          break;
19          case WM_DESTROY:
20             DeleteObject (hPenMiddle);
21             DeleteObject (hPenLane) ;
22             DeleteObject(hBlackPen) ;
23             DeleteObject(hGrayPen) ;
24             DeleteObject(hCarBitMap) ;
25             DeleteObject(hFrogBitMap) ;
26             PostQuitMessage(0);
27          break;
28          case WM_PAINT: {
29             PAINTSTRUCT ps;
30             hdc=BeginPaint(hwnd, &ps);
31             DrawLanes(hwnd) ;
32             EndPaint (hwnd, &ps);
33             if (frogExists)
34                 RedrawFrog(hwnd) ;
35             return FALSE;
36          }
37          case WM_COMMAND: {
38             switch(LOWORD(wParam)){
39               case IDM_START:
40                  StartWorkers(hwnd) ;
41                  FrogStart(hwnd) ;
42               break ;
43               case IDM_QUIT:
44                  PostMessage(hwnd, WM_DESTROY, 0, 0L) ;
45                  break ;
46               default:
47                  break ;
48             }
49          }
50          break ;
51          case IDM_FROGHIT:
```

```
 52              KillAllWorkers() ;
 53              frogExists = 0 ;
 54              switch (MessageBox(hwnd, "Frog dead; Another Game?",
 55                      lpszTitle, MB_YESNO|MB_ICONQUESTION)) {
 56                case IDYES:
 57                   InvalidateRect(hwnd, NULL, TRUE) ;
 58                   StartWorkers(hwnd) ;
 59                   FrogStart(hwnd) ;
 60                break ;
 61                case IDNO:
 62                   PostMessage(hwnd, WM_QUIT, 0, 0L) ;
 63                   break ;
 64                default:
 65                   break ;
 66              }
 67          break ;
 68          case IDM_GAMEWON:
 69             KillAllWorkers() ;
 70             frogExists = 0 ;
 71             switch (MessageBox(hwnd, "Congratulations; Another Game?",
 72                     lpszTitle, MB_YESNO|MB_ICONQUESTION)) {
 73                case IDYES:
 74                   InvalidateRect(hwnd, NULL, TRUE) ;
 75                   StartWorkers(hwnd) ;
 76                   FrogStart(hwnd) ;
 77                break ;
 78                case IDNO:
 79                   PostMessage(hwnd, WM_QUIT, 0, 0L) ;
 80                break ;
 81                default:
 82                break ;
 83             }
 84          break ;
 85          case WM_KEYDOWN:
 86             switch (wParam) {
 87                case VK_UP:
 88                   MoveFrogUp(hwnd) ;
 89                   break ;
 90                case VK_DOWN:
 91                   MoveFrogDown(hwnd) ;
 92                break ;
 93                case VK_LEFT:
 94                   MoveFrogLeft(hwnd) ;
 95                break ;
 96                case VK_RIGHT:
 97                   MoveFrogRight(hwnd) ;
 98                break ;
 99             }
100          return (DefWindowProc(hwnd, message, wParam, lParam));
101          default:
102             return (DefWindowProc(hwnd, message, wParam, lParam));
103       }
104    return FALSE ;
105 }
```

The `MainWndProc` function moves the frog up, left, or right based on the arrow keys pressed by the user. The `StartWorkers` function's implementation follows:

```
1     void StartWorkers(HWND hwnd)
2     {
3       RECT rect ;
4       int i ;
5
6       GetClientRect (hwnd, &rect);
7
8       for (i=0; i< nCars; i++) {
9         WaitForSingleObject(threadArg[i].hMutex, INFINITE) ;
10        threadArg[i].hwnd = hwnd ;
11        threadArg[i].speed = 4 ;
12        threadArg[i].carY = rect.bottom*(2*(i % 6)+1)/12 ;
13        if (i % 2)
14          threadArg[i].direction = 1 ;
15        else
16          threadArg[i].direction = -1 ;
17        threadArg[i].hThread=CreateThread(NULL,0,
18                    (LPTHREAD_START_ROUTINE) RunCar, &(threadArg[i]),
19                    0, &(threadArg[i].dwThreadId)) ;
20        ReleaseMutex(threadArg[i].hMutex) ;
21      }
22    }
```

Each worker thread receives the identity of a car to run, a particular lane to run it on, and the direction in which to run it. It then runs the car, using the `RunCar` procedure.

```
1     void RunCar(struct ThreadArg *threadArg)
2     {
3
4       loopForEver:
5       GetClientRect (threadArg->hwnd, &(threadArg->rect));
6
7       threadArg->carX = rand() % threadArg->rect.right ;
8       threadArg->endReached = FALSE ;
9       threadArg->hitFrog = FALSE ;
10
11      while (!(threadArg->endReached) && !(threadArg->hitFrog)){
12        WaitForSingleObject(threadArg->hMutex, INFINITE) ;
13        DrawCar(threadArg->hwnd, threadArg->carX, threadArg->carY) ;
14        if (threadArg->direction > 0)
15          threadArg->carX += threadArg->speed ;
16        else
17          threadArg->carX -= threadArg->speed ;
18        Sleep((int) 20) ;
19        if (threadArg->direction > 0)
20          threadArg->endReached = (threadArg->carX >
21                          threadArg->rect.right + threadArg->speed) ;
22        else
23          threadArg->endReached = (threadArg->carX < -bmCar.bmWidth) ;
24        threadArg->hitFrog = CarHitFrog(threadArg->direction,
25                      threadArg->speed, threadArg->carX,
```

```
26                              threadArg->carY) ;
27             ReleaseMutex(threadArg->hMutex) ;
28         }
29         if (threadArg->hitFrog) {
30             PostMessage(threadArg->hwnd, IDM_FROGHIT, 0, 0L) ;
31             ExitThread(0) ;
32         }
33         goto loopForEver ;
34     }
```

Before moving the car, each worker thread checks to see if the frog has been hit. If so, then the FrogExists variable is set to false, thereby terminating the game. To simplify the presentation, we have not presented the entire code here; however, the code is available in our source code distribution.

As another illustration of the workgroup programming model, consider multiple threads in a text editor. Suppose the text to be edited is maintained in a shared data structure, usually called a text buffer, with several threads operating on it. One worker thread can accept user input and modify this buffer (e.g., to delete and add characters), while a second worker thread can take information from the buffer and display it on a screen. Finally, a third thread could periodically save the contents of the buffer in a file. Figure 8-3 depicts this organization.

8.2 Manager-Worker Model

Unlike the workgroup model, in which all threads have the same capabilities, the manager-worker[1] model has two different kinds of threads:

1.   Manager—the main thread of computation, which is responsible for creating worker threads as necessary and coordinating them
2.   Worker—a thread created in order to perform a subtask

In this model, an application must have at least one manager, but it may or may not have workers. Typically, a manager thread responds to a service request by creating a worker thread and assigning it the job of providing the requested service. Each worker operates independent of others, but it must coordinate with its manager by putting data in a shared variable, then notifying the manager of the data's presence. Before a manager can exit, it must ensure that all worker threads have terminated.

The manager-worker model is appropriate in programs that must handle multiple concurrent requests, such as user inputs or other I/O events. For example, if an application expects input from multiple windows on a monitor screen, each window can be handled by a separate thread. Or, if the application is a server to which multiple clients send requests, each request can be handled by a separate worker thread. Unlike the workgroup model, the number of threads created in the manager-worker model dynamically changes depending on the application workload.

Let us now demonstrate this concept using an example in which we write a simple multithreaded "grep" program to find all occurrences of a character string in a set of text files within a directory. Using the manager-worker model, we designate the program's main thread to be the manager, and for each file in the directory we can create a worker thread to look for

---

[1.] Also known as *master-slave*.

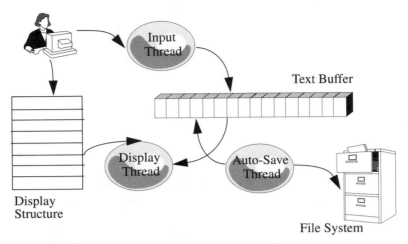

Text Buffer

Display
Structure

File System

Figure 8-3. A Workgroup of Three Threads for a Text Editor Application.

the string in that file. Each worker searches only one file and, when it finishes, reports its result to the manager. The manager then collates all results and displays them to a user.

```
1    // Manager Thread
2    void ManagerGrep(ManagerArgType *arg_p)
3    {
4        int i;
5        LPHANDLE ThHnd;
6        DWORD*TID;
7        Buffer **WorkerArg;
8
9        // create arrays of TH's and argument objects for Worker threads
10       ThHnd = (LPHANDLE) malloc (arg_p->numFiles * sizeof(HANDLE));
11       TID = (DWORD *) malloc (arg_p->numFiles * sizeof(DWORD));
12       WorkerArg = (Buffer **) malloc(arg_p->numFiles*sizeof(Buffer *));
13
14       // initialize Workers' argument objects and create Workers
15       for (i=0; i < arg_p->numFiles; i++) {
16         WorkerArg[i] = newBuffer();
17         strcpy(WorkerArg[i]->filename, arg_p->fileArray[i]);
18         strcpy(WorkerArg[i]->pattern, arg_p->pattern);
19         ThHnd[i] = CreateThread(NULL, 0,
20                      (LPTHREAD_START_ROUTINE)WorkerGrep,
21                      WorkerArg[i], 0, (LPDWORD)&(TID[i]));
22       }
23
24       // wait for everyone to finish
25       WaitForMultipleObjects((DWORD)arg_p->numFiles, ThHnd, TRUE,
26                    INFINITE);
27
28       // print out grep buffer
29       for (i=0; i < arg_p->numFiles; i++)
```

```
30          printBuffer(WorkerArg[i]);
31   }
```

Each worker thread executes a function named `WorkerGrep`, which sequentially searches a file to find all lines matching the given pattern.

```
1   void WorkerGrep(Buffer *arg_p)
2   {
3       Grep(arg_p->filename, arg_p->pattern, arg_p);
4   }
```

The `Grep` function, called in this fragment, is implemented as follows:

```
1   void Grep(char *fileName, char *pattern, Buffer *arg_p)
2   {
3       FILE *fptr;
4       char *lineStr, *matchStr;
5       char buf[1024];
6
7       fptr = fopen(fileName, "r")) ;
8       lineStr = fgets(buf, sizeof(buf), fptr);
9       while (lineStr != NULL) {
10          matchStr = (char *) strstr(buf, pattern);
11          if (matchStr != NULL)
12              addBuffer(buf, arg_p);
13          lineStr = fgets(buf, sizeof(buf), fptr);
14      }
15  }
```

The main advantage of this model is the use of concurrency to expedite the solution to a particular problem. Since all the text files are being searched concurrently in this case, an inaccessible single file will not block the entire process. Moreover, on a multiprocessor machine the search will proceed in parallel and can be much faster.

8.3 Deferred-Computation Model

The *deferred-computation* model is a variation of the manager-worker model in which the main manager thread creates other threads to perform work, but the worker's execution may be deferred if processor time is not readily available. Meanwhile, the manager thread returns to its task without waiting for the completion of any subtask—this is what distinguishes the deferred-computation model from the manager-worker model. Clearly, this model applies only to tasks without firm deadlines. As a result of the create-and-forget nature of worker threads, an application using this model can be very responsive to a user, since the manager can spend most of its time handling user interaction.

To demonstrate this model, we create a sample application to maintain a red-black (balanced) binary search tree. For look-up time to remain predictable, the defining property of a red-black tree requires that the entire tree be rebalanced when a new node is added or removed. Using the deferred computation model, when the main thread creates or deletes a node, it also creates a new thread to balance the tree. It then quickly returns to its interaction with a user while the new thread balances the tree in the background. As a result, the application is very responsive.

Below is our sample program in which we only support node creation operation, and node deletion is left as an exercise for the reader. The main thread is responsible for interacting with a user and initiating insertion. Tree balancing is deferred to a thread that executes in the background. The implementation is simple—all we need is a mutex to protect access to the search tree. Let's define the tree and its mutex as:

```
1    struct Tree {
2        struct Tree *left, *child, *parent ;
3        int key ;
4    } ;
5    HANDLE hTreeMutex ;
```

To insert an element in the tree, we define the function `Insert`, which takes a pointer to the root of a tree and an integer to be inserted in it. The multithreaded version of this can be written as follows.

```
1    void Insert(struct Tree *tree, int value)
2    {
3        HANDLE hThread ;
4        struct Tree *node ;
5        DWORD dwThreadId ;
6
7        WaitForSingleObject(hTreeMutex, INFINITE) ;
8        node = InsertValue(tree, value) ;
9        ReleaseMutex(hTreeMutex) ;
10       hThread = CreateNewThread(NULL, 0,
11                   (LPTHREAD_START_ROUTINE) FixTree, node,&dwThreadId) ;
12   }
```

`InsertValue` and `FixTree` functions are defined as follows.

```
1    struct Tree *InsertValue(struct Tree *tree, int value)
2    {
3        struct Tree *x, *y, *z ;
4
5        y = NULL ;
6
7        if (!(z = malloc(sizeof(struct Tree)))) {
8            fprintf(stderr, "Could not get memory!\n") ;
9            exit(1) ;
10       }
11
12       z->left = z->right = z->parent = NULL ;
13       z->key = value ;
14       x = tree ;
15       while (x) {
16           y = x ;
17           if (value < x->key)
18               x = x->left ;
19           else
20               x = x->right ;
21       }
22
23       z->parent = y ;
24       if (!y)
25           tree = z ;
26       else if (value < y->key)
```

```
27        y->left = z ;
28     else
29        y->right = z ;
30     return z ;
31  }

1   FixTree(struct Tree *x)
2   {
3      struct Tree *y ;
4
5      WaitForSingleObject(hTreeMutex, INFINITE) ;
6      x->color = RED ;
7      while ((x != tree) && (x->parent->color == RED)) {
8         if (x->parent->parent->left == x->parent) {
9            y = x->parent->parent->right ;
10           if (y && y->color == RED) {
11              x->parent->color = BLACK ;
12              y->color = BLACK ;
13              x->parent->parent->color = RED ;
14              x = x->parent->parent ;
15           }
16           else if (x->parent->right == x) {
17              x= x->parent ;
18              LeftRotate(x) ;
19           }
20           else {
21              x->parent->color = BLACK ;
22              x->parent->parent->color = RED ;
23              RightRotate(x->parent->parent) ;
24           }
25        }
26        else {
27           y = x->parent->parent->left ;
28           if (y && y->color == RED) {
29              x->parent->color = BLACK ;
30              y->color = BLACK ;
31              x->parent->parent->color = RED ;
32              x = x->parent->parent ;
33           }
34           else if (x->parent->left == x) {
35              x= x->parent ;
36              RightRotate(x) ;
37           }
38           else {
39              x->parent->color = BLACK ;
40              x->parent->parent->color = RED ;
41              LeftRotate(x->parent->parent) ;
42           }
43        }
44     }
45     tree->color = BLACK ;
46     ReleaseMutex(hTreeMutex) ;
47  }
```

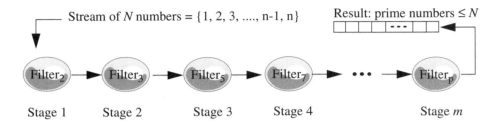

Figure 8-4. A Pipeline to Compute Prime Numbers.

[Cormen et al., 1990] discuss red-black tree algorithms, including their performance. Here we note only that there is one thread fixing the height of the tree at any given time, so creating extra threads in such applications is not very expensive.

As a further example, a text editor can create deferred threads to perform many tasks in parallel. For example, when a user pulls down a menu to select *save*, the editor can start a thread to perform this operation in the background, while allowing the user to continue editing. This same technique can be applied to other time-consuming operations, such as updating cross references, tables, and indices, which can all be performed by background threads while the program maintains a high degree of responsiveness to its users.

8.4 Pipeline Model

A different way to organize multithreaded applications is the *pipeline* model [Birrel, 1991], which is useful when we have a problem that can be divided into stages, each of which transforms data passing through. As an example, the UNIX© operating system provides a mechanism called a "pipe" that connects the output of one program to the input of another. When we cascade a set of programs in this fashion, a "pipeline" is created, where each program processes information flowing through it. Threads let this model be implemented in a single program, using shared memory for information exchange at low cost.

This model is particularly suited to applications that perform signal processing and data filtering. Using it, we may be able to reduce the complexity of program logic and capitalize on the parallelism of multiprocessor machines. Let's demonstrate the concept using a sample program that finds all prime numbers less than or equal to a number N. There are many ways to solve this problem, but an easy one is to filter out all nonprime numbers between 2 and N in a pipeline (Figure 8-4) using a strategy commonly known as the "Sieve of Eratosthenes." The filtering strategy is as follows:

1.   Organize each subtask as a distinct stage.
2.   A sequence of integers between 2 and N, inclusive, is fed to the first stage.
3.   Each stage retains the first number that it receives as a seed, then uses it to filter multiples of that number from the incoming stream. The first number that each stage receives is thus guaranteed to be a prime, and all other incoming numbers are forwarded to the next stage.

4.   This continues until the end of the input stream, at which time each stage reports its
      seed number. The seeds are then the set of all prime numbers less than or equal to *N*.

This pipeline is implemented as follows:

```
1     char Result[400]; // handles first 400 primes
2     void PipeNode(bb_monitor *fromMon)
3     {
4        int p;
5        int myPrime = 0;
6        bb_monitor *toMon;
7        HANDLE nextStage;
8        DWORDnextStageID;
9
10       fromMon->get(p);
11       while (p){ // while there is data to process
12          if (myPrime == 0){ // first number received, it's a prime
13             myPrime = p;
14             // create next stage of pipeline
15             toMon = new bb_monitor; // create shared buffer
16             nextStage = CreateThread(NULL, 0,
17                       (LPTHREAD_START_ROUTINE)PipeNode,
18                       toMon, 0, (LPDWORD)&nextStageID);
19          }
20          else {
21           // pass on if not divided evenly
22           // (else definitely not a prime)
23           if (p % myPrime) toMon->put(p);
24          }
25          fromMon->get(p);
26       } // end while loop
27
28       // end of input stream, report result
29       if (myPrime) {
30          SaveResultBuf(Result, myPrime);
31          toMon->put(p); // forward the sentinel
32          WaitForSingleObject(nextStage, INFINITE); // exit cleanly
33          delete toMon;
34       }
35       else
36          ExitThread(0);
37    }
38
39    void FindPrime(int number)
40    {
41       bb_monitor *toMon;
42       HANDLE nextStage;
43       DWORD nextStageID;
44       if (number<2) return; // no prime number < 2, return
45       // create buffer to feed to next pipe node
46       toMon = new bb_monitor;
47
48       // create next pipe node
49       nextStage = CreateThread(NULL, 0,
```

```
50                        (LPTHREAD_START_ROUTINE)PipeNode, toMon,
51                        0, (LPDWORD)&nextStageID);
52      // feed the pipe
53      for (int i = 2; i<=number; i++)
54         toMon->put(i);
55      toMon->put(0); // indicate the end of input stream
56      WaitForSingleObject(nextStage, INFINITE); // exit cleanly
57      delete toMon; // clean up
58   }
59
60   void main(int argc, char** argv)
61   {
62      if (argc < 2){
63         printf("Usage: prime <n>\n");
64         return;
65      }
66      InitResultBuf(Result);
67      FindPrime(atoi(argv[1]));
68      PrintResultBuf(Result);
69   }
```

This implementation uses a global array, named Result, to store resulting prime numbers. The main thread initializes the Result buffer (line 66), then begins filling the pipeline by calling the function, FindPrime (line 67). FindPrime establishes the first stage of the pipeline by creating a thread for it, asking it to execute the procedure PipeNode (line 16), and feeding it integers from 2 to N (lines 23–25), followed by 0 to indicate the end of data. Note that we use a monitor, described in Chapters 4 and 5, for sharing data between threads. FindPrime waits for the first stage to terminate (line 56), after which it exits.

Each stage of the pipeline is a thread executing the PipeNode function, which accepts the address of the monitor used to share data with the previous stage. When any stage must pass data down the pipe, it creates a new stage and begins filling it, as described above. If any stage reads the value 0 (end of data), it registers its prime number and waits for its successors to terminate.

This program is an example in which an otherwise complex task is simplified by dividing it into stages, each with simple processing logic, that can execute concurrently. In practice, this example will not be efficient for large N, since it will create too many threads. We will learn more about this problem in the following sections, using other models to control the number of threads. Nevertheless, the pipeline model is suitable for some applications, and threads allow these to be built efficiently.

8.5 WorkCrew Model

In all of the programming models presented so far, the number of threads that can be created by an application is unbounded. This has the disadvantage that if there are significantly more threads than the number of CPUs in the computer, performance will degrade due to the overhead of thread management. In this section, we describe two programming models that bound the number of threads: the *ForkWhenIdle* model and the WorkCrew model. These operate on the premise that the user or programmer can determine the maximum number of threads based on system load and processing power.

If we think of each thread as having a "virtual processor" on which to execute, then the ForkWhenIdle model, as its name suggests, creates a new thread only when an application is sure that there is an idle "processor" to run that thread. Once the number of threads in an application reaches a prescribed limit, all virtual processors are deemed "busy," and no new threads are created until existing threads terminate and release some virtual processors.

The WorkCrew model goes one step further to improve efficiency:

> In the WorkCrew paradigm, a set of worker threads cooperate to perform divisible tasks. When a worker has a task that can be subdivided into two possibly concurrent sub-tasks, it begins work on one of the sub-tasks and queues a help request for the other. When it finishes the first sub-task, it checks to see if its help request was answered by another worker. If so, the original worker assumes that the operation is in good hands and returns. If not, the pending request is cancelled, and the original worker completes the remainder of the task itself [Vandervoorde and Roberts, 1988, pp. 352].

We use a sorting algorithm to demonstrate what can happen when we overload too many threads on too few processors, based on [Vandervoorde and Roberts, 1988]. We first present the algorithm using a *ForkAlways* implementation in which threads are created liberally, and then compare it against versions using the ForkWhenIdle and WorkCrew models.

8.5.1 Quicksort Example

Quicksort is a popular and efficient sorting algorithm, which operates by dividing data into two partitions, called low and high, then recursively sorting each partition. This divide-and-conquer algorithm naturally lends itself to parallelism. In a multiprocessing environment, each recursive call is a subtask that can be handled by a separate thread, which operates concurrently with other subtasks.

Let's first examine a basic, sequential implementation of Quicksort:

```
1    void QuickSort(int a[], int low, int high)
2    {
3        if (low < high) {
4            int boundary = partition(a, low, high) ;
5            QuickSort(a, low, boundary);
6            QuickSort(a, boundary+1, high);
7        }
8    }
9    int partition(int a[], int low, int high)
10   {
11       int i, j, pivot;
12
13       pivot = a[low];
14       i = low - 1;
15       j = high + 1;
16
17       while (1) {
18           while (a[--j] > pivot)
19               ;
20           while (a[++i] < pivot);
21           if (i < j)
22               exchange(a, i, j);
```

```
23              else
24                  return j;
25      }
26  }
```

This `QuickSort` function accepts an array of integers to be sorted, named a, and two integers, low and high, indexing its first and last elements. If the array has more than one element, the algorithm divides the array into two parts: one containing all elements less than a selected pivot element, and the other containing elements greater than the pivot element. The function then recursively calls itself to sort each partition.

8.5.2 ForkAlways Quicksort

Since each of the two recursive calls within our `QuickSort` function manipulates a separate part of the array, they can be done in parallel without requiring mutual exclusion. In a naive and straightforward implementation, one would create a new thread to handle each `Quick-sort` call. This approach, which we label *ForkAlways Quicksort,* can be written as follows:

```
1   void QSort(struct ArgBlock *args)
2   {
3      int boundary;
4      struct ArgBlock *part1, *part2;
5
6      HANDLE child;
7      DWORD dwThreadId;
8
9      if (args->low < args->high) {
10        boundary = partition(args->a, args->low, args->high);
11
12        // create argument blocks for new threads
13        part1 = CreateArgBlock(args->a, args->low, boundary);
14        part2 = CreateArgBlock(args->a, boundary+1, args->high);
15
16        // create a new thread to execute sort partition: part1
17        child = CreateThread(NULL, 0,
18                    (LPTHREAD_START_ROUTINE) QSort,
19                    (DWORD *) part1,
20                    0, &dwThreadId);
21
22        if (child == NULL)
23           ErrorExit("Error creating a thread\n");
24
25        QSort(part2); // call QSort on partition "part2"
26
27        WaitForSingleObject(child);
28     }
29  }
30
31  void QuickSort(a, low, high)
32     int a[], low, high;
33  {
34     QSort(CreateArgBlock(a, low, high));
35  }
```

Notice that we defined a new function named `QSort`, which accepts one argument, to replace the original `QuickSort` function of three arguments. This is because the thread creation subroutine can pass only one argument to the function that a new thread will execute. Hence, we define a structure, named `ArgBlock`, containing a pointer to the array and indices of its lowest and highest elements.

```
1    struct ArgBlock {
2        int *a;
3        int low, high;
4    };
```

For convenience, we define a function, named `CreateArgBlock`, that accepts these values and builds an `ArgBlock` structure:

```
1    struct ArgBlock *CreateArgBlock(int b[], int i, int j)
2    {
3        struct ArgBlock *arg_block;
4
5        if ((arg_block = malloc(sizeof(struct ArgBlock))) == NULL) {
6            fprintf(stderr, "Could not get memory for arguments,
7                        exiting\n");
8            exit(1);
9        }
10       arg_block->a = b;
11       arg_block->low = i;
12       arg_block->high = j;
13       return arg_block;
14   }
```

If the number of unique values in the array is N, then this algorithm will create $N/2$ threads. For numbers N much greater than the number of processors in the system, we expect performance to degrade due to the overhead of thread management. We will compare this implementation to the ForkWhenIdle and WorkCrew models below.

8.5.3 ForkWhenIdle Quicksort

For a ForkWhenIdle QuickSort, we maintain a state variable, name `nIdle`, indicating the number of idle "virtual processors," which is shared by all threads in our program. When an opportunity arises to create a new thread, the program checks `nIdle` to determine if there is an idle virtual processor. If so, it decrements the value of `nIdle` by 1 and creates a new thread to sort one part of the array. If there is no idle processor (`nIdle` equals zero), then the thread does all of the extra sorting itself.

```
1    HANDLE hnIdleMutex;
2    int nIdle = 4;
3    void QSort(struct ArgBlock *args)
4    {
5        int boundary;
6        struct ArgBlock *part1, *part2;
7
8        HANDLE child;
9        DWORD dwThreadId;
10       int shouldfork;
```

```
11      DWORD waitresult;
12
13      if (args->low < args->high) {
14
15      boundary = partition(args->a, args->low, args->high);
16      part1 = CreateArgBlock(args->a, args->low, boundary);
17      part2 = CreateArgBlock(args->a, boundary+1, args->high);
18
19      if (!(waitresult = WaitForSingleObject(hnIdleMutex, 5000L)) {
20         shouldfork = (nIdle > 0);
21         if (shouldfork)
22            nIdle-- ;
23         if (ReleaseMutex(hnIdleMutex))
24            ErrorExit("Error releasing nIdleMutex\n");
25      }
26      else
27         ErrorExit("Error getting nIdleMutex\n");
28
29      if (shouldfork) { // determine if new thread should be created
30         child = CreateThread(NULL, 0,
31                 (LPTHREAD_START_ROUTINE) QSort,
32                 (DWORD *) part1, 0, &dwThreadId);
33
34         if (child == NULL)
35            ErrorExit("Error creating a thread\n");
36         QSort(part2);
37         if (!(waitresult = WaitForSingleObject(hnIdleMutex, 5000L)) {
38            nIdle++ ;
39            if (ReleaseMutex(hnIdleMutex))
40               ErrorExit("Error releasing nIdleMutex\n");
41         else
42            ErrorExit("Error getting nIdleMutex\n");
43         WaitForSingleObject(child);
44      }
45      else {
46         QSort(part1);
47         QSort(part2);
48      }
49   }
```

In order for this to work, we must introduce a mutex, hnIdleMutex, and a variable, nIdle, to keep track of the number of processors in use. Notice that these are global variables, shared by all threads in the program. The main QuickSort function must be modified to initialize the mutex.

```
1    void QuickSort(int a[], int low, int high)
2    {
3       hnIdleMutex = CreateMutex(NULL, FALSE, NULL);
4       if (!hnIdleMutex)
5          ErrorExit("Error creating nIdleMutex\n");
6
7       QSort(CreateArgBlock(a, low, high));
8    }
```

A slight inefficiency exists using the ForkWhenIdle model, because the decision to parallelize a task is made at only a few specific points in the program. In our example, there is one such point at line 20, following partition of the array. If the program decides not to create a new thread (because the number of existing threads has reached a limit), it loses the opportunity to parallelize if one or more virtual processors become available shortly thereafter. The best that a program can do is try to parallelize at the next decision point, which may not be reached for some time. Meanwhile, the idle "virtual processors" remain idle, even though they could handle some work.

8.5.4 WorkCrew Quicksort

The WorkCrew model improves upon the ForkWhenIdle model by allowing more dynamic parallelism. Recall that in this model a thread can break a task into several independent subtasks, place them in a common job queue, then proceed to execute a subtask. If other threads finish their work, these can immediately help out by picking and executing subtasks on the job queue. In the worst case where no threads become available, the first thread eventually finishes its subtask and picks the other subtasks that it enqueued. This is equivalent to executing them sequentially.

The following is an implementation of Quicksort using the WorkCrew model:

```
1    void QSort(args)
2        struct ArgBlock *args;
3    {
4        int boundary;
5        struct ArgBlock *part1, *part2;
6
7        if (args->low < args->high) {
8            boundary = partition(args->a, args->low, args->high);
9            part1 = CreateArgBlock(args->a, args->low, boundary);
10           part2 = CreateArgBlock(args->a, boundary+1, args->high);
11
12           RequestHelpWorkCrew(QSort, part2);
13           QSort(part1);
14
15           if (!WorkCrewGotHelp())
16               QSort(part2);
17       }
18   }
```

This example partitions the array like the ForkWhenIdle example, but rather than checking for an idle processor, the thread requests help (by placing a job on the queue) to sort on one partition of the array; then it continues working on the other partition. While this is happening, another thread could become available to perform the requested work, but if not, the thread that requested help can perform the work itself.

To use this model, the main QuickSort function must first initialize the crew of worker threads, add the main task of sorting array a, and then wait for all of the crew threads to finish (at which time the array is sorted).

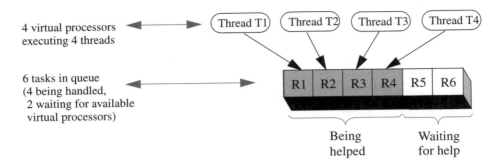

Figure 8-5. A WorkCrew's Request Queue.

```
1    void QuickSort(int a[], int low, int high)
2    {
3        struct WorkCrew *crew;
4
5        crew = CreateWorkCrew(nWorkers);
6        AddTaskWorkCrew(crew, QSort, CreateArgBlock(a, low, high));
7        JoinWorkCrew(crew);
8    }
```

Since the implementation of the WorkCrew model is complicated, we present it in Appendix A. Figure 8-5 illustrates the high-level behavior of a WorkCrew request queue. Threads T1, T2, and T3 are currently handling subtasks R1, R2, and R3, respectively. Thread T4 breaks its task into R4, R5, and R6, handles R4 itself, and requests help for R5 and R6. If any one of T1, T2, or T3 completes its task, it can pick up and execute one of the waiting tasks. If no thread picks up the work, T4 will eventually finish R4 and perform R5 and R6 in turn, as though it had not asked for help.

8.5.5   Performance Assessment

Multithreaded programming generally allows us to modularize programs as well as parallelize them. Care must be taken not to greatly exceed the number of processors available; otherwise, performance may degrade because the system spends too much time swapping threads. If an array containing 100,000 elements were sorted using our sample ForkAlways implementation of QuickSort, up to 50,000 threads may be created, which is likely to bring most computer systems to a halt. But if the number of threads is limited using the ForkWhenIdle or WorkCrew models, we can have predictable performance. Table 8–1 is from a study done by [Vandervoorde and Roberts, 1988] using several array sizes to compare the efficiency of various programming models on DEC's Firefly computer with five MicroVax-II processors.

As we can see, even with an array size of 10,000, the ForkAlways implementation performs very poorly (six times slower) compared to a straightforward serial implementation. On the other hand, the ForkWhenIdle model is about three times faster than the serial implementation with input size of one million data points. By further optimizing the process of

Table 8–1. Performance Comparison of Various Programming Models.

Strategy	Array Size (N)	Time (sec)	Speedup (serial = 1)
Serial	10K	3.7	1.00
ForkAlways	10K	21.8	0.17
ForkWhenIdle	10K	1.6	2.31
WorkCrew	10K	1.3	2.85
Serial	100K	46.4	1.00
ForkWhenIdle	100K	16.3	2.85
WorkCrew	100K	14.4	3.22
Serial	1M	560.3	1.00
ForkWhenIdle	1M	183.1	3.06
WorkCrew	1M	157.7	3.55

generating and handling subtasks, the WorkCrew model improves performance slightly over the ForkWhenIdle model. The implementation of the WorkCrew model, however, is more complicated than the ForkWhenIdle model; so the effort to implement it may outweigh its benefit.

Since both the ForkWhenIdle and WorkCrew models limit the number of threads according to the number of available processors, applications using them may not be portable unless they can be easily retuned to accommodate the load and processing power of different operating environments.

8.6 Summary

In this chapter, we examined several programming models from which the designer of a multithreaded application may choose, including the workgroup, manager-worker, deferred-computation, pipeline, ForkAlways, ForkWhenIdle, and WorkCrew models. In the manager-worker, deferred computation, workgroup, pipeline, and ForkAlways models, the number of threads spawned is independent of the number of available processors. In the ForkWhenIdle and WorkCrew models, a maximum number of threads in an application prevents the system from being overloaded by too many threads.

8.7 Bibliographic Notes

Andrew Tanenbaum briefly mentions thread programming models in chapter 12 of his book [Tanenbaum, 1992]. Birrel [1991] describes several programming models. Our discussion of the WorkCrew model and its use is based on [Vandervoorde and Roberts, 1988].

8.8 Exercises

1. Describe a programming problem for which each of the following programming models would be an appropriate solution: (a) manager-worker; (b) pipeline; (c) workgroup.

2. In the pipeline example on page 159, consider the effect of switching lines 30 and 31 in the `PipeNode` function to:

   ```
   toMon->put(p); // forward the sentinel
   SaveResultBuf(Result, myPrime);
   ```

   Is the program still correct? What kind of potential synchronization problem have we just introduced? What else should we do to make the program correct? Hint: Consider synchronization with respect to a shared object.

3. Enhance the MultiGrep example on page 154 to spawn a slave thread that doubles as a manager thread when it finds a subdirectory. The new manager should create a worker thread for each file/subdirectory in the new subdirectory.

8.9 References

1. Birrel, A. D. (1991). An Introduction to Programming with Threads. In Nelson, G., editor, *Systems Programming with Modula-3*, pp. 88–118. Prentice Hall, Englewood Cliffs, NJ.
2. Cormen, T. H., Leiserson, C. E., and Rivest, R. L. (1990). *Introduction to Algorithms*. McGraw-Hill, New York, NY.
3. Tanenbaum, A. (1992). *Modern Operating Systems*. Prentice Hall, Englewood Cliffs, NJ.
4. Vandervoorde, M. T. and Roberts, E. S. (1988). WorkCrews: An Abstraction for Controlling Parallelism. *International Journal of Parallel Programming*, 17(4):347–366.

Threads in Distributed Applications

*I*n this chapter, we examine the use of threads in distributed computing, where parts of the system run on different devices or computers. For example, a bank's network of automatic teller machines (ATMs) is a large distributed application, parts of which reside on local automatic teller machines to interact with users, and other parts in more powerful computers where customers' records are stored.

Although an in-depth study of distributed computing is beyond the scope of this book, our goal is to introduce you to this important topic, and to illustrate the key role that threads play in it. We start with an introduction to the popular distributed object system and *client-server* architectures, then show how to use threads in building a simple distributed RPC-based client-server application. Next, we briefly describe Microsoft's DCOM model and show you what it's like to implement our sample application using threads and DCOM.

9.1 The Client-Server Model

Distributed computing is a popular and important modern programming paradigm. With the rapid increase in the power of personal computers and workstations, organizations can replace traditional mainframe computers with clusters of smaller, much cheaper

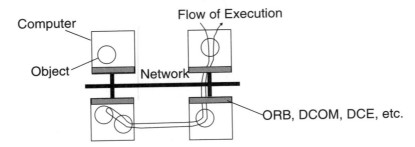

Figure 9-1. A typical distributed object system.

computers. Each of the computers participating in a distributed application runs a part of the application. Emerging standards like Open Group's Distributed Computing Environment (DCE), OMG's Common Object Request Broker Architecture (CORBA), Java's Remote Method Invocation (RMI), and Microsoft's DCOM provide the necessary "plumbing" for such application components to talk to each other. Each pair of distributed objects participate in a **client-server** relationship. A distributed application can consist of many such client-server relationships, forming an **n-tiered** architecture. In the following, we will focus on a **two-tiered** client-server architecture, without loss of generality.

The client-server model is a popular choice for migration from a centralized mainframe computer to a distributed network of workstations and personal computers. An instance of this model has two software components—*client* and *server*—which are independent programs (often running on separate machines) that communicate with each other using a predefined interface. Usually, a single server program services one or more client programs, but in a large distributed computing environment with many clients, server processes can be replicated to share the load and improve response time. Figure 9-2 shows the high-level client-server architecture of a distributed application.

One reason for the client-server model's popularity is that it provides a natural and effective way to modularize an application. For example, instead of running many instances of a large, interactive program (which requires many powerful computers), we can implement the core of the application as a server program, and implement the user interface as a client program. Then we need only one powerful computer to run the usually compute-intensive server program, while lighter-weight client programs can run effectively on less powerful and less expensive machines.

Another benefit of the client-server model is reduced development time. Once the client and server interface is specified, they can be developed independently. Once deployed, improvements can be made to either a client or server program without disturbing the other, as long as the interface remains unchanged. This greatly simplifies program maintenance.

Threads can play an essential role in client-server distributed computing, since both clients and servers can benefit greatly by using threads. The minimal architecture of a server process may include a thread to receive and dispatch client requests, a thread to handle signals and exceptions, and one or more threads to carry out the computation for each client request. On the client side, threads can be very effectively used to improve the responsiveness

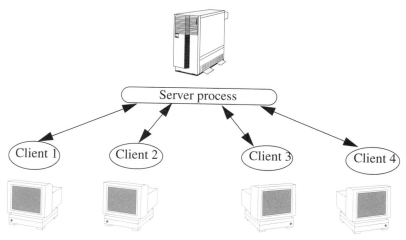

Figure 9-2. Client-Server Architecture of a Distributed Application.

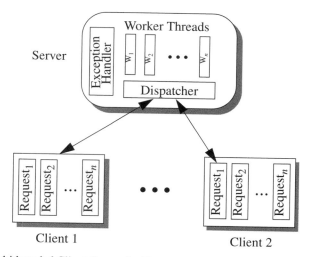

Figure 9-3. Multithreaded Client-Server Architecture.

of applications: with dedicated threads handling the user interface, while the others pre-fetch, load, and compute data in the background. Figure 9-3 shows typical threads in a distributed application.

9.2 Remote Procedure Call (RPC)

On a Windows platform, you can construct the inter-process communication between clients and servers using one of many **middleware** technologies: DCOM, RPC, CORBA, RMI, etc. In this book, we'll illustrate the use of threads in distributed applications using two

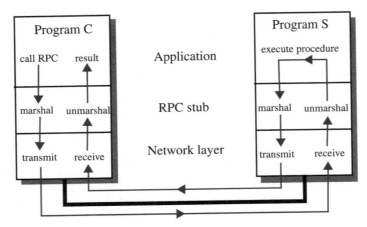

Figure 9-4. How RPC Works.

approaches: Microsoft RPC and DCOM. We describe the use of RPC's in this section and Section 9.3. We'll describe the use of DCOM in Section 9.4. The idea behind RPC is that invoking a service on a remote computer should be as simple as calling a local procedure. This concept emerged in the mid-1970s, and several implementations were available in the early 1980s [Birrel and Nelson, 1984].

Figure 9-4 illustrates how RPC works. Assuming that a client program C and a server program S agree on an interface, if program C on one machine would like to execute a procedure in program S on another machine, it calls a remote procedure "stub" (like calling any local procedure) with the appropriate number of arguments. The RPC mechanism, in an activity known as *marshaling*, translates the procedure call "stub" arguments into a sequence of data packets to be sent across a communication network. The network interface layer of program C then transmits the packets to program S. When the network layer of program S receives the packets, it passes them to another RPC stub, which unmarshals and reconstructs the procedure call arguments. Program S executes the procedure, and it returns results to the RPC stub, which marshals the result. The network layer transmits the data packets back to program C, which receives them, then unmarshals and returns the result of the procedure call. Although the steps are elaborate, the calling program views them as simply a function call returning a result.

RPC is important in distributed computing because it eases the programming burden by hiding details of the networking layer. To implement the communication between software processes using RPC, you need not know network details. Like calling a local procedure, calling a remote procedure is a synchronous activity. This means that a single-threaded client application may face an indefinite delay if a server is busy or deadlocked. This problem is easily resolved using threads and RPC: by executing each remote procedure call in the context of a new thread, the client program can continue to execute even when a remote server is busy.

The implementation of servers usually relies on threads. Even when the user doesn't explicitly use threads in server code, an effective server almost always is composed of at least one thread to listen for and dispatch client requests, and another to carry out each job. In

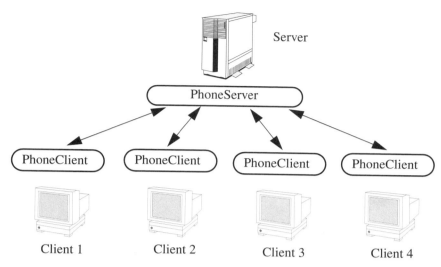

Figure 9-5. Client-Server Architecture of a Distributed Phone Directory.

addition, the server's runtime library may use threads and RPC to avoid blocking. For example, in the process of handling a client request, a server process may need to make an RPC call to another server. While this call is in progress, the first server continues to accept and handle more client requests.

9.3 An RPC-Based Distributed Application Example

As an example, we'll build a simple client-server application that provides a phone directory service. The server component, called *PhoneServer*, maintains the names and phone numbers of people and provides the following functions:

1. **Update**: Given a person's name and a phone number, the server inserts them in the phone directory. For simplicity, we assume that a person can only have one phone number; so a new phone number will overwrite an existing one.

2. **Retrieve**: Given a person's name, the server finds the person's phone number.

3. **Shutdown**: Upon receiving this command, the server terminates.

Figure 9-5 illustrates the structure of the *Phones* distributed application. The *PhoneServer* program serves many *PhoneClient* clients. Each client interacts with a user, and it may call the server to retrieve or update phone numbers, or to request that the server shutdown.

The steps for constructing a client-server distributed application using Microsoft's RPC are shown in Figure 9-6. To interact with each other, the client and server must agree upon a common communication interface, which is defined using the Interface Definition Language (IDL) in a file with the extension *.idl*. Next, we use the Microsoft IDL compiler (MIDL) to compile this file, generating the necessary include files (extension .h), and RPC **stub files** to be compiled and linked with the respective client and server software.

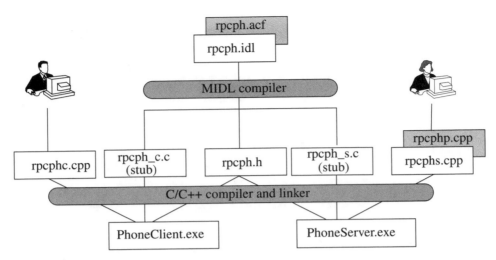

Figure 9-6. The Construction Steps for the Distributed Phones Application Using RPC.

Once the interface is defined, the development of client and server components can proceed independently. When these components are coded, we compile and link them with the respective RPC stubs to generate client and server programs. As long as the client and server components comply with the interface, the resulting programs will work with each other as a distributed application.

In the following sections, we will walk through each of the implementation steps for the interface, client, and server components of our distributed phone directory application.

9.3.1   Interface Definition

An IDL interface consists of a universal unique identifier (UUID), a version number, an interface name, and a collection of server-supported function prototypes, using which a client can request service. For example, the interface for our distributed **Phones** application is:

```
1    [
2        uuid(2F5F6520-CA46-1067-B319-00DD010662DA),
3        version(1.0)
4    ]
5
6    interface rpcph {
7        void Update([in, string] unsigned char *name,
8                    [in, string] unsigned char *phone) ;
9        [string] unsigned char
10               *Retrieve([in, string] unsigned char *name) ;
11       void Shutdown(void) ;
12   }
```

In addition to the IDL file that describes the contract between clients and the server, you can also use the ACF file to describe data structures and types local to the client or the server. For example, we use the following ACF file to define a **binding handle**, hPhones, that will be used by the clients to refer to the server.

```
1    [implicit_handle(handle_t hRpcph)]
2    interface rpcph
3    {
4    }
```

You can generate a unique UUID, for example, 2F5F6520-CA46-1067-B319-00DD010662DA, by using the **uuidgen** command of the Software Development Kit (SDK). Uuidgen ensures that an interface will be uniquely identified in the distributed computing environment. The version number of an interface (line 3) contains two parts: a *major* and a *minor* number. The major number indicates whether the interface is compatible with a previous version. With the same major number, the minor number indicates that although there are changes to the interface, it is fully compatible with previous versions having smaller minor numbers. For example, suppose version 1.0 of a calculator server provides the operations ADD and SUBTRACT, and the next release of the server, version 1.1, supports ADD, SUBTRACT, and MULTIPLY. A server implementing the version 1.1 interface is compatible with clients using the version 1.0 interface, since those clients can still call ADD or SUBTRACT operations. Now, suppose that a new release of the server supports only the operations ADD, MULTIPLY, and DIVIDE. This server is not compatible with clients using interface version 1.0 or version 1.1, since clients can no longer call the SUBTRACT operation, so it must carry a different major version number (e.g., 2.0).

Line 6 contains the full name of the interface. The server "publishes" this name along with the binding information via the name service provider, so client applications can use the name to obtain a handle for calling the server.

The rest of the interface definition is a collection of procedure declarations that specify the services provided. The declaration of each procedure resembles a function prototype, including the procedure name, argument types, and return types. In addition, each argument type has an attribute [in] or [out], indicating the direction of data movement.

When the interface definition is complete, we compile the IDL file, to generate the necessary include files and RPC stubs for server and client code. Specifically, the MIDL compiler processes the file phone.idl to generate header file phone.h, plus the client and server stub files phone_c.c and phone_s.c. At this point, the development of client and server components can proceed independently.

9.3.2 Server Implementation

A sever's job is to publish its interfaces and service all client requests. To construct a server application, we must implement the services specified by the interfaces in the IDL file, write server initialization code, then compile and link all of this with the RPC stubs.

At runtime, a server application publishes its interface (hence its services) by registering with a name service. The memory-resident name service is called the **Microsoft Locator**. Server registration requires the following steps: choose a protocol sequence, register the interface, then listen for client requests. Optionally, a server may need to initialize internal data or clean up upon termination. The following code implements server registration for our phone server.

```
1   void _CRTAPI1 main(int argc, char *argv[]) {
2     RPC_STATUS status;
3     unsigned char *pszProtocolSequence = (unsigned char *) "ncacn_np";
4     unsigned char *pszSecurity         = NULL;
5     unsigned char *pszEndpoint = (unsigned char *) "\\pipe\\rpcph";
6     unsigned int   cMinCalls           = 1;
7     unsigned int   cMaxCalls           = 20;
8     unsigned int   fDontWait           = FALSE;
9
10  // register server endpoints so that clients can find
11  // the ports for this server on the server machine.
12
13      status = RpcServerUseProtseqEp(pszProtocolSequence,
14                        cMaxCalls,   // max # of concurrent clients
15                        pszEndpoint, // end points for this server
16                        pszSecurity); // Security descriptor
17      if (status) {
18        printf("ERROR: RpcServerUseProtseqEp returned 0x%x\n", status);
19        exit(status);
20      }
21
22      // register server interface so that clients can find
23      // the service provider
24      status=RpcServerRegisterIf(rpcph_v1_0_s_ifspec,
25                                  // interface to register
26                        NULL,    // MgrTypeUuid
27                        NULL);   // MgrEpv; null means use default
28      if (status) {
29        printf("ERROR: RpcServerRegisterIf returned 0x%x\n", status);
30        exit(status);
31      }
32
33      // initialize the server database
34      InitPhones() ;
35
36      // go into listening loop to accept client calls
37      // and dispatch thread to process them.
38      status = RpcServerListen(cMinCalls, cMaxCalls, fDontWait);
39
40      // if ServerListen loop is gracefully terminated,
41      // we reach this point.
42      if (status)
43        exit(status);
44
45      // synchronize before exiting
46      if (fDontWait) {
47        status = RpcMgmtWaitServerListen();  //  wait operation
48        if (status)
49          exit(status);
50      }
51      RpcServerUnregisterIf(NULL,NULL,FALSE);
52      // clean up server before exiting
53      ClosePhones() ;
54  }
```

1. **Choose a protocol sequence:** The function `RpcServerUseProtocolSeqEp` (line 13) selects a communication protocol, maximum number of concurrent calls allowed, an endpoint, and a security descriptor. The server advertises its services on a given set of communication protocols: the underlying inter-process communication protocols that will be used by the RPC runtime mechanisms. For example, on Windows platform, a server can choose to use a named pipe, a mailslot, TCP/IP, NetBIOS, and so forth. We choose a named pipe, `nacn_np`, as the communication protocol for the RPCServer. This implies that only clients who are willing and able to support the named pipe protocol will be able to use this server. The endpoint, `\\pipe\\rpcph`, indicates a port at which the server process listens for calls from client programs. The (optional) security descriptor informs the security subsystem of the desired security level. Finally, the number set by `cMaxCalls` is a hint about the number of RPC calls that the server is expected to handle concurrently. We chose an arbitrary number, 20, for our example. You must choose the number carefully—each client request creates a new thread, if this number is large a server may create too many threads, resulting in poor server performance.

2. **Register interface:** The function `RpcServerRegisterIf` expects an interface specification, a manager-type UUID, and the manager entry point vector (EPV). The interface specification, a data structure generated by the MIDL compiler, identifies the particular interface that this server is exporting. One server can advertise multiple interfaces. The manager-type UUID and the manager EPV combine to allow multiple interfaces and object types to be supported by an RPC server. To keep it simple, our server example registers its interface specification, `rpcph_v1_0_s_ifspec`, with no manager-type UUID, and uses the default manager EPV, also generated by the MIDL compiler.

3. **Initialize data (optional):** This optional step initializes the server to receive client requests. In our example, the function `InitPhones` initializes the phone database by reading a file of phone numbers. We also create a mutex object here that we use to synchronize accesses to the server's functions.

4. **Listen to requests:** The server calls the function `RpcServerListen` to wait for incoming RPC requests from clients. Note that in this call we also specify the minimum and maximum concurrency for client requests.

5. **Clean up:** Servers must clean up their registration with the RPC runtime system upon exit. When the function `RpcServerListen` returns, usually as a result of a call to `RpcServerStopListen`, we can call procedures to clean up the state of the server and remove it from the network. In the above code, we call the function `RpcServerUnregisterIf` to remove the server from the network. Since we do not want to loose the phone numbers created during this session, we also call the `ClosePhones` procedure to save memory-resident data in secondary storage while the server is shutting itself down.

The `InitPhones` and `ClosePhones` functions load and save disk file data.

```
1     typedef map<string, string> t_PhoneDir ;
2     t_PhoneDir g_PhoneDir ;
3     char szName[MAX_NAME], szPhone[MAX_NAME] ;
4
5     void InitPhones(void)
6     {
7       ifstream phStream("E:\\Dist Apps\\Phones") ;
8       if (phStream)
9         while (!phStream.eof()) {
10          phStream >> szName >> szPhone ;
11          //insert in m_PhoneDir
12          g_PhoneDir.insert(t_PhoneDir::value_type(szName, szPhone)) ;
13        }
14      g_hPhonesMutex = CreateMutex(NULL,FALSE,NULL);
15    }
16
17    void ClosePhones(void)
18    {
19      t_PhoneDir::iterator p ;
20      ofstream phStream("E:\\Dist Apps\\Phones") ;
21
22      if (phStream) {
23        WaitForSingleObject(g_hPhonesMutex, INFINITE) ;
24        for (p = g_PhoneDir.begin(); p != g_PhoneDir.end(); p++)
25          phStream << (p->first).c_str() << ' ' <<
26                      (p->second).c_str() << endl ;
27        ReleaseMutex(g_hPhonesMutex) ;
28      }
29    }
```

Once the server is operational, it provides the operations Update, Retrieve, and Shutdown.

```
1     void Update(unsigned char *name, unsigned char *phone) {
2       if (strlen((char *)name) && strlen((char *)phone)) {
3         WaitForSingleObject(g_hPhonesMutex,INFINITE);
4         g_PhoneDir.erase((char *)name) ;
5         g_PhoneDir.insert(
6             t_PhoneDir::value_type((char *)name, (char *)phone)) ;
7         ReleaseMutex(g_hPhonesMutex);
8       }
9     }
10
11    unsigned char *Retrieve(unsigned char *name) {
12      t_PhoneDir::iterator r ;
13      WaitForSingleObject(g_hPhonesMutex,INFINITE);
14      r = g_PhoneDir.find((char *)name) ;
15      ReleaseMutex(g_hPhonesMutex);
16      if (r != g_PhoneDir.end())
17        return (unsigned char *) (r->second).c_str() ;
18      else
19        return (unsigned char*) "No Entry!" ;
20    }
21
```

```
22   void Shutdown(void) {
23      RpcMgmtStopServerListening(NULL);
24   }
```

The Shutdown procedure performs a graceful exit by calling the function RpcMgmt-
StopServerListening. The latter causes the server to stop accepting new RPC calls
and wait for all current calls to complete before exiting. At this point, you can provide code to
clean up, remove the server name from the name service database, and retract all RPC end-
points so that new clients do not receive a stale binding handle after it is no longer in service.

9.3.3 Client Application

Once a server application announces its availability in the environment, client applications can invoke its services using remote procedure calls. The following is the top-level code
for our *Phones* client. We've omitted code that creates the application window, for brevity of
presentation.

```
1     long APIENTRY MainWndProc(HWND   hWnd, UINT   message, WPARAM wParam,
2                               LPARAM lParam) {
3        switch (message) {
4          case WM_CREATE:
5            Bind(hWnd);
6            break;
7          case WM_COMMAND:
8            switch (LOWORD(wParam)) {
9              case IDM_DIALOG1:
10               hWndDlg = CreateDialog(ghInst,   "PERSONBOX",
11                               hWnd, (DLGPROC) PersonDlgProc);
12               break;
13             case IDM_QUIT_SERVER:
14               if (fBound)
15                 RpcTryExcept {
16                   Shutdown();
17                 }
18                 RpcExcept (1) {
19                 } RpcEndExcept;
20               UnBind(hWnd) ;
21               break;
22             case IDM_QUIT:
23               DestroyWindow(hWnd);
24               break;
25            }
26            break;
27          case WM_DESTROY:     // message: window being destroyed
28            UnBind(hWnd) ;
29            PostQuitMessage(0);
30            break;
31          default:
32            return(DefWindowProc(hWnd, message, wParam, lParam));
33        }
34     return(0);
35   }
```

To connect to the server program, our client application calls the function Bind (line 5), in response to the WM_CREATE message when the application's window is created. As the following code for the Bind function shows, we construct a string binding using the function RpcStringBindingCompose. The binding handle to the server is then obtained by passing it to RpcBindingFromStringBinding. This binding handle is implicitly used by the RPC stub functions when making calls for the client to the server.

```
1    RPC_STATUS Bind(HWND hWnd)
2    {
3      RPC_STATUS status ;
4      UnBind(hWnd) ;
5      status = RpcStringBindingCompose(pszUuid,
6                                       pszProtocolSequence,
7                                       pszNetworkAddress,
8                                       pszEndpoint,
9                                       pszOptions,
10                                      &pszStringBinding);
11     if (status != RPC_S_OK) {
12       MessageBox(hWnd, "Could not compose binding string",
13               "RPC Phones", MB_OK);
14       return(status);
15     }
16     status = RpcBindingFromStringBinding(pszStringBinding,
17                                   &hRpcph);
18     if (status) {
19       MessageBox(hWnd, "Failed to get binding",
20         "RPC Runtime Error", MB_ICONEXCLAMATION);
21       return(status);
22     }
23     fBound = TRUE;   // bind successful; reset flag
24     return(status);
25   }
26   void UnBind(HWND hWnd)
27   {
28     RPC_STATUS status;
29
30     if (fBound == TRUE) {   // unbind only if bound
31       status = RpcStringFree(&pszStringBinding);
32       if (status) {
33         MessageBox(hWnd, "RpcStringFree failed",
34                         "RPC Error", MB_ICONSTOP);
35         return ;
36       }
37       status = RpcBindingFree(&hRpcph);
38       if (status) {
39         MessageBox(hWnd, "RpcBindingFree failed",
40                         "RPC Error", MB_ICONSTOP);
41         return ;
42       }
43       fBound = FALSE;   // unbind successful; reset flag
44     }
45   }
```

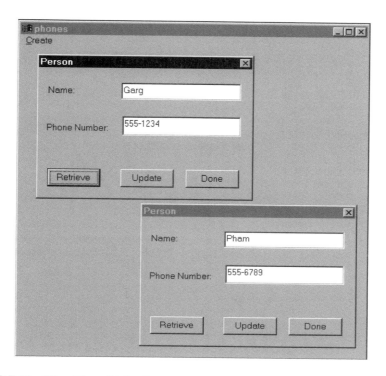

Figure 9-7. The Client Phone Dialog Box.

The binding handle contains information for the client's RPC libraries to locate the server process in the computer network, including a protocol sequence, a host machine name, a process ID, an endpoint, and so forth. The binding handle is used by the RPC stub functions and is opaque to the client code (much like any other handle to a kernel object such as a thread or a process). The application must free the binding handle when its done using the server's services. We will now look at how the client makes RPC calls to its server.

Our sample application creates a dialog box, which displays the name and phone number of a person, plus three buttons that allow a user to either retrieve or update a phone number, or to close the box (see Figure 9-7).

Once the dialog box is created, when the user pushes the Update or Retrieve buttons the client program invokes the corresponding RPC function. The following code shows the implementation of the procedure that is called whenever the user pushes one of the Retrieve, Update, or Done buttons of the dialogue box. In line 38 we start a thread to invoke the RPC Update call, so that if the server is not responsive, our client application does not block. We pass a new memory block with the update parameters to the each update thread. This way, there is no synchronization problems among the main thread and the update threads. The update thread frees this memory block when it is done with the update. These RPC calls actually invoke the corresponding functions in the server using marshalling and unmarshalling, as described in Section 9.2. Note that the client makes the RPC calls within

the RPCTryExcept and RPCEndExcept blocks. This is a Microsoft extension that allows
clients to gracefully exit from any failures in the network or the server.

```
1    struct threadArg {
2       HWND hwnd;
3       unsigned char name[256];
4       unsigned char phone[256];
5    } *namePhone;
6
7    LRESULT APIENTRY PersonDlgProc(
8          HWND hwnd, UINT message, UINT wParam, LPARAM lParam)
9    {
10      HWND hNameWnd;
11      unsigned char nameText[256];
12      unsigned char phoneText[256];
13
14      switch (message) {
15        case WM_INITDIALOG:
16           DlgExists = 1;
17           return FALSE;
18        case WM_COMMAND:
19           switch (wParam) {
20             case IDM_Update:
21                hNameWnd = GetDlgItem(hwnd, IDM_Name);
22                hPhoneWnd = GetDlgItem(hwnd, IDM_PhoneNumber);
23                namePhone = (struct threadArg *)
24                malloc(sizeof(struct threadArg)) ;
25
26                if (!namePhone) {
27                   MessageBox(hwnd, "Could not get memory!",
28                            "Dialog Proc", MB_OK);
29                   break ;
30                }
31                if (GetWindowText(hNameWnd, namePhone->name,
32                    GetWindowTextLength(hNameWnd)+1) == 0)
33                break;
34                if (GetWindowText(hPhoneWnd, namePhone->phone,
35                    GetWindowTextLength(hPhoneWnd)+1) == 0)
36                break;
37                namePhone->hwnd = hwnd;
38                if (_beginthread(UpdateServer, 0, namePhone) == -1)
39                   MessageBox(hwnd, "Could not create update thread!",
40                            "Dialog Proc", MB_OK);
41                break;
42             case IDM_Retrieve:
43                hNameWnd = GetDlgItem(hwnd, IDM_Name);
44                hPhoneWnd = GetDlgItem(hwnd, IDM_PhoneNumber);
45                if (GetWindowText(hNameWnd, nameText,
46                    GetWindowTextLength(hNameWnd)+1) == 0)
47                break;
48                RpcTryExcept {
49                   strcpy(phoneText, Retrieve(nameText));
50                   SetWindowText(hPhoneWnd, phoneText);
51                }
```

```
52                        RpcExcept (1) {
53                            MessageBox(hwnd, "Retrieve call didn't go through!",
54                                         "RPC Error", MB_OK);
55                        } RpcEndExcept;
56                        break;
57                    case IDM_Done:
58                        SendMessage(hwnd, WM_CLOSE, 0, 0);
59                        break;
60                }
61            return TRUE;
62        case WM_CLOSE:
63            DlgExists = 0;
64            DestroyWindow(hwnd);
65            return TRUE;
66        }
67    return FALSE;
68 }
69
70 void __cdecl UpdateServer(struct threadArg *Arg)
71 {
72    RpcTryExcept {
73        Update(Arg->name, Arg->phone);
74    }
75    RpcExcept (1) {
76        MessageBox(Arg->hwnd, "Update call didn't go through!",
77                    "RPC Error", MB_OK);
78    } RpcEndExcept;
79    free(Arg) ;
80 }
```

To terminate the server program a user must select "Terminate Server" from the pull-down menu, at which point the client application calls the RPC function Shutdown (line 16 on page 179). This informs the server that it can shut itself down as we don't expect any more clients to connect to it.

As we can see from this example, threads play an essential role in a distributed application, in both the server and the client components. In the server, threads are implicitly used to handle signals, listen for RPC's, and execute different client requests. Each new incoming request creates an additional server thread. An interface function of a server, of course, can also create its own additional threads as needed. You should remember to always make server interface functions thread safe! On the client side, clients can invoke different server requests in different threads, to prevent the application from blocking if the server is not responsive.

This completes our discussion of RPC-based client and server distributed applications. We will now look at a more modern approach for building distributed applications, using a "distributed objects" paradigm.

9.4 Distributed Applications Using DCOM

On many modern platforms (Win32, MacOS, and various flavors of UNIX), you can build distributed applications using "software components," each of which works as part of the overall application. One technology for creating such components is Microsoft's COM and DCOM. The COM architecture enables you to write applications as separable binary

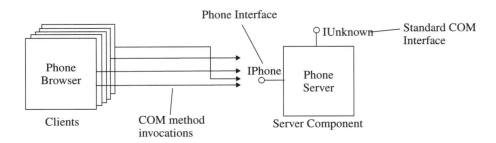

Figure 9-8. A DCOM Client-Server application.

modules that client programs combine at runtime to provide an application's services. A COM component is a binary module, much as a RPC server in a client-server model. A component exports a set of **interfaces** which define a set of methods (functions, services) that clients can invoke. A component's interface is different from a traditional C++ object in that a client cannot access any data from a component directly, everything has to be done through an interface.

Figure 9-8 shows a typical COM component and clients, arranged in a client-server relationship. A component provides one or more interfaces. Clients access the methods of a component's interface through an **interface pointer**. Note that this client-server relationship can be used recursively in COM—a component can be a client of another component in its client or a client of another component. A component is shown as a box and its interfaces as small circle-tipped lines protruding from the box.

Multiple clients can access a given component concurrently. COM clients and components can be programmed in different languages. You can have a directory server written in C++ being accessed by clients written in Java, Visual Basic, C++, and so forth. Another important feature of COM/DCOM is that a component can be co-located with a client in the same address space, or in a different address space on the same or different machine. Since we are concerned with distributed applications in this chapter, the rest of the discussion will only focus on components executing on a different address space from the client programs.

9.4.1 Thread Models in DCOM

The basic model of thread safety in DCOM is the **apartment** thread model.

Each thread of an application that uses DCOM must initialize the DCOM library using `CoInitializeEx` or `CoInitialize`. In this call, the thread specifies whether it will be using a single-threaded apartment (STA) or a multithreaded apartment (MTA). The nature of concurrent access to DCOM components is different depending on whether the thread that created the component asked DCOM for an MTA or STA. Similarly, the scope of visibility of interface pointers is different in DCOM client threads, depending on whether the threads asked DCOM for an STA or MTA. We'll explain this using a simple example, depicted in Figure 9-9. Suppose we have a DCOM client with three threads, T_1 through T_3, and a server component with three threads T_A through T_C. We will now describe the behavior and choices

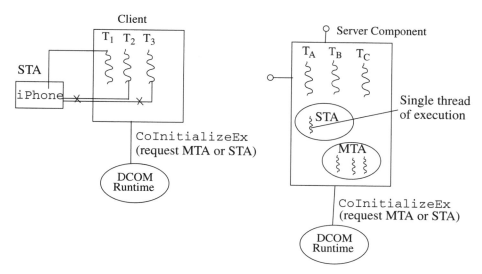

Figure 9-9. Apartment threading model in DCOM.

for the apartment models from first the client's perspective and then from the server component's perspective. Note that a process can have multiple STAs but only one MTA.

9.4.1.1 Client's Perspective

From the client's perspective, we can choose for each of the threads T_1 through T_3 whether we will share DCOM interface pointers among them or not. If we decide not to share the interface pointers, then each of the threads T_1 and T_3 can have interface pointers that are visible solely within that thread. Say T_1 uses an interface pointer, iPhone, that accesses a DCOM component, PhoneServer. If T_1 has told DCOM that it wants to be in an STA, then the variable iPhone will not be accessible from T_2 or T_3. (Even though you may declare it as a global variable. If T_2 or T_3 try to access a method of iPhone, you will get a DCOM runtime error.) T_2 and T_3 can behave as T_1 with regards to other interface pointers, i.e., they can ask for an STA and access a server component solely within themselves. If T_1 wants to share the interface pointer iPhone with T_2 and T_3, then it must ask DCOM to use an MTA. T_2 and T_3 also must initialize DCOM requesting an MTA. Once all three threads have initialized DCOM with a request for an MTA, they can all share the interface pointers among themselves, much as they would share any other global variable. You can also have the situation where T_1 and T_2 are sharing an interface pointer via an MTA and T_3 is using a STA and does not have access to interface pointers of T_1 or T_2. Finally, you can also explicitly share interface pointers between threads in different STAs. You do that by marshalling and unmarshalling the interface pointer in each of the threads. See the SDK or [Eddon and Eddon 98] for details on how to do this.

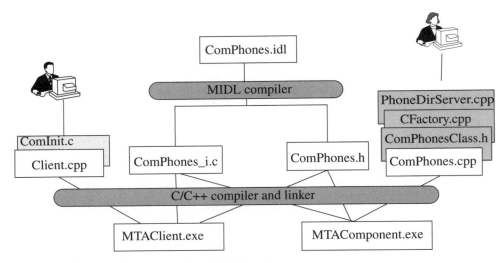

Figure 9-10. Construction steps for a DCOM application.

9.4.1.2 Server Component Perspective

Threads T_A through T_C have a choice of whether they want to allow concurrent access to components provided by them. If they do not want to allow concurrent access to a component, then the thread that creates the component should initialize DCOM with a request for an STA. DCOM ensures that all accesses to a component in an STA are serialized. This is a quick and easy way of obtaining synchronized access to a DCOM component. If you have a thread-unsafe component that you want to make available through DCOM, you should create that component using an STA. If, on the other hand, you have built a thread-safe component then you should allow concurrent access to the component using an MTA.

We now describe an implementation of the phone directory server as a multithreaded DCOM component.

9.5 DCOM-Based Phone Application

The construction steps for a DCOM application are similar to the construction steps for an RPC-based application. Figure 9-10 shows the steps involved: you first create an IDL file specifying the interface between the client and the server programs. Compile the IDL file using Microsoft's IDL (MIDL) compiler. MIDL generates two main files:[1] ComPhones.h, and ComPhones_i.c. You write the client and server programs and compile and link with these files to produce the client and server parts of your distributed application.

9.5.1 DCOM Interface Definition

Our component, shown in Figure 9-8, provides two interfaces: IUnknown and IPhone. (By convention interface names begin with a capital I.) The IUnknown interface

---

[1.] MIDL also generates a couple of additional files, dlldata.c, ComPhones.tlb, and ComPhones_p.c. Their use is beyond the scope of the current discussion. See the SDK for more information.

is a standard interface that all components must provide. The interface IPhone is similar to the RPC interface we've seen earlier which provides methods for looking up a phone number or updating a phone number. The interfaces of a component are described in IDL, similar to the RPC interfaces. (An interface pointer in DCOM clients serves the purpose of a binding handle in RPC clients.) The following IDL code shows the DCOM interface for the phone directory server:

```
1    import "unknwn.idl" ;
2    [object,
3       uuid(1604591e-ef42-11d1-8413-080009dd432d),// interface ID
4       oleautomation]
5    interface IPhone : IUnknown {
6       HRESULT Update([in, string] BSTR name, [in, string] BSTR phone) ;
7       HRESULT Retrieve([in, string] BSTR name,
8                        [out, string, retval] BSTR *phone) ;
9    } ;
10
11   [uuid(52e25874-f58a-11d1-8414-080009dd432d),// Library ID
12      helpstring("Multithreaded Book Phone Example"),
13      version(1.0)]
14   library ComPhones {
15       importlib("stdole32.tlb") ;
16       interface IPhone ;
17       [uuid(642c8bd4-ef47-11d1-8413-080009dd432d)]// Class ID
18       coclass CPhoneExample {
19          interface IPhone ;
20       }
21   };
```

This code is similar to the RPC interface code we've seen so far, with three main additions: (1) the IUnknown interface, (2) the attribute object attached to the interface (line 2), and (3) the use of a library (line 14). The IUnknown interface is a standard COM interface that all components must provide. We'll see its use in the client and component codes shortly. The attribute object instructs the MIDL compiler that the interface is a COM interface. Finally, the library is used to ensure that components built with this interface can be accessed by clients written in other programming languages like Visual Basic, Java and so forth.

9.5.2 DCOM Client

We'll now show the main parts of our DCOM-based phone directory application. We'll implement a multithreaded version of the client and server.

Here's the code for the main window procedure for the DCOM phone directory client.

```
1    long APIENTRY MainWndProc(HWND   hWnd, UINT   message, WPARAM wParam,
2                                        LPARAM lParam)
3    {
4       switch (message) {
5         case WM_CREATE:
6            // initialize the COM stuff here
7            g_pPhones = InitializePhoneServer(hWnd) ;
8            break;
9         case WM_COMMAND:
```

```
10              switch (LOWORD(wParam)) {
11                 case IDM_DIALOG1:
12                    if (!g_pPhones)
13                        MessageBox(hWnd,
14                        "COM Phone Directory Server Object not available!",
15                        "PhoneDir Error", MB_OK);
16                    else
17                        g_hWndDlg = CreateDialog(ghInst,
18                        "PERSONBOX", hWnd, (DLGPROC) PersonDlgProc);
19                    break;
20                 case IDM_QUIT_SERVER:
21                    if (g_pPhones)
22                        ReleaseComponent(hWnd, &g_pPhones) ;
23                    break;
24                 case IDM_QUIT:
25                    DestroyWindow(hWnd);
26                    break;
27              }
28              break;
29           case WM_DESTROY:     // message: window being destroyed
30              if (g_pPhones)
31                 ReleaseComponent(hWnd, &g_pPhones) ;
32              PostQuitMessage(0);
33              break;
34           default:
35              return(DefWindowProc(hWnd, message, wParam, lParam));
36       }
37    return(0);
38 }
```

Much of this code in terms of window management and dialogue creation is the same as in the case of the RPC client. We call the function InitializePhoneServer when the application's window is first created (line 7). (Similar to the Bind call we made in the RPC client.) Similarly, we call the function ReleaseComponent (like UnBind), to release the server component once we are done with it (lines 22 and 31). The code for the InitializePhoneServer and ReleaseComponents functions is as follows:

```
1  IPhone* InitializePhoneServer(HWND hwnd)
2  {
3     IUnknown* pUnknown ;
4     IPhone* pPhones = NULL ;
5     HRESULT hr = CoInitializeEx(NULL, COINIT_MULTITHREADED) ;
6
7     hr = CoCreateInstance(CLSID_CPhoneExample,
8                    NULL, CLSCTX_SERVER, IID_IUnknown,
9                    (void **) &pUnknown) ;
10
11    hr = pUnknown->QueryInterface(IID_IPhone, (void **) &pPhones) ;
12
13    pUnknown -> Release() ;
14    return pPhones ;
15 }
16
17 void ReleaseComponent(HWND hWnd, IPhone** pPhones) {
```

```
18      RpcTryExcept {
19         *pPhones->Release() ;
20      } RpcExcept(1) {
21         MessageBox(hWnd, "Release call didn't go through!",
22                    "RPC Error", MB_OK);
23      } RpcEndExcept ;
24      *pPhones = NULL ;
25      CoUninitialize() ;
26   }
```

As the code shows, here we initialize the COM library using the function CoInitializeEx (line 5). The first argument to this function is a reserved void pointer and must be NULL. Using the second argument we specify the apartment type for the current thread of execution. This can be one of: COINIT_MULTITHREADED or COINIT_APARTMENTTHREADED. The COINIT_MULTITHREADED value informs the COM library that this thread and its interface pointers will reside in a multithreaded apartment. The COINIT_APARTMENTTHREADED indicates to the COM library that this thread and its interface pointers will reside in a single-threaded apartment. Since we are currently creating a multithreaded client, we use the value COINIT_MULTITHREADED. The next step in a DCOM client is to look for a component that provides the required IPhone interface. We do this by issuing the call CoCreateInstance. The first parameter of this calls specifies the class identifier of the desired component. This identifier is the same one that we used in the IDL file (line 17). The constant variable CLSID_CPhoneExample is declared in the MIDL-generated file ComPhones_i.c. The third parameter specifies the desired type of server. This can be either an in-process server (CLSCTX_INPROC_SERVER), a local server (CLSCTX_LOCAL_SERVER, a different process on the same machine), or a remote server (CLSCTX_REMOTE_SERVER). We have specified CLSCTX_SERVER to get any one of the above. DCOM will optimize this call and provide us with the closest server component available. The next parameter to CoCreateInstance specifies that we are looking for a pointer to the IUnknown interface. This is the standard protocol for obtaining interface pointers: we obtain the IUnknown interface first, as all DCOM components must provide this interface. Finally, as the last parameter, we pass the address of the pointer where we want CoCreateInstance to return the interface pointer to the component.

Once we get an interface pointer to a DCOM component providing the IUnknown interface (in pUnknown), we query the component for the IPhone interface pointer (line 11). The query returns an interface pointer to a DCOM component providing the IPhone interface in g_pPhones variable. As the following implementation of the new dialogue procedure shows, we use the g_pPhones interface pointer to access the Update (line 112) and Retrieve (line 84) functions of the component's interface. Note that we use the Rpctry block to catch any possible runtime exceptions from either the network or the server component. This is very important in DCOM applications, otherwise your application will not gracefully exit from networking errors.

```
1    BSTR g_bsName, g_bsPhone ; // current name and number information
2    TCHAR g_szName[MAX_NAME], g_szPhone[MAX_PHONE] ;
3
4    class threadArg {
5    public:
```

```
6      HWND hwnd ;
7      TCHAR szName[MAX_NAME] ;
8      TCHAR szPhone[MAX_PHONE] ;
9      threadArg() {} ;
10     ~threadArg() {} ;
11  } ;
12
13  threadArg *g_ptA ;
14
15  LRESULT APIENTRY PersonDlgProc(HWND hwnd, UINT message,
16                    UINT wParam, LPARAM lParam) {
17     HWND g_hNameWnd;
18     DWORD ThreadID ;
19     HRESULT hr ;
20     wchar_t wcszName[MAX_NAME] ;
21
22     switch (message) {
23       case WM_INITDIALOG:
24         DlgExists = 1;
25         return FALSE;
26       case WM_COMMAND:
27         switch (wParam) {
28           case IDM_Update:
29             g_hNameWnd = GetDlgItem(hwnd, IDM_Name);
30             g_hPhoneWnd = GetDlgItem(hwnd, IDM_PhoneNumber);
31             if (!(g_ptA = new threadArg())) {
32                 MessageBox(hwnd, "Not enough memory!",
33                     "Dialog Proc", MB_OK) ;
34             break ;
35             }
36             if (GetWindowText(g_hNameWnd,
37                               g_ptA->szName, MAX_NAME)==0)
38                break;
39             if (GetWindowText(g_hPhoneWnd, g_ptA->szPhone,
40                          MAX_PHONE) ==0)
41                break;
42             g_ptA->hwnd = hwnd ;
43             // make the COM call in a separate thread
44             CreateThread(NULL, 0, (LPTHREAD_START_ROUTINE)
45                 UpdateServer, g_ptA, 0, &ThreadID);
46             break;
47           case IDM_Retrieve:
48             g_hNameWnd = GetDlgItem(hwnd, IDM_Name);
49             g_hPhoneWnd = GetDlgItem(hwnd, IDM_PhoneNumber);
50             if (GetWindowText(g_hNameWnd, g_szName, MAX_NAME) == 0)
51                break;
52             SetWindowText(g_hPhoneWnd, TEXT("")) ;
53             g_bsPhone = 0 ;
54             mbstowcs(wcszName, g_szName, MAX_NAME) ;
55             g_bsName = SysAllocString(wcszName) ;
56             RetrieveFromServer(hwnd) ;
57             if (FAILED(hr))
58                 MessageBox(hwnd, "Could not retrieve phone number??",
59                     "COM Error", MB_OK) ;
```

```
60                   else if (g_bsPhone) {
61                       wcstombs(g_szPhone, g_bsPhone, MAX_PHONE) ;
62                       SetWindowText(g_hPhoneWnd, g_szPhone) ;
63                       SysFreeString(g_bsPhone) ;
64                       SysFreeString(g_bsName) ;
65                   }
66                   break;
67                 case IDM_Done:
68                   SendMessage(hwnd, WM_CLOSE, 0, 0);
69                   break;
70             }
71         return TRUE;
72       case WM_CLOSE:
73         DlgExists = 0;
74         DestroyWindow(hwnd);
75         return TRUE;
76     }
77     return FALSE;
78 }
79
80 HRESULT RetrieveFromServer(HWND hwnd) {
81     HRESULT hr ;
82
83     RpcTryExcept {
84         hr = g_pPhones->Retrieve(g_bsName, &g_bsPhone) ;
85     } RpcExcept(1) {
86     MessageBox(hwnd, "RPC Error in calling retrieve",
87             "COM Error", MB_OK) ;
88     } RpcEndExcept ;
89     return hr ;
90 }
91
92 void UpdateServer(threadArg *tA)
93 {
94     wchar_t wcszPhone[MAX_PHONE], wcszName[MAX_NAME] ;
95
96     // Each thread has register itself with COM library
97     HRESULT hr = CoInitializeEx(NULL, COINIT_MULTITHREADED) ;
98
99     if (FAILED(hr)) {
100        MessageBox(tA->hwnd,  "Failed to Initialize COM!",
101                    "Com Error", MB_OK) ;
102        return ;
103    }
104
105    mbstowcs(wcszPhone, tA->szPhone, MAX_PHONE) ;
106    mbstowcs(wcszName, tA->szName, MAX_NAME) ;
107
108    g_bsPhone = SysAllocString(wcszPhone) ;
109    g_bsName = SysAllocString(wcszName) ;
110
111    RpcTryExcept {
112        hr = g_pPhones->Update(g_bsName, g_bsPhone) ;
113    } RpcExcept(1) {
```

```
114        MessageBox(tA->hwnd, "RPC Error in Update!",
115                   "COM Error", MB_OK) ;
116    } RpcEndExcept ;
117
118    if (FAILED(hr))
119        MessageBox(tA->hwnd, "Could not do Update??",
120                   "COM Error", MB_OK) ;
121    SysFreeString(g_bsName) ;
122    SysFreeString(g_bsPhone) ;
123    delete tA ;
124    CoUninitialize() ; // done with the call
125
126 }
```

This finishes our description of the DCOM client for the phone directory. Now we'll show you how to implement the DCOM server component.

9.5.3 DCOM Component (Server)

A component must provide two classes: (1) a **factory** class that creates new instances of an **server** class, and (2) a server class that provides the functions of an interface. We will explain the construction of a DCOM component in three parts:

1.   Constructing the server class,
2.   Constructing the factory class, and
3.   Registering the factory and component.

Object instances of the server class implement the functions provided by the IPhone interface. Object instances of the factory class, on the other hand, create server objects. A DCOM component registers each of its factory objects with DCOM, giving a class ID for which the factory object can create server objects. Then, when a client requests DCOM for a server object of a particular class, DCOM asks the appropriate registered factory object to create a server object. Let's look at the server object class first.

9.5.3.1 Phone Server Class

Here is the definition of the CPhoneExample class that provides the functions of the interface IPhone.

```
1     using namespace std ;
2     typedef map<string, string> t_PhoneDir ;
3     class CPhoneExample : public IPhone {
4         char *szPhoneFile ;
5     public:
6         // IUnknown
7         ULONG __stdcall AddRef() ;
8         ULONG __stdcall Release() ;
9         HRESULT __stdcall QueryInterface(REFIID rid, void** ppv) ;
10
11        //IPhone
12        HRESULT __stdcall Update(BSTR bsName, BSTR bsPhone) ;
13        HRESULT __stdcall Retrieve(BSTR bsName, BSTR *bsPhone) ;
```

```
14
15     CPhoneExample();
16     ~CPhoneExample() ;
17 private:
18     HANDLE m_hMutex ;
19     t_PhoneDir m_PhoneDir ;
20 };
```

The definition specifies that the CPhoneExample class will implement the IPhone interface (line 11) and the IUnknown interface (line 6). The IPhone interface is the one that our server had promised to provide clients. In addition, we have to implement the IUnknown interface, because COM requires all component objects to provide this interface. This interface will be used by clients at runtime to dynamically query the component for a particular interface and for reference counting. The server object manages three data items: (1) m_hMutex: handle to a mutex object that will be used to synchronize access to shared data by multiple threads (of multiple requests), (2) m_PhoneDir: an STL map object to store the phone database, and (3) m_cRef: to count the references to the server object. Here's the implementation of the IUnknown interface for our server object class, CPhoneExample:

```
1  ULONG CPhoneExample::AddRef() {
2      return CoAddRefServerProcess() ;
3  }
4
5  ULONG CPhoneExample::Release() {
6      ULONG cRef ;
7      if ((cRef = CoReleaseServerProcess()) == 0)
8          InitiateComponentShutdown() ;
9      return cRef ;
10 }
11 HRESULT CPhoneExample::QueryInterface(REFIID iid, void** ppv) {
12     if(iid == IID_IUnknown)
13         *ppv = (IUnknown*)this;
14     else if(iid == IID_IPhone)
15         *ppv = (IPhone*)this;
16     else {
17         *ppv = NULL;
18         return E_NOINTERFACE;
19     }
20     AddRef();
21     return S_OK;
22 }
```

Each of the methods in this class has to be thread safe, because we are expecting concurrent, multiple threads to access these methods. The functions AddRef and Release manage the references to this object. Since we are using one server object in the whole DCOM component, we can use the functions CoAddRefServerProcess and CoReleaseServerProcess to keep a reference count for the entire component. These functions provide a threadsafe mechanism for DCOM component reference counting and shutdown. CoAddRefServerProcess increments a process-wide reference count. CoReleaseServerProcess decreases the same process-wide reference count. In addition, `CoReleaseServerProcess` calls `CoSuspendClassObjects` when the reference count reaches 0. `CoSuspendClassObjects` tells DCOM to suspend any new requests for factory or server objects for this component. In this way, we can safely initiate a component shutdown when the reference count reaches 0. This saves us from the unsafe race condition when one thread could be initiating a component shutdown while another thread could be handing out interface pointers.

In response to the `QueryInterface` method invocation, the object returns a pointer to itself if the request is for an `IUnknown` or an `IPhone` interface. This way, a client can query this object at runtime to find out which interfaces it supports.

The implementation of the `IPhone` interface is some ways similar to the corresponding RPC-based server functions. On start-up (object creation), we load the directory contents from the file. When the server object is shutting down, it writes the contents of its in-memory directory to a file. The following constructor and destructor functions for the object class illustrate this. Note that the destructor has to be thread safe to ensure that it synchronizes with any outstanding client requests.

```
1    TCHAR szName[MAX_NAME], szPhone[MAX_NAME] ;
2
3    CPhoneExample::CPhoneExample(): m_cRef(0) {
4      m_hMutex = CreateMutex(NULL, FALSE, NULL) ;
5      if (!m_hMutex) {
6        cout << "Could not obtain mutex!!" << endl ;
7        SetEvent(g_hEvent) ;
8      }
9
10     ifstream phStream("E:\\Dist Apps\\Phones") ;
11     if (phStream)
12       while (!phStream.eof()) {
13         phStream >> szName >> szPhone ;
14         //insert in m_PhoneDir
15         m_PhoneDir.insert(t_PhoneDir::value_type(szName, szPhone)) ;
16       }
17   }
18
19   CPhoneExample::~CPhoneExample() {
20     t_PhoneDir::iterator p ;
21     ofstream phStream("E:\\Dist Apps\\Phones") ;
22     if (phStream) {
23       WaitForSingleObject(m_hMutex, INFINITE) ;
24       for (p = m_PhoneDir.begin(); p != m_PhoneDir.end(); p++)
25         phStream << (p->first).c_str() << ' ' <<
26                     (p->second).c_str() << endl ;
27       ReleaseMutex(m_hMutex) ;
28     }
29   }
30
31   HRESULT CPhoneExample::Retrieve(BSTR bsName, BSTR *bsPhone)
32   {
33     t_PhoneDir::iterator r ;
34     wchar_t wcszPhone[MAX_PHONE] ;
```

```
35      if (bsName) {
36         WaitForSingleObject(m_hMutex, INFINITE) ;
37         wcstombs(szName, bsName, MAX_NAME) ;
38         r = m_PhoneDir.find(szName) ;
39         if (r != m_PhoneDir.end()) {
40            mbstowcs(wcszPhone, (r->second).c_str(), MAX_PHONE) ;
41            *bsPhone = SysAllocString(wcszPhone) ;
42         }
43         ReleaseMutex(m_hMutex) ;
44      }
45      if (bsPhone)
46         return S_OK ;
47      else
48         return S_FALSE ;
49   }
50
51   HRESULT CPhoneExample::Update(BSTR bsName, BSTR bsPhone) {
52      if (bsName && bsPhone) {
53         WaitForSingleObject(m_hMutex, INFINITE) ;
54         wcstombs(szName, bsName, MAX_NAME) ;
55         wcstombs(szPhone, bsPhone, MAX_NAME) ;
56         // insert bsName and bsPhone in m_PhoneDir ;
57         // take out anything that already exists
58         m_PhoneDir.erase(szName) ;
59         m_PhoneDir.insert(t_PhoneDir::value_type(szName, szPhone)) ;
60         ReleaseMutex(m_hMutex) ;
61         return S_OK ;
62      }
63      else
64         return S_FALSE ;
65   }
```

This completes our description of the server object class, that provides objects to service client requests for phone numbers. Now, we'll describe the factory class, that will create server objects on request.

9.5.3.2 Phone Server Factory Class

The factory class provides three main functions: `CreateInstance` and `QueryInterface`. The `CreateInstance` function will return a pointer to a server object on demand. Since in our case we can handle all requests for directory service with one server object, we create a server object only once. As the following code shows, `CreateInstance` requests will simply return a pointer to the same server object. Depending on your situation, you may want to create a new server object each time this request is made. In any case, we call the `QueryInterface` function on the server object. This way, each time we return a pointer to the server object, its reference count will be incremented by one. As we described in the previous discussion, we maintain a process-wide reference counting mechanism. In the case of the factory object, DCOM will invoke the function `LockServer` with a boolean value of `true` or `false`, depending on whether it needs the factory object or not. Hence, we increment or decrement the process-wide reference count for each of these invocations. Here's the code for implementing the factory class.

```
1    class CFactory : public IClassFactory {
2    public:
3      // IUnknown
4      ULONG __stdcall AddRef() { return (ULONG) 0 ;} ;
5      ULONG __stdcall Release() { return (ULONG) 0 ;} ;
6      HRESULT __stdcall QueryInterface(REFIID iid, void** ppv) ;
7
8      // IClassFactory
9      HRESULT __stdcall CreateInstance(IUnknown *pUnknownOuter,
10                           REFIID iid, void** ppv) ;
11     HRESULT __stdcall LockServer(BOOL bLock) ;
12
13     CFactory() { m_piPhoneExample = new CPhoneExample() ;} ;
14     ~CFactory() { delete m_piPhoneExample ; };
15   private:
16     CPhoneExample *m_piPhoneExample ;
17   } ;
18
19   HRESULT CFactory::QueryInterface(REFIID iid, void** ppv) {
20     if((iid == IID_IUnknown) || (iid == IID_IClassFactory))
21        *ppv = (IClassFactory *)this;
22     else {
23        *ppv = NULL;
24        return E_NOINTERFACE;
25     }
26     return S_OK;
27   }
28
29   HRESULT CFactory::CreateInstance(IUnknown *pUnknownOuter,
30                          REFIID iid, void** ppv) {
31     if(pUnknownOuter != NULL)
32        return CLASS_E_NOAGGREGATION;
33     // we'll use a singleton instance for all clients
34     return m_piPhoneExample->QueryInterface(iid, ppv);
35   }
36
37   HRESULT CFactory::LockServer(BOOL bLock) {
38     if (bLock)
39        CoAddRefServerProcess() ;
40     else if (CoReleaseServerProcess() == 0)
41        InitiateComponentShutdown() ;
42     return S_OK;
43   }
```

This completes our discussion of the factory class. Now, we'll describe the third aspect of writing a DCOM server component: registering the component with DCOM.

9.5.3.3 Component Registration

As in the case of RPC, a DCOM server component has to register itself with a location service (called **Service Control Manager (SCM)** for DCOM). There are two aspects of registering a DCOM component: (1) registering the component with the registry, and (2) registering the factory class with the DCOM runtime. We must register the component in the registry so that DCOM can find the appropriate executable (for different process components) or the library (for in-process components). We have to register the factory class with the DCOM runtime so that DCOM can ask the factory to create new server objects of a given class. You register the component in the registry once the server is built. The factory object, on the other hand, must be registered each time a component executes.

For registering our component with, we use the simplified API for registering server components described in Eddon and Eddon (1998). The `RegisterServer` function registers our server (`MTAComponent.exe`) with the registry, giving it details like the class ID for which we provide the component. The `UnRegisterServer` will remove the appropriate registry entries. When you first build the component, you must invoke the component with the `RegServer` switch. This will register your component in the registry until you execute the component with the `UnRegServer` switch. For details of the actual registry entries made, see the source code accompanying the book.

Once the component has been started by DCOM (in response to a request from a client), it must register a runtime factory class object with DCOM. We do this using the `Co-RegisterClassObject` function (line 55). This is how DCOM knows the factory from whom it can ask for a server object. Once we have registered the factory object, our component waits for a shutdown event (line 61). This is the event that is set by the `Initiate-ComponentShutdown` function. Remember that the `InitiateComponentShutdown` was called by either the factory (line 41) or the server (line 8) object when the process-wide reference count reaches 0. For proper component shutdown, we revoke the class factory's registration with DCOM and delete the factory object itself.

```
44   HANDLE g_hEvent ;
45
46   void InitiateComponentShutdown() {
47      SetEvent(g_hEvent) ;
48   }
49   void main(int argc, char** argv)
50   {
51      CommandLineParameters(argc, argv);
52      CoInitializeEx(NULL, COINIT_MULTITHREADED);
53      CFactory *pFactory = new CFactory();
54      DWORD dwRegister;
55      CoRegisterClassObject(CLSID_CPhoneExample,
56         pFactory, CLSCTX_SERVER, REGCLS_MULTIPLEUSE,
57         &dwRegister);
58
59      g_hEvent = CreateEvent(NULL, FALSE, FALSE, NULL) ;
60      if (g_hEvent)
61         WaitForSingleObject(g_hEvent, INFINITE) ;
62      else
63         cout << "Could not obtain an Event object." << endl ;
64      CoRevokeClassObject(dwRegister);
65      delete pFactory ;
66      CoUninitialize();
67   }
68
69   void CommandLineParameters(int argc, char** argv)
70   {
```

```
71    if(argc < 2) {
72       cout << "Usage: [/Register /UnRegister]" << endl;
73       exit(false);
74    }
75    char* szToken = strtok(argv[1], "-/");
76    if(_stricmp(szToken, "RegServer") == 0) {
77       RegisterComponent();
78       exit(true);
79    }
80    if(_stricmp(szToken, "UnregServer") == 0) {
81       UnRegisterTypeLib(LIBID_ComPhones, //unregister library
82                         1, 0, LANG_NEUTRAL,
83                         SYS_WIN32);
84       UnregisterServer(CLSID_CPhoneExample,
85                        "PhoneExample.NTBook",
86                        "PhoneExample.NTBook.1") ;
87       exit(true);
88    }
89    if(_stricmp(szToken, "Embedding") != 0) {
90       cout << "Invalid parameter" << endl;
91       exit(false);
92    }
93 }
94 void RegisterComponent()
95 {
96    ITypeLib* pTypeLib;
97
98    LoadTypeLibEx(L"ComPhones.tlb", REGKIND_DEFAULT, &pTypeLib);
99    if (pTypeLib) {
100      pTypeLib->Release();
101      RegisterServer("MTAComponent.exe", CLSID_CPhoneExample,
102              "Phone Directory",
103              "PhoneExample.NTBook", "PhoneExample.NTBook.1", NULL) ;
104   }
105   else
106      cout << "Unable to load type library!" << endl ;
107 }
```

9.6 Summary

In this chapter, we described how to use threads in distributed applications. Distributed applications are becoming popular as low-cost workstations replace mainframe systems. The most common structure for a distributed application is a multi-tiered client-server architecture, in which part of an application acts as a server to which clients can send requests. Remote Procedure Calls (RPC's) are one currently used paradigm for communication between clients and the server. Threads are used in a server to process multiple RPC requests concurrently, and clients use them to make asynchronous RPC calls, which are inherently synchronous. Microsoft's DCOM builds on top of RPC to provide object-oriented access to a server's functions. In addition, DCOM provides location transparency (a server component can be an in-process component, or in a different address space either on the same or different machine) and language independence (the same server component can be accessed by a Java,

Visual Basic, or C++ client). In this chapter, we presented a simple phone distributed service using both RPC and DCOM, illustrating some of these points.

9.7 Bibliographic Notes

Distributed computing has been a popular topic of computer science research since the 1970s. Early distributed applications were built using an input–output paradigm, in which parts of an application communicate with others by sending messages. The Remote Procedure Call paradigm allowed distributed applications to be written just like applications in a single address space. Birrel and Nelson [1984] provided the first efficient RPC implementation. Williams and Kindel (1994) and Box (1998) provide some insights into the multilingual features of COM. Eddon and Eddon (1998) give a good tutorial on how to build distributed applications using DCOM. Microsoft's Visual C++ product contains several articles on the architecture and use of DCOM.

9.8 Exercises

1. Why is the distributed computing paradigm popular?

2. What roles can threads play in a distributed client-server application? Are threads necessary for building client-server applications?

3. Modify the phone directory sample RPC application so that the server allows one person to have several phone numbers. Does this require you to change the version number of the server?

4. Convince yourself that the server does indeed invoke different threads for each service call. [One way to do this is to put a sleep call in each service procedure.]

5. What is the purpose of the function calls CoInitializeEx and CoUninitialize? Do you have to make these calls for each client thread?

6. What is the difference between a single-threaded and a multithreaded apartment? If you are building a new component, which apartment model will you choose for it? If you have an existing server that you want to make available through DCOM, which apartment model will you choose for it?

7. What is the relationship between a DCOM component's factory object and server object?

9.9 References

1. Birrel, A. and Nelson, B. (1984). Implementing Remote Procedure Calls. *ACM Transactions on Computer Systems*, 2(1):39–59.

2. Box, D. (1998). *Essential COM*. Addison-Wesley, Reading, MA.

3. Eddon, G. and Eddon, H. (1998). *Inside Distributed COM*. Microsoft Press, Redmond, WA.

4. Rosenberry, W. and Teagle, J. (1993). *Distributed Applications Across DCE and Windows NT*. O'Reilly and Associates, Inc.

5. Williams, S. and Kindel, C. (1994). The Component Object Model: A Technical Overview, *Dr. Dobbs Journal*, December 1994.

WorkCrew Implementation

*I*n this appendix, we present an implementation of the WorkCrew multithreaded programming model discussed in Chapter 8. Our implementation is derived directly from [Vandervoorde and Roberts, 1988].

A.1 WorkCrew Implementation

The implementation uses two important data structures: a `Crew` structure and a `Worker` structure, which we describe below.

```
1    struct Crew {
2        struct Worker *workers; // A set of workers for this workcrew
3        struct TaskQueue *taskQueue; // A queue of tasks to be done
4        BOOL noMoreTasks; // A boolean indicating no more tasks
5        int nForked; // Number of workers created
6        int nRetired; // Number of workers that have exited
7        int nIdle; // Number of workers waiting for a task
8        HANDLE hallDone; // Condition indicating all tasks done
9        HANDLE hwakeWorker; // Condition to wake a worker
10       HANDLE hcrewMutex; // Mutex to protect access to all this
11   } ;
```

A `Crew` data structure records information about a particular WorkCrew. Workers forming the WorkCrew are represented by a linked-list anchored in it. The set of tasks that have been assigned to the WorkCrew is maintained as a queue using two structures, `TaskElem` and `TaskQueue`.

```
1   struct TaskElem {
2     void (*func)() ;
3       struct ArgBlock *args ;
4       struct TaskQueue *prev, *next ;
5   }
6
7   struct TaskQueue {
8       struct TaskElem *first, *last ;
9   } ;
```

Each element of a `TaskQueue` identifies a function that must be invoked in order to perform a particular task, plus its arguments. The `ArgBlock` data structure is the same as described on page 163.

Three variables, named `nForked`, `nRetired`, and `nIdle`, record the number of workers that are created, have exited, and are currently waiting for work. A boolean variable, `noMoreTasks`, indicates that a join operation should be performed among threads representing this WorkCrew, and that no more tasks should be assigned to it. The `Crew` structure contains three synchronization variables, named `hallDone`, `hwakeWorker`, and `hcrew-Mutex`. `hallDone` is an event object used to signal that all the crew workers have finished. `hwakeWorker` is an event object to signal that there is more work to be done. `hcrew-Mutex` is a mutex used to synchronize concurrent access to various parts of the crew data structure.

Next, we describe the `Worker` data structure, which keeps track of a worker's requests for help:

```
1   struct Worker {
2     struct TaskElem *requests; // A stack of requests made
3                                // by this worker
4     struct TaskElem *SP; // Top of stack pointer
5     struct TaskElem *helpedPtr; // Pointer to requests that have been
6                                // helped (from bottom of stack)
7     HANDLE hworkerMutex; // Mutex to protect access to all this
8     struct Crew *crew; // Back pointer to the crew which this
9                        // worker belongs
10    struct Worker *next; // next element in a set of workers
11  } ;
```

Requests are maintained as a stack in the `request_stack` data structure.

```
1   struct request_stack {
2     void (*func)() ;
3       struct ArgBlock *arg ;
4       struct request_stack *prev, *next ;
5   } ;
```

Each stack entry identifies a function that must be invoked to satisfy an associated request, plus a pointer to the function's arguments.

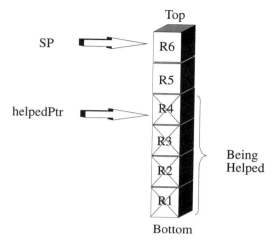

Figure A–1. A Worker's Request Stack.

The `Worker` data structure maintains two pointers into the request stack, `SP` and `helpedPtr` (Figure A–1). `SP` points to the top of the stack, while `helpedPtr` points to a request, such that all other requests between the bottom of the stack and the one identified by `helpedPtr` have been serviced.

Concurrent access to elements of the Worker data structure are synchronized by a mutex, named `hworkerMutex`.

A.1.1 WorkCrew Interface Functions

Next, we describe interface functions that manipulate our WorkCrew representation. The function `CreateWorkCrew` accepts an argument, `n`, and creates *n* workers in the WorkCrew.

```
1    struct Crew *CreateWorkCrew(int n)
2    {
3      int i ;
4      struct Crew *crew;
5
6      if ((crew=(struct Crew *) malloc(sizeof(struct Crew))) == NULL)
7        ErrorExit("Could not get memory to start crew!\n") ;
8      crew->taskQueue   = NULL ;
9      crew->noMoreTasks = FALSE ;
10     crew->nRetired    = 0 ;
11     crew->hcrewMutex  = NULL;
12     crew->hallDone    = NULL;
13     crew->hwakeWorker = NULL;
14     crew->workers     = NULL;
15     if (!(crew->hcrewMutex = CreateMutex(NULL, FALSE, NULL)))
16       ErrorExit("Error creating the crew mutex\n") ;
17     if (!(crew->hallDone = CreateEvent(NULL, TRUE, FALSE,
```

```
18                                    "AllDoneEvent")))
19        ErrorExit("Error creating allDone event\n") ;
20        if (!(crew->hwakeWorker = CreateEvent(NULL, TRUE, FALSE,
21                                      "WakeWorkerEvent")))
22          ErrorExit("Error creating wakeWorker event\n") ;
23        InitializeQueue(crew) ;
24        if ((dwTlsIndex = TlsAlloc()) == 0xffffffff)
25          ErrorExit("Error creating a thread local storage\n") ;
26        WaitForSingleObject(crew->hcrewMutex, INFINITE) ;
27        for (i=1; i<=n; i++)
28          createWorker(crew) ;
29        crew->nForked = n ;
30        crew->nIdle = n ;
31        ReleaseMutex(crew->hcrewMutex) ;
32        return crew ;
33    }
```

The CreateWorkCrew function allocates a new Crew data structure and initializes it. In order to initialize the queue of tasks, it calls the InitializeQueue function (line 23).

```
1     void InitializeQueue(struct Crew *crew)
2     {
3        if ((crew->taskQueue = (struct TaskQueue *)
4            malloc(sizeof(struct TaskQueue))) == NULL)
5          ErrorExit("Error getting memory for task queue") ;
6        crew->taskQueue->first = crew->taskQueue->last = NULL ;
7     }
```

The variable dwTlsindex (line 24) is used to create an index that will be used to store data belonging to each thread. We will return to this when we describe functions used by each worker.

The CreateWorkCrew function calls the createWorker function in order to create each of the *n* workers.

```
1     static void createWorker(struct Crew *crew)
2     {
3        struct Worker *worker ;
4        HANDLE hworker ;
5        DWORD ThreadID;
6
7        if ((worker = (struct Worker *)
8            malloc(sizeof(struct Worker))) == NULL)
9          ErrorExit("Could not get memory for worker!\n") ;
10       worker->requests = worker->SP = worker -> helpedPtr = NULL ;
11       worker->crew = crew ;
12       if (!(worker->hworkerMutex = CreateMutex(NULL, FALSE, NULL)))
13         ErrorExit("Error creating a worker mutex\n") ;
14       hworker = CreateThread(NULL, 0,
15                       (LPTHREAD_START_ROUTINE) WorkerRoot,
16                       worker, 0, &ThreadID) ;
17       // the crew structure is already protected for multithreaded access
18       worker->next = crew->workers ;
19       crew->workers = worker ;
20    }
```

The `CreateWorker` function allocates and initializes a `Worker` data structure for each worker thread. It also arranges for that thread to call `WorkerRoot` function, which we will describe shortly. Two functions help workers make requests for help: `RequestHelp-WorkCrew` and `WorkCrewGotHelp`.

```
1    void RequestHelpWorkCrew(void (*func)(struct ArgBlock *args),
2                            struct ArgBlock *args)
3    {
4      LPVOID tlvariable ;
5      struct Worker *currentWorker ;
6      tlvariable = TlsGetValue(dwTlsIndex) ;
7      currentWorker = (struct Worker *)tlvariable ;
8      WaitForSingleObject(currentWorker->hworkerMutex, INFINITE) ;
9      push(currentWorker, func, args) ;
10     ReleaseMutex(currentWorker->hworkerMutex) ;
11     if (!SetEvent(currentWorker->crew->hwakeWorker))
12        ErrorExit("Error trying to signal request available\n") ;
13     Sleep(0) ;
14   }
```

The `RequestHelpWorkCrew` function accepts a pointer to a function to call when help is provided, along with arguments to that function. It determines the identity of its caller using a thread-private variable named `currentWorker`. Observe that we could not have used a local variable for `currentWorker` since C uses static lexical scoping, and we cannot pass it as an argument if we wish to keep the WorkCrew functions' interfaces simple. A help request is pushed on a stack that is maintained for the current worker, and then the worker signals the `hwakeWorker` condition so that any idle worker can examine the stack and help out. The `Sleep` call at the end ensures that any idle worker is given a chance to run.

A worker can call the `WorkCrewGotHelp` function in order to determine whether help has been provided.

```
1    int WorkCrewGotHelp()
2    {
3      int gotHelp = 0 ;
4      LPVOID tlvariable ;
5      struct Worker *currentWorker ;
6      tlvariable = TlsGetValue(dwTlsIndex) ;
7      currentWorker = (struct Worker *)tlvariable ;
8      WaitForSingleObject(currentWorker->hworkerMutex, INFINITE) ;
9      if (currentWorker->helpedPtr == currentWorker->SP) {
10        gotHelp = 1 ;
11        currentWorker->helpedPtr = currentWorker->helpedPtr->prev ;
12     }
13     currentWorker->SP = currentWorker->SP->prev ;
14     if (currentWorker->SP)
15       if (currentWorker->SP->next) {
16          free(currentWorker->SP->next) ;
17          currentWorker->SP->next = NULL ;
18       }
19     ReleaseMutex(currentWorker->hworkerMutex) ;
20     return gotHelp ;
21   }
```

The `WorkCrewGotHelp` function uses a thread local variable, named `tlvari-able`, in order to identify its caller. It checks to see if it got help for its last request by testing whether `helpedPtr` refers to the top of the stack, `SP`. In either case, the request is popped from the stack, since it will be serviced by the calling thread if it hasn't been serviced already.

The function `AddTaskWorkCrew` can be used to add tasks for the WorkCrew.

```
1    void AddTaskWorkCrew(struct Crew *crew, void (*task)
2                           (struct ArgBlock *args),
3                           struct ArgBlock *arguments)
4    {
5       WaitForSingleObject(crew->hcrewMutex, INFINITE) ;
6       enqueue(crew, task, arguments) ;
7       ReleaseMutex(crew->hcrewMutex) ;
8       if (!SetEvent(crew->hwakeWorker))
9          ErrorExit("Error signalling a new task addition\n") ;
10   }
```

The `AddTaskWorkCrew` function accepts a pointer to a function that must be invoked in order to accomplish the desired task, together with its arguments. It adds a new task to the queue of tasks being maintained for the WorkCrew, then signals the condition `hwake-Worker` so that any idle worker can perform the task.

Finally, the `JoinWorkCrew` function waits for all workers to finish their tasks.

```
1    void JoinWorkCrew(struct Crew *crew)
2    {
3       WaitForSingleObject(crew->hcrewMutex, INFINITE) ;
4       crew->noMoreTasks = TRUE ;
5       ReleaseMutex(crew->hcrewMutex) ;
6       WaitForSingleObject(crew->hallDone, INFINITE) ;
7    }
```

This completes our description of the WorkCrew interface functions. Now we describe functions used by each worker.

A.1.2 Worker Implementation

The initial function for each worker is `WorkerRoot` (see line 14 of `Create-Worker`).

```
1    void WorkerRoot(struct Worker *me)
2    {
3       struct TaskElem *task;
4       struct Crew *crew ;
5       LPVOID lpvData ;
6       lpvData = (LPVOID) LocalAlloc(0, sizeof(struct Worker *)) ;
7       lpvData = me ;
8       if (!TlsSetValue(dwTlsIndex, lpvData))
9          ErrorExit("TlsSetValue Error") ;
10      crew = me->crew ;
11      block(crew) ;
12      while (1) {
13         if (FindTask(me, &task))
14            DoTask(me,task) ;
```

```
15      else {
16        if (AllTasksDone(crew)) {
17          terminate(crew) ;
18          WaitForSingleObject(crew->hcrewMutex, INFINITE) ;
19          crew->nRetired++ ;
20          ReleaseMutex(crew->hcrewMutex) ;
21          ExitThread(0) ;
22        }
23        else
24          block(crew) ;
25      }
26    }
27  }
```

The WorkerRoot function loops forever, waiting when there is no work to be done until it is terminated with a call to ExitThread. Before entering the loop, this function initializes a thread-private variable with which to subsequently determine the identity of the calling thread, and blocks to allow for initial tasks to be added to the crew. When the thread is awakened by an hwakeWorker signal, it calls the FindTask function to check if there is work to be done. If so, the thread calls the DoTask function; otherwise, it checks whether all of the WorkCrew's tasks are done, in which case it can terminate. If not, it calls the block function to await more work.

```
1   int FindTask(struct Worker *worker, struct TaskElem **task)
2   {
3     struct Crew *crew ;
4     int foundTask = 0;
5     crew = worker->crew ;
6     WaitForSingleObject(crew->hcrewMutex, INFINITE) ;
7     if (*task = deQueue(crew)) // a task exists in the queue
8       foundTask = 1 ;
9     else { // no tasks in crew, check workers
10      worker = crew->workers ;
11      while ((worker != NULL) && (!foundTask)) {
12        if (CheckWorkerForTask(worker, task))
13          foundTask = 1 ;
14        worker = worker->next ;
15      }
16    }
17    ReleaseMutex(crew->hcrewMutex) ;
18    return foundTask ;
19  }
```

The FindTask function searches the crew's task queue. If the queue contains a task, it is dequeued and returned; otherwise, FindTask checks each worker by calling the Check-WorkerForTask function.

```
1   int CheckWorkerForTask(struct Worker *worker,struct TaskElem **task)
2   {
3     int foundTask = 0 ;
4     struct TaskElem *newtask;
5
6     WaitForSingleObject(worker->hworkerMutex, INFINITE) ;
```

```
7       if (worker->SP) {
8          if (worker->helpedPtr)
9             newtask = worker->helpedPtr->next ;
10         else
11            newtask = worker->requests ;
12         if (newtask) { // a task exists
13            *task = newtask;
14            worker->helpedPtr = newtask ;
15            foundTask = 1 ;
16         }
17      }
18      ReleaseMutex(worker->hworkerMutex) ;
19      return foundTask ;
20   }
```

The CheckWorkerForTask function searches a worker's request stack, if one exists. If the stack is not empty, the next task requiring help is above the one pointed to by helpedPtr. If the stack has only one element, this pointer will be NULL. If helpedPtr is NULL but the stack is not empty, the request at the bottom of the stack is serviced first.

The DoTask function is called in order to perform a dequeued task.

```
1    void DoTask(struct Worker *worker, struct TaskElem *task)
2    {
3       WaitForSingleObject(worker->crew->hcrewMutex, INFINITE) ;
4       worker->crew->nIdle-- ;
5       ReleaseMutex(worker->crew->hcrewMutex) ;
6       (task->func)(task->args) ;
7       WaitForSingleObject(worker->crew->hcrewMutex, INFINITE) ;
8       worker->crew->nIdle++ ;
9       ReleaseMutex(worker->crew->hcrewMutex) ;
10   }
```

If FindTask (called in WorkerRoot) cannot find any work to do, a worker thread then checks whether all of the crew's tasks have been done by calling the AllTasksDone function.

```
1    int AllTasksDone(struct Crew *crew)
2    {
3       BOOL allDone ;
4
5       if (allDone = crew->noMoreTasks)
6          if (crew->nForked == crew->nRetired + 1)
7             //last one out signals main thread
8             if (!SetEvent(crew->hallDone))
9                ErrorExit("Error trying to signal all done\n") ;
10      return allDone ;
11   }
```

There are no more tasks for the crew if JoinWorkCrew has been called, that is, the boolean noMoreTasks is true. In addition, if all workers but one have finished, the condition hallDone is signaled so that JoinWorkCrew can peacefully exit. If the main loop of the WorkerRoot function discovers that there are no more tasks, it calls the terminate function, which terminates other members of the crew.

```
1   void terminate(struct Crew *crew)
2   {
3     if (!SetEvent(crew->hwakeWorker))
4       ErrorExit("Error signalling termination") ;
5   }
```

Finally, if a worker finds no work but more tasks may arrive, it calls the `block` function in order to await new requests.

```
1   void block(struct Crew *crew)
2   {
3     WaitForSingleObject(crew->hwakeWorker, INFINITE) ;
4     ResetEvent(crew->hwakeWorker) ;
5   }
```

A.2 References

1. Vandervoorde, M. T. and Roberts, E. S. (1988). WorkCrews: An Abstraction for Controlling Parallelism. *International Journal of Parallel Programming*, 17(4):347–366.

Bibliography

1. Anderson, T. E., Bershad, B. N., Lazowska, E. D., and Levy, H. M. (1991). Scheduler Activations: Effective Kernel Support for User-Level Management of Parallelism. In *Proceedings of the Thirteenth Symposium on Operating System Principles*, pp. 95–109.

2. Anderson, T. E., Lazowska, E., and Levy, H. (1989). The Performance Implications of Thread Management Alternatives for Shared Memory Multiprocessors. *IEEE Transactions on Computers*, 38(12):1631–1644.

3. Andrews, G. (1991). *Concurrent Programming: Principles and Practice*. Benjamin-Cummings, Redwood City, CA.

4. Bach, M. J. (1986). *The Design of the UNIX Operating System*. Prentice Hall, Inc., Englewood Cliffs, NJ.

5. Barton-Davis, P., McNamee, D., Vaswani, R., and Lazowska, E. (1993). Adding Scheduler Activations to Mach 3.0. In *Proceedings of the 3rd Mach Symposium*, pp. 119–136. USENIX Association.

6. Box, D. (1998). *Essential COM*. Addison-Wesley, Reading, MA.

7. Ben-Ari (1990). *Principles of Concurrent and Distributed Programming*. Prentice Hall, New York, NY.

8. Bensoussan, A., Clingen, C. T., and Daley, R. C. (1972). The Multics Virtual Memory: Concepts and Design. *Communications of the ACM*, 15(5):308–318.

9. Birrel, A. and Nelson, B. (1984). Implementing Remote Procedure Calls. *ACM Transactions on Computer Systems*, 2(1):39–59.

10. Birrel, A. D. (1991). An Introduction to Programming with Threads. In Nelson, G., ed., *Systems Programming with Modula-3*, pp. 88–118. Prentice Hall.

11. Burks, A. W., Goldstine, H. H., and von Neumann, J. (1946). Preliminary discussion of the logical design of an electronic computing instrument. Report to the U.S. Army Ordnance Department. Also appears in *Papers of John von Neumann*, W. Aspray and A. Burds, eds., The MIT Press, Cambridge, MA, and Tomash Publishers, Los Angeles, California, 1987, 97-146.

12. Cheriton, D. (1988). The V Distributed System. *Communications of the ACM*, 31(3):314–333.

13. Cheriton, D. R., Malcolm, M. A., Melen, L. S., and Sager, G. R. (1979). Toth, a Portable Real-Time Operating System. *Communications of the ACM*, 22(2):105–115.

14. Coffman, Jr., E. G., Elphick, M. J., and Shoshani, A. (1971). System Deadlocks. *Computing Surveys*, 3(2):67–78.

15. Corbató, F. J., editor (1963). *The Compatible Time-Sharing System: A Programmer's Guide*. MIT Press, Cambridge, MA.

16. Corbató, F. J. and Vyssotsky, V. A. (1965). Introduction and Overview of the Multics System. In *Proceedings of the AFIPS Fall Joint Computer Conference*, pp. 185–196.

17. Cormen, T. H., Leiserson, C. E., and Rivest, R. L. (1990). *Introduction to Algorithms*. McGraw-Hill, New York, NY.

18. Crisman, P. A., editor (1964). *The Compatible Time-Sharing System*. MIT Press, Cambridge, MA.

19. Custer, H. (1993). *Inside Windows NT*. Microsoft Press, Seattle, WA.

20. Dahl, O. J. (1972). Hierarchical Program Structures. In *Structured Programming*. Academic Press, New York, NY.

21. DEC (1990). *Concert Multithread Architecture*. Digital Equipment Corporation.

22. Deitel, H. M. (1990). *An Introduction to Operating Systems*. Addison-Wesley, Readings, MA.

23. Dijkstra, E. W. (1968). Cooperating Sequential Processes. In Genuys, F., editor, *Programming Languages*. Academic Press, New York, NY.

24. Eddon, G. and Eddon, H. (1998). *Inside Distributed COM*. Microsoft Press, Redmond, WA.

25. Fontao, R. O. (1971). A Concurrent Algorithm for Avoiding Deadlocks. In *Proceedings of the third ACMP Symposium on Operating System Principles*, pp. 72–79.

26. Gehani, N. H. and Roome, W. D. (1989). *Concurrent C*. Silicon Press.

27. Gold, E. M. (1978). Deadlock Prevention: Easy and Difficult Cases. *SIAM Journal of Computing*, 7(3):320–336.

28. Goldberg, A. and Robson, D. (1983). *Smalltalk-80: The Language and its Implementation*. Addison-Wesley, Reading, MA.

29. Haberman, A. N. (1969). Prevention of System Deadlocks. *Communications of the ACM*, 12(7):373–377.

30. Haberman, A. N. (1978). System Deadlocks. In *Current Trends in Programming Methodology*, pp. 256–297. Prentice Hall, Englewood Cliffs, N. J.

31. Hansen, P. B. (1973a). Concurrent Programming Concepts. *Computing Surveys*, 5(4):223–245.

32. Hansen, P. B. (1973b). *Operating System Principles*. Prentice Hall, Englewood Cliffs, NJ.

33. Hansen, P. B. (1975). The Programming Language Concurrent Pascal. *IEEE Transactions on Software Engineering*, SE-1(2):199–207.

34. Havender, J. W. (1968). Avoiding Deadlock in Multitasking Systems. *IBM Systems Journal*, 7(2):74–84.

35. Hoare, C. A. R. (1974). Monitors: An Operating System Structuring Concept. *Communications of the ACM*, 17(10):549–557.

36. Holt, R. C. (1972). Some Deadlock Properties of Computer Systems. *ACM Computing Surveys*, 4(3):179–196.

37. Howard, J. (1976). Signaling in Monitors. In *Proceedings of the 2nd International Conference on Software Engineering*, pp. 47–52, San Francisco, CA.

38. Lampson, B. W. and Redell, D. D. (1980). Experience with Processes and Monitors in Mesa. *Communications of the ACM*, 23(2):105–117.

39. Lett, A. S. and Konigsford, W. L. (1968). TSS/360: A Time-Shared Operating System. In *Proceedings of the AFIPS Fall Joint Computer Conference*, vol. 33, pp. 15–28, Montvale, NJ.

40. Marovich, S. B. (1990). Interprocess Concurrency under UNIX. Technical Report HPL-90-02, Hewlett-Packard Labs, Palo Alto, CA 94304.

41. McJones, P. R. and Swart, G. F. (1987). Evolving the UNIX System Interface to Support Multi-threaded Programs. Technical Report 27, Digital Equipment Corporation, Systems Research Center, 130 Lytton Avenue, Palo Alto, CA 94301.

42. Microsoft. *RPC Programming Guide and Reference (part of Microsoft Win32 SDK)*. Microsoft Corporation.

43. Microsoft (1992). *Windows NT Programmer's Reference: Application Programming Interface, Part 1 and 2*. Microsoft Corporation.

44. Murphy, J. E. (1968). Resource Allocation with Interlock Detection in a Multitask System. In *Proceedings of the AFIPS Fall Joint Computer Conference*, vol. 33, pp. 1169–1176.

45. Newton, G. (1979). Deadlock Prevention, Detection, and Resolution: An Annotated Bibliography. *ACM Operating Systems Review*, 13(2):33–44.

46. OSF (1993). *OSF DCE Application Development Guide*. Prentice Hall, Englewood Cliffs, NJ.

47. Pham, T. Q. and Garg, P. K. (1992). On Migrating a Distributed Application to a Shared-Memory Multi-Threaded Environment. In *Proceedings of the Summer USENIX*, San Antonio, TX. USENIX.

48. Powell, M. L., Kleiman, S. R., Barton, S., Shah, D., and Weeks, M. (1991). SunOS Multithread Architecture. In *Proceedings of the 1991 USENIX Winter Conference*, pp. 65–79, Dallas, TX.

49. Rashid, R. F. (1986). Threads of a new system. *Unix Review*, pp. 37–49.

50. Rosenberry, W. and Teagle, J. (1993). *Distributed Applications Across DCE and Windows NT*. O'Reilly and Associates, Inc.

51. Saltzer, J. H. (1966). *Traffic Control in a Multiplexed Computer System*. PhD thesis, Massachusetts Institute of Technology.

52. Stein, D. and Shah, D. (1992). Implementing Lightweight Threads. In *Proceedings of the 1992 USENIX Summer Conference*, pp. 1–9, San Antonio, TX.

53. Stroustrup, B. (1994). *The Design and Evolution of C++*. Addison-Wesley, Reading, MA.

54. Tanenbaum, A. (1992). *Modern Operating Systems*. Prentice Hall, Englewood Cliffs, NJ.

55. Tevanian, A., Rashid, R. F., Golub, D. B., Black, D. L., Cooper, E., and Young, M. W. (1987). MACH Threads and the UNIX Kernel: The Battle for Control. Technical Report CMU-CS-87-149, Carnegie Mellon University.

56. Thacker, C., Stewart, L., and Satterthwaite, Jr., E. (1988). Firefly: A Multiprocessor Workstation. *IEEE Transactions on Computers*, 37(8):909–920.

57. Vandervoorde, M. T. and Roberts, E. S. (1988). WorkCrews: An Abstraction for Controlling Parallelism. *International Journal of Parallel Programming*, 17(4):347–366.

58. Vyssotsky, V. A., Corbató, F. J., and Graham, R. M. (1965). Structure of the Multics Supervisor. In *Proceedings of the AFIPS Fall Joint Computer Conference*, pp. 203–212.

59. Weiser, M., Demers, A., and Hauser, C. (1989). The Portable Common Runtime Approach to Interoperability. In *Proceedings of the Twelfth ACM Symposium on Operating System Principles*, pp. 114–122.

60. Williams, S. and Kindel, C. (1994). The Component Object Model: A Technical Overview, *Dr. Dobbs Journal*, December 1994.

61. Wirth, N. (1985). *Programming in MODULA-2*. Springer-Verlag, New York, NY.

Index

A

address space 3
Amoeba 135
Anderson, T. E. 142
apartment threading model 184
ATM 169
auto reset event 43
automatic teller machines 169

B

banker's algorithm 127
Barton, S. 141
Barton-Davis, P. 143
base priority 46
Ben-Ari 109
Bensoussan, A. 3

Bershad, B. N. 142
binary semaphore 41
Birrel, A. D. 158, 172, 199
bounded-buffer
    file copy 65
    problem 61
    using monitors 85, 102
buffer monitor 100
Bundy 87, 88
Burks, A. W. 2

C

C++ 5, 95
central processing unit 134
Cheriton, D. 4
Chorus 135, 139
circular wait 113

ForkAlways model 162
ForkWhenIdle model 163

G

Gehani, N. H. 96
Goldberg, A. 5
Goldstine, H. H. 2
graph reduction 123

H

Hansen, P. B. 5, 79, 93
Hauser, C. 137
Hoare, C. A. R. 5, 79, 93
hold and wait 113
Holt, R. C. 122

I

IBM 3
IDL 173, 174
IEEE P1003.4A 138
Interface Definition Language 173
interface pointer 184

J

Java 184, 187

K

kernel 134
kernel-level threads 133, 139
    advantages 139
    drawbacks 140
kernel-supported user-level threads 133
keyboards 134
Kleiman, S. R. 141
Konigsford, W. L. 3

L

Lampson, B. W. 96
Lazowska, E. D. 142, 143
Leiserson, C. E. 158
Lett, A. S. 3
Levy, H.M. 142
lightweight process 4, 6, 140
livelock 16
LWP 140

M

Mach 4, 135, 139, 143
    threads 4
Mach 3.0 4
mailslot 177
manager-worker model 148, 153
manual reset event 43
Marovich, S. 140
marshaling 172
McJones, P. R. 137
McNamee, D. 143
memory 134
Mesa 96
microkernel 135
Microsoft IDL compiler 173
Microsoft Locator 175
middleware 171
MIDL 173
MIT 3
Modula2 96
monitors 5, 79
    benefits 85
    declaration 80
    implementation 95
    initialization 80
    procedures 80
    shared buffer 81
    use 85
MTA 184
Multics 3
multiple-readers/single-writer locking
        protocol 71
multiplexed threads 133, 140

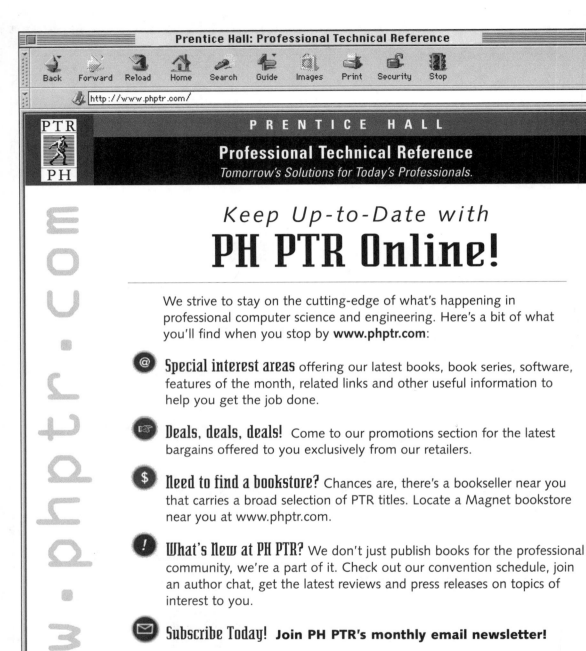

7.   **MISCELLANEOUS:** This Agreement shall be construed in accordance with the laws of the United States of America and the State of New York and shall benefit the Company, its affiliates, and assignees.

8.   **LIMITED WARRANTY AND DISCLAIMER OF WARRANTY:** The Company warrants that the SOFTWARE, when properly used in accordance with the Documentation, will operate in substantial conformity with the description of the SOFTWARE set forth in the Documentation. The Company does not warrant that the SOFTWARE will meet your requirements or that the operation of the SOFTWARE will be uninterrupted or error-free. The Company warrants that the media on which the SOFTWARE is delivered shall be free from defects in materials and workmanship under normal use for a period of thirty (30) days from the date of your purchase. Your only remedy and the Company's only obligation under these limited warranties is, at the Company's option, return of the warranted item for a refund of any amounts paid by you or replacement of the item. Any replacement of SOFTWARE or media under the warranties shall not extend the original warranty period. The limited warranty set forth above shall not apply to any SOFTWARE which the Company determines in good faith has been subject to misuse, neglect, improper installation, repair, alteration, or damage by you. EXCEPT FOR THE EXPRESSED WARRANTIES SET FORTH ABOVE, THE COMPANY DISCLAIMS ALL WARRANTIES, EXPRESS OR IMPLIED, INCLUDING WITHOUT LIMITATION, THE IMPLIED WARRANTIES OF MERCHANTABILITY AND FITNESS FOR A PARTICULAR PURPOSE. EXCEPT FOR THE EXPRESS WARRANTY SET FORTH ABOVE, THE COMPANY DOES NOT WARRANT, GUARANTEE, OR MAKE ANY REPRESENTATION REGARDING THE USE OR THE RESULTS OF THE USE OF THE SOFTWARE IN TERMS OF ITS CORRECTNESS, ACCURACY, RELIABILITY, CURRENTNESS, OR OTHERWISE.

IN NO EVENT, SHALL THE COMPANY OR ITS EMPLOYEES, AGENTS, SUPPLIERS, OR CONTRACTORS BE LIABLE FOR ANY INCIDENTAL, INDIRECT, SPECIAL, OR CONSEQUENTIAL DAMAGES ARISING OUT OF OR IN CONNECTION WITH THE LICENSE GRANTED UNDER THIS AGREEMENT, OR FOR LOSS OF USE, LOSS OF DATA, LOSS OF INCOME OR PROFIT, OR OTHER LOSSES, SUSTAINED AS A RESULT OF INJURY TO ANY PERSON, OR LOSS OF OR DAMAGE TO PROPERTY, OR CLAIMS OF THIRD PARTIES, EVEN IF THE COMPANY OR AN AUTHORIZED REPRESENTATIVE OF THE COMPANY HAS BEEN ADVISED OF THE POSSIBILITY OF SUCH DAMAGES. IN NO EVENT SHALL LIABILITY OF THE COMPANY FOR DAMAGES WITH RESPECT TO THE SOFTWARE EXCEED THE AMOUNTS ACTUALLY PAID BY YOU, IF ANY, FOR THE SOFTWARE.

SOME JURISDICTIONS DO NOT ALLOW THE LIMITATION OF IMPLIED WARRANTIES OR LIABILITY FOR INCIDENTAL, INDIRECT, SPECIAL, OR CONSEQUENTIAL DAMAGES, SO THE ABOVE LIMITATIONS MAY NOT ALWAYS APPLY. THE WARRANTIES IN THIS AGREEMENT GIVE YOU SPECIFIC LEGAL RIGHTS AND YOU MAY ALSO HAVE OTHER RIGHTS WHICH VARY IN ACCORDANCE WITH LOCAL LAW.

ACKNOWLEDGMENT

YOU ACKNOWLEDGE THAT YOU HAVE READ THIS AGREEMENT, UNDERSTAND IT, AND AGREE TO BE BOUND BY ITS TERMS AND CONDITIONS. YOU ALSO AGREE THAT THIS AGREEMENT IS THE COMPLETE AND EXCLUSIVE STATEMENT OF THE AGREEMENT BETWEEN YOU AND THE COMPANY AND SUPERSEDES ALL PROPOSALS OR PRIOR AGREEMENTS, ORAL, OR WRITTEN, AND ANY OTHER COMMUNICATIONS BETWEEN YOU AND THE COMPANY OR ANY REPRESENTATIVE OF THE COMPANY RELATING TO THE SUBJECT MATTER OF THIS AGREEMENT.

Should you have any questions concerning this Agreement or if you wish to contact the Company for any reason, please contact in writing at the address below.

Robin Short
Prentice Hall PTR
One Lake Street
Upper Saddle River, New Jersey 07458

About the CD

The CD-ROM contains the source code covered in the book. For your convenience, we have included all the executable programs so that you can run them without having to build the code.

Platforms: Windows 95/98/NT.

Software: Microsoft Visual Studio is required. We recommend Microsoft Visual Studio 5.0 or later to build the DCOM example in Chapter 9.

Note: When you copy the code from the CD to your local hard disk, the operating system may set the file permissions as Read-Only. Change the permissions to Read-Write if you want to compile the examples. You can execute the binaries unchanged.

Please note: Prentice Hall does not offer technical support for this software. However, if there is a problem with the media, you may obtain a replacement copy by emailing us with the problem at disc_exchange@prenhall.com